My
Own
Life

My
Own
Life

◇

AN AUTOBIOGRAPHY

Hazel Hawke

THE TEXT PUBLISHING COMPANY
MELBOURNE AUSTRALIA

The Text Publishing Company Pty Ltd
220 Clarendon Street
East Melbourne Victoria 3002
Australia

First published 1992

Typeset on Quark Xpress 3.1 by Mark Carter
Text setting in Janson, chapter heads in Bembo
Printed and bound at Griffin Press

National Library of Australia
Cataloguing-in-Publication data:
Hawke, Hazel.
My own life.
ISBN 1 86372 101 0
1.Hawke,Hazel. 2.Hawke,Bob,1929- . 3.Prime ministers' wives -
Australia - Biography. 4. Prime ministers - Australia -
Biography. I. Title.
994.063092

Designed by Chong Weng-Ho

Stephen Hawke's essay 'Class War', an extract from which appears
on pages 102-4, appears with his permission. It was first published
in *The Independent Monthly*, December 1990.

The extract on pages 205-6, from Peter Bowers' article, appeared
in full in the *Sydney Morning Herald* on 4 March 1989 and is
quoted with his permission.

The author's report of the Newcastle earthquake on pages 208-9
first appeared in full in the *Daily Telegraph* in January 1990.

Every effort has been made to credit photographers but the
publisher would welcome additional information.

ACKNOWLEDGEMENTS

◇

I am grateful to Bob for his encouragement and his trust in me doing my own thing, then when I had done it, checking the accuracy of events, dates and names. I also thank my sister Edith, my children Susan, Stephen and Rosslyn for their support and cooperation and my dear, ninety-seven-year-old mother who in earlier years transferred to me the flavour of her life and her own life's values. My six very special grandchildren have unwittingly helped me feel it was worth doing.

My thanks are also due to: Peter Redlich, friend and family lawyer, who always gives me a good hearing and good advice; Sue Spence, fact-checker with unerring judgment and a sense of humour which makes every task good fun; Di Gribble, my publisher, who has become another of my women friends; Richard Super, VHF (Very Helpful Friend); Sharon Massey my invaluable helper and friend for our nine years in Canberra; Jill Hickson, an early encourager, who became my literary agent; and Les Kossatz for the use of his studio in Melbourne. Numerous other friends and colleagues have supplied, corrected or confirmed facts, and I thank them.

The Grand Hyatt hotel, Melbourne, The Ritz-Carlton hotel, Double Bay and IBM have all given generous assistance. And I couldn't have done without the tiny, pocket *Collins English Gem Dictionary*, labelled in pink texta 'Roz Hawke, 5a', which has been my constant companion.

This book has been written at a disorientated time in my life – between houses, between surgeries and between occupations. My files, books, photographs and cuttings have not been easily accessible, so the ready support of all the above is especially appreciated.

CONTENTS

◇

A STREET AT THE EDGE OF THE BUSH

◇

A childhood I still treasure equipped me to make choices which opened great possibilities for me. The most momentous choice I made was to join Bob for our life's journey.

◆

I grew up in Mount Hawthorn, Western Australia, a working-class suburb exactly three miles from the Perth General Post Office, and had never a care, at least for the first decade of my life. Somehow, I always felt I was just a bit luckier than those around me.

My father and mother, James Masterson and Edith Laura Clark, married in 1923 and built one of the first houses in Coogee Street, then just a stony and sandy road with a last scatter of houses as the suburbs gave way to the edge of the bush. The house was weatherboard, with one central room where visitors ate which we called the dining-room; the carved sideboard, the good table and tall-backed chairs were there. The room had an open fireplace backing onto the woodstove in the kitchen. Three sides of the house were verandah, most of which Dad enclosed over the years for various uses. At first the house sat in a sandpatch – black, loose sand as only Perth can provide, on the coastal plain before the escarpment of the Darling Ranges rises to bushier vegetation and red, loamy soil (we are not called Sandgropers for nothing!). But Dad had built the fences, made the red concrete paths and had the lawns growing before I was born.

Dad and Mum were both homemakers and gardeners. Their maxim was that you did things for yourself. If you did not know how, then you found out, and that was money saved, new skills learned, and a sense of satisfaction. I cannot recall there ever being a tradesman or help at home, unless it was family or friends giving us a hand with some project – help which would be reciprocated.

My mother was the second child of George Clark and Laura Louise Beamer. She was born in South Melbourne in 1895 and had a childhood which must have taken her to the limits of her endurance. She learnt very young to accept responsibility and to work hard. All this was laced with the fear and love of God, learnt from her devout mother. Her father, George, worked as a wharf labourer and by all accounts was a troublesome character. When she was five years old, Mum went by sailing ship to Perth with her mother and infant sister Maud. Grandpa, with the oldest child George, had gone ahead to try his luck and to pursue a dalliance with a woman in Western Australia, some say. I remember visiting that woman in Perth with Mum and sensing the discomfort. She had an imperious manner, a matriarchal air, and she lived more comfortably than us. She felt she was above us, and we felt inferior.

My mother's childhood was spent as a mainstay for her mother. She took responsibility for the care of her four younger siblings. She picked up and delivered the laundry which her mother took in and would wash toiling over a wood-fired copper in the backyard of the house in Myrtle Street, North Perth, where they lived at that time. One morning she set off to collect the laundry, leaving her mother bending over the copper crying. When young Edith arrived back later with her load, there was a baby. It was Nell. She had no idea how. She was eight years old.

George Clark found work as a timber-logger at Keysbrook, thirty-seven miles south of Perth in the Darling Ranges. He cut huge logs four miles up on the scarp, which his Irish mate, Mick Frawley, hauled down the bush tracks by bullock train. One favourite family story is of George and Mick in those days. There were four logger's cottages up in the hills, and one of the wives took ill with appendicitis. George and Mick tied a mattress on top of one huge log and then tied the sick woman to it. It was a hair-raising ride for the poor woman, as with the downward slope the bullocks' slow lumbering turned to a lurching trot propelled by the weight of the logs.

The family lived on the Keysbrook flats in a house Grandpa built. He stood the trunks of blackboy plants side-by-side for walls, sealed them with mud, and made a roof of bagging. Then the whole house was given many coats of whitewash. Gran told my sister it was the coolest house she had ever lived in. My mother had only spasmodic schooling – there were, after all, younger children to be raised and the family was often on the move. There was no school at Keysbrook but young Edith travelled three or four miles by push-pull trolley along the railway line to Serpentine for her lessons. She struck up friendships with the fettlers who were 'running along the railway' to maintain the tracks. They were mostly Irish and sang catchy ditties to the rhythm of the push-pull. She used to collect coal that had fallen from passing trains and take it for use at home.

But even here, living in the most modest of circumstances, Gran insisted on dignity. Her grandfather, Jacob Beamer, had been a convict. When he was twenty-two he had joined a rebellion against the British in his birthplace in Canada and was sentenced to transportation for life. He was sent to Van Diemen's Land on HMS *Canton* in 1838. After seven years, he was one of a small group of eight to be granted a full pardon. His craft was timber work and he started a new family and life for himself in the lower central table-lands of Tasmania. I have been delighted to discover an ancestor with political commitment and the courage to involve himself in the risky business of rebellion.

As a young woman, Gran left Tasmania with her mother to work in Melbourne. They became dressers and hairdressers to the ladies of the Gilbert and Sullivan Opera Company in the late 1880s. Working in the theatre in those Dickensian times was regarded by some as a job for 'scarlet women'. Gran was sensitive about it and was always at pains to behave with extra decorum. At one stage she did not allow mirrors in her house because they denoted vanity, and vanity was frowned upon as a sin.

At Keysbrook, Gran and her daughters starched and goffered the frills on the girls' petticoats. When a teacher came to Keysbrook and taught Edith to crochet, she made lacy curtains for their bush home. Sometimes there were no boots to wear to school so the children stayed at home – Gran considered the respectability of button-up boots a necessity. They always lived by the discipline of good manners and the duty of family members to each other.

◆

At our house in Coogee Street, I shared a three-quarter-sized bed with my older sister Edith (whom I called 'Sis' until we were grown women). We slept on the front verandah which was enclosed with mosquito wire and canvas blinds. There were three years and four months between us and my sister was well ahead of me in competence and maturity. I can remember asking her endless questions, each answer prompting another question ... and why ... but why ... with the persistence of an irritating younger sister testing the older's patience and her superior knowledge. We were not physically alike – Sis was brunette and I was blonde. She had the longer-boned body of the Clark family while I was shorter – 'like a Masterson,' Mum said. My sister was an organiser and would get things going without the fear of failure that would have stopped me. Once, for instance, she had me and the local kids practising songs and learning poetry for a neighbourhood concert. I thought it was a bit much to ask our parents, and our aunts, and to charge them a penny each in aid of the Missionary Society. But she did ask them, and they did come, and sat on stools in the summerhouse with the back verandah as a stage.

In the backyard Dad built a cubby house in which we and other kids in the street could play. It had a concrete floor, a real glass window and a hip roof of corrugated iron painted dark red. It was furnished with child-sized table and chairs, a dresser and shelves, all of which Dad had made and painted bright blue. Behind the cubby house (no doubt to save a wall) was his workshop which doubled as a woodshed. We had a swing on the back lawn too. Dad and his brother-in-law, Uncle Sid, built it – a sturdy jarrah frame, strong chains and a wooden seat which, with time, became satin-smooth and shiny from polishing by many bottoms.

My father was born in Perth in 1898. His mother, born Edith Moss, had come from a Jewish-Czechoslovakian family who went to Lancashire to make their fortune in the cotton mills. When she fell in love with and married William Masterson, an Irish goy from Belfast, they disowned and disinherited her. When William and his brother decided to leave troubled Ireland, they tossed a coin – one would go to Australia and one to America. Family lore has it that the brother who won America was the father of Bat Masterson, the 'Robin Hood' of the Midwest. I am grateful for the fall of the penny, so long ago, that brought my grandfather to Australia.

My grandmother, Edith Masterson, died when my father was an infant. Grandfather raised his four children, a daughter and three sons of whom Dad was the youngest, with the help of his only daughter and oldest child, Mary. She mothered the boys and remained motherly to Dad until he died. William was always talked of as a sensitive, almost mystical man. He was a green-thumbed gardener and was renowned for 'fixing people up' – the bush healer for the district around the tiny town of Ajana, where there were no doctors. There was a sterner side to him though – when his sons began working, he made them give all their wages to him. Released from the burden of raising his children, he revisited Ireland, funded at least in part by their earnings. His passport for that trip declared his occupation as 'Gentleman' – a source of some amusement to his children.

My father was dux of Newcastle Street Boys' High in Perth and wore the prize, an elegant silver map of Australia set on a gold laurel wreath, on his waistcoat chain for all the years I remember him. He went on studying at night-school while employed by Westralian Farmers, then worked for them at Geraldton before he set up his own business as an accountant and auditor in Perth. Dad had a chubby face and figure. His expression was open and kindly, Mum's sisters used to say, 'Jimmy would never hurt a fly.' But he was rather a worrier and as he grew older his face often registered concern. His portly figure belied his physical energy – I remember seeing him as a young man training on the beach with the Leighton lifesavers. When I was growing up, he would get home from work each evening at about half past five and was quickly off with his shoes and socks and into khaki shorts to dig, mow, chop or build – always busy.

◆

So much about our house and yard at Coogee Street was from an era of Australian family life that has vanished. It was all typical for its time and purpose, and full of the practical necessities for a house-hold of the 1920s: the obligatory rainwater tank, a lemon tree, the chooks' yard, and the shed where we cut the lucerne Dad grew and mixed with bran and pollard for their feed. Dad dug holes for kitchen scraps. When one was filled he would cover it with the sand from the next hole, and the pile would soon rot down to ground level. Very little rubbish was put out for collection. Most of the fruit and vegetables for the family were home-grown and the rest was bought in bulk from the markets. Grains came in sacks from the grain merchant. Tins and bottles were few, and plastic unheard of. At the back of the house was an outhouse bathroom and wash-house. The lavatory was a fair walk away at the back fence, where the pan was collected once a week by a nightman who came up the back lane in a horse-drawn cart.

The kitchen door led straight into a wonderful summer-house, built by Dad, with an aviary and trellises for wisteria to scramble on. The memory of that place still fills me with skin-tingling pleasure. It was almost as wide as the house, with a red concrete floor, walls of criss-cross lattice and a high-hip tin roof. Around three sides were dado-height shelves for potplants, and in the centre an old, covered billiard table where many family meals were eaten. I remember Mum ironing out there to avoid the worst of the heat on summer days, standing carefully on a rubber mat so she wouldn't get a shock. Behind the summerhouse was a pergola to support grapevines, sheltering the eastern side from the hot morning sun and making it a cool retreat in Perth's hot summers. Nasturtiums ran riot under the vines, and sometimes we ate their leaves in sandwiches.

By day we would hear the tweeting and chirruping of Mum's birds. The aviaries – one for canaries and one for finches – could be seen through the trellis, and so could the post with three-inch nails all the way up for Peter, the free-roving pink and grey galah, to climb up. Mum had tamed him and taught him to talk – 'Hello Peter, pretty boy, and how are you today?'

When my sister and I were about nine and six, Dad sent us to piano lessons with a teacher who lived just across the road from our primary school. To go to her house we would plod through the thick, loose, black sand of the schoolyard and climb through a post and wire fence. We took to the piano from the beginning and would play for singsongs or perform duets together at family and church gatherings.

Unlike most of the families nearby, we had a car, and there were lots of outings to family and friends, bush and beach. We had also acquired a fretwork and cloth-fronted radio which became a gathering place for neighbours. We would all sit on the lino floor and listen to serials – 'Dad and Dave' with its theme, 'There's a track, winding back to an old-fashioned shack, along the road to Gundagai' was the favourite. Another possession shared with the neighbourhood was a second-hand pushbike which Dad bought for us girls. We learnt to ride with all the kids from round about, taking turns pushing each other from the back of the seat.

I always walked to and from school with the other kids my own age, Florrie from next door and Audrey from over the road. We would 'sing out' to each other from our front gates. After school, we dawdled home stopping to pick and eat 'puddin's', the sweet, juicy, green seedpods of the Guildford weed which grew in tight carpets over the sand. In summer, when the temperature soared over a hundred degrees Fahrenheit, we were let out from school early. On the way home we would burst with our fingers the tar bubbles rising along the edge of the scorching bitumen road.

I love to remember how welcoming the house felt after the hot walk home from school. We would come down the side of the house under the wisteria and along beside shelves of potted ferns, and the lilies planted below, into this cool, quiet place. On really hot days, when Mum had just watered all the plants, there was a delicious cool dampness.

Mount Hawthorn was by-and-large a battlers' suburb. Florrie's father was away from home a lot; he worked as a sustenance labourer on the Canning Dam, which was being built some thirty miles away in the hills. The breadwinner for our other next-door family was a french-polisher who worked from a shed in the backyard. Audrey's dad was a tuck-pointer. Another man in the street was a clerk, and we saw him in his dark, serge suit plodding wearily the half mile to and from the tramstop each morning and evening. One neighbour was sometimes out of work but sometimes delivered milk in the dark morning hours to billies left near the gate. Next to Audrey's house lived a shrivelled woman who seemed one hundred years old to me and on the corner of the street, behind a huge, overgrown hedge, was mysterious, bearded old Mr. Kelly who we seldom saw and half feared.

Us kids, as we called ourselves, were a large part of each other's lives as we played the now old-fashioned games after school: skippy, hoppy, hidey and endless ball games against the best bit of brick wall we could find. A tennis ball was a very personal possession, well marked with our initials in indelible pencil to last at least a season. The games came and went as the weather or fad dictated. Our playthings were simple, portable and cheap: a length of rope for skipping, a piece of chalk to draw hoppy on the now-tarred road, alleys (marbles) in a small drawstring cloth bag. We saved knucklebones from the weekly roast of mutton to play jacks with as we squatted on the verandah floor or the footpath. Our play was left to our own resourcefulness.

There was a girl who lived nearby who was spoken of in lowered tones. She never went to school and it was rare to see her on the street, and then only with her family. When she became an adult she would sometimes wander about alone. I realise now she was a Down's Syndrome child. I have worked with Down's Syndrome parents in recent years and know the special capacity for learning these affectionate children have. It was never suspected fifty years ago and I have often thought of the sad isolation of that girl in our neighbourhood.

Sis and I had an extended family of aunts and uncles, as well as the church community, all woven into our everyday existence.

◆

My mother worked as a clerk in the shipping department of the Foy & Gibson store until her marriage. She always seemed to me to be a quiet, unassuming woman who was born to care for others and did it lovingly and constantly. Her expression and demeanour came from a childhood where she had to 'be seen and not heard'. She met my father through the Congregational Church and it is probably true to say that, when they were getting to know each other and were part of that church family, it was the first time either of them really had fun. They played in a banjo band, joined in singsongs, church concerts and social nights, beach holidays and picnics. There was lots of laughing, and the happiness of belonging in a group of good friends. There are some snapshots of Mum and her sisters at the beach in neck-to-knee bathing costumes or dressed in the Girls' Club uniform of navy-blue tunics with large white sailor collars. There was lots of physical activity. Mum and her sister Maud would sometimes bind their wooden swinging clubs in kerosene-drenched rags and set them alight. At church concerts they would swing great patterned arcs with their clubs blazing away around them in the darkness.

In the 1920s, my grandfather, George Clark, won a lottery. While keeping some land at Keysbrook, he built a house in Coogee Street, just a few minutes walk from where my mother and father later settled. He and Gran and their children lived there as a family, but at some time during the 1930s he built himself a large shed from split logs at the back of that suburban block and moved in. He lived a separate life from then on, the social focus of which was the Mount Hawthorn pub. His main distinction in family memory seems to be that he was often drunk and not well-liked – he had certainly not treated my grandmother well. Family duty prevailed, though. My sister remembers that our mother would walk down the street to rub her father's bad back.

Grandpa Clark was a tall, big-boned man with large hands, hooded eyes and a strong, dark moustache drooping at the ends as I remember him, though he used to wax it to stand out stiff when he was younger. When I was a little girl, he invited me into his shed home on three or four occasions. There was always a sense of conspiracy about these invitations because of his reputation in the family. I wondered whether his awfulness had been exaggerated and really wanted to know for myself what my grandfather was like. I was reluctant to accept the bitterness and anger he had caused as the whole truth about him.

There was a distinct air of order and homeliness about Grandpa's shed. Tanned kangaroo skins lay on the floor of jarrah sleepers, a coloured woollen blanket was spread neatly over his bed and his favourite things were displayed around the room. He especially drew my attention to the rabbit's foot hanging there for good luck. It made me shudder. I thought it sinister and sensed that, although he wanted me to like him, he took some pleasure in my feeling scared and uncertain, even a bit afraid of him. There was a strong smell of pipe tobacco, which he slivered from a hard block with his very sharp pocket knife. And I noticed the glass and open beer bottle on his table.

One day, when I was about twelve years old, he waited for me coming up the street and gave me a gold watch. I took it in confusion and he quickly turned back from the gate as I walked on to our house further up the street. The watch was old and beautiful. His daughters said he'd first given it to his barmaid girlfriend who had returned it when they fell out. I wore this watch every day until I was nearly forty, when I lost it. I still regret its loss – it was a mysterious symbol of a family's sadness and division, still a puzzle to me.

After their family grew up, George and Laura Louise finally parted. She went back to Keysbrook with her youngest son, Frank, to work the land there. My mother's two younger sisters, Maud and Nell, stayed on in the Coogee Street house and were constant figures in our lives when I was growing up. They were working girls with an air of glamour for me and my sister because they were usually dressed up in smart black for work. They also spoiled us. They would curl our hair with pins, rags or tongs and make special treats at Christmas. At lunchtime on Saturdays my sister and I would walk the two blocks to their house, each of us carrying a plate of hot roast dinner for them to have when they got home from the morning's work. Better still, on Tuesday nights, they would come to our house for tea, always bringing a bag of lollies from the Foy & Gibson store where they worked. On Tuesday evenings in summer, Dad would drive all six of us to the wonderful Scarborough beach for a swim and to play on the sand after tea. In winter, we sat around the wood fire talking and embroidering or playing cards (Dad said card games helped us learn our numbers).

When I was eight or nine, I took one of my embroideries to school for 'show'. It was a table-centre of yellow grub-stitched daisies and blue lazy-daisy lupins. My mother had added a crocheted edge, starched and ironed it and tacked it to a backing paper. I remember my teacher sending me around the other rooms to show it off. Such encouragement fuels one's efforts! By the time I was fourteen I was making all my dresses.

When I was nine and Edith was twelve, the family set off to visit Dad's sister Mary and her husband, Sid Atkinson, at Ajana, beyond the northern railhead, four hundred miles from Perth. We were up at three o'clock in the morning and left home at five in the grey Essex car with its button-on celluloid windows and a waterbag hung on the front bumper bar. The car was packed to the limit. We drove all day at forty miles per hour, stopping only for thermos and sandwiches and calls of nature.

Sid had built their house of four small rooms from flattened kerosene tins, lined inside with hessian bagging and roofed with corrugated iron. It was remarkably homely, even though it was so modest and lacking in the services of city living. Mary made us laugh by suggesting we would no doubt like to take a bath, putting the kettle on to boil. That was all the water that might be drawn from the tank for bathing in this arid country, way out on the fringe of the wheat belt.

After a day or two seeing relations at Ajana, trekking around with Mary tending and milking her goats, and gathering hard, round quandong nuts for craft work, we set off for the coast. Sid had borrowed a T-model Ford truck which could do the trip over trackless sandhills. It had very high axles and our luggage was stacked on its long tray and covered with a tarpaulin. A nest was moulded in the top of all this, where my sister and I rode with Tom, a family friend who had his rifle at the ready in case he spotted a kangaroo. His eyes were as sharp as a desert hawk's.

'The Mouth', as the locals call it, is where the Murchison River flows into the Indian Ocean, first widening and lingering in a huge lagoon, stilled by the enclosing reef. It became a popular holiday spot when a sealed bitumen road was built during the Second World War. But in pre-war 1939, we bumped and droned and at times got out and pushed the old truck over the miles of white sand supporting only low brush and scrubby growth on the coastal plain.

At The Mouth, Uncle Sid and Dad erected a large square tent and laid an old carpet square for a floor, and that was headquarters. Sid had built a pontoon of two airtight cylinders topped by a small wooden platform on which Edith and I could float about the lagoon to fish, or just lie and look at coral and creatures in the clear water below us. And we always took the dog.

The adults fished seriously. Aunty Mary's regular dress in the bush was blue denim bib-and-brace overalls – about thirty years ahead of the trend for women! One day, when we were all knee-deep pulling in the lead-line of the fishing net full of herring, Mary fell right into the water. I still smile to recall the sight of her, soaked and laughing. We ate a lot of the catch and smoked the rest to take back to Ajana. On a couple of nights we walked the long curve of the beach to a headland of layers of red rock, pocked by blowholes. Dad and Sid lay flat, faces down, and when the waves receded under the blowholes, grabbed crayfish by the feelers and tossed them back over their shoulders. Later we cooked them in a kerosene tin over a campfire and ate them with hot damper cooked by Sid in a hole dug on the beach and filled with glowing coals.

◆

It was not long after this holiday that we moved into a brick house Mum and Dad had built on the other half of their double block in Coogee Street. The big gum-trees had to go! Dad owned a block of land in the smarter suburb of Nedlands, over near the Swan River, but Mum was too attached to Mount Hawthorn to leave. It was where she felt comfortable and it was near her sisters. Social status was not part of her thinking. We were excited at the move to next-door and Sis and I emptied our money boxes to buy pink and gold satin eiderdowns for our new bedroom, where we had a single bed each. All over again Dad built paths, enclosed the large back veran-dah and built a summerhouse the width of the block for Mum to fill with wondrous ferns and flowering exotics. The clipped lantana and plumbago hedges of the old house were eclipsed in this new garden, as Dad became a rosarian. Bush roses were mass-bedded, polyan-thus made the borders, and climbing roses were trained on trellises and fences. Rose names became part of our vocabulary – Ophelia and later the new rose, Peace, were favourites. There was a huge, flat lawn at the back to play on and a curved wall on the front veran-dah where for years to come all the family photos were taken in the afternoon sun.

◆

Until I was about fifteen years old, we spent many weekends, and all the school holidays at Keysbrook where Mum's younger brother Frank and his mother had gone back to work the family's sixty-acre farm. They grew potatoes and peas and ran a small dairy herd, milking about twenty jerseys. My grandmother must have been in her seventies as I remember her best. She always took care of her appearance. She curled her long hair each night on two long, crinkled pins that clipped shut, and each morning brushed it out and wound it into a soft top-knot. She often wore pearl earrings, and pinned a brooch with the blue-and-white colours of her dead son George's regiment on whatever she was wearing, even on her black, Fuji cotton work dresses. George had fought in the battle of the Somme in 1917 and was presumed killed in action in that ghastly debacle where so many Anzacs died in the muddy fields of France. He was her much-loved, first-born son. One of my mother's saddest memories is of standing on Fremantle wharf on her twenty-first birthday, waving goodbye to George as he sailed away in a troopship. It was the last time she saw him.

When we visited Keysbrook, Dad used to help Frank with ploughing and other tasks while Mum helped my grandmother in the house with cooking and cleaning. We kids were given lesser chores, like collecting freshly dug potatoes from mounds of red crumbly loam, or picking and bagging peas then holding the sacktops while the grown-ups sewed them up with huge curved needles and coarse Bind-O-Twine. One of our jobs was to take morning and afternoon tea to Frank and anyone else who might be working with him. We carried a big, scalding hot billy of tea – on a stick between us if it was a really big one – and a basket of fresh-baked scones or cakes from the woodstove, wrapped in a tea towel to keep warm. Sis and I would sit with the men in the corner of a paddock, or on the edge of a plough furrow of freshly turned earth. I loved the sound of their soft voices as they yarned on. Mickey, the stolid, white plough horse welcomed the break and could be reluctant to start work again. That was when Frank called upon some farmer's language! Sis and I would stay on, playing on the banks of the creek.

Frank had trained as a motor mechanic in his Mount Hawthorn days and had pieced together a peculiar old Whippet truck with a corrugated iron roof – rather like a shed on wheels. It made a terrible noise. We sometimes went with him while he drove the four winding miles through the hills, down to the township of Keysbrook. The town consisted of a railway siding with a loading platform and small signal shed, a weatherboard hall for functions, a one-room wooden school house and a general store attached to the storekeeper's house. There Frank would pick up provisions, newspapers and mail. The reading matter I recall was *News of the World*, the pink-paged *Bulletin* and the local newspapers. When the mail was expected to include cheques in payment for produce sent to the metropolitan markets, there was sometimes anxiety. If there had been a glut, prices would drop to just about what it cost to get the crop there, or less. At such times the grown-ups would mutter and shake their heads.

When I was a little older Sis and I loved fetching the cows from the paddocks to bring them to the milking shed and, later still, I would help with the milking. We carried hay to the chaffcutter, measured the buckets of feed into the bale boxes, then slipped the wooden rails across the cows' necks to hold them while they were milked. I felt very important being a milker, and especially enjoyed the sensual pleasure of sitting on the small wooden stool, resting my head against the warm, soft belly of the cow, and squirting two warm jets of creamy milk into the bucket. Then a brisk slap on her haunch to 'be off', to make way for the next cow. But I wasn't allowed to milk Rosie, she was a real kicker. When we finished, the men would carry the cans of milk down through a long wisteria-clad pergola built of tree-trunks to the summerhouse.

Wherever there was a branch of the Clark family there was a summerhouse. They were an extension of the house and the coolest place to be in summertime. The Keysbrook summerhouse was a beauty. It had a gravel floor and was built of young saplings set vertically for the walls and meeting in a peak for the high roof. There were sapling rails round the three sides, for sitting on, and in the centre a long narrow table and stools, all made from rough timber and unpainted. On each side of the wide doorway-without-a-door there was a wooden barrel lying on its side and lined with an old bag, where the two farm dogs, Paddy and Mut, slept and were fed. And of course this whole huge summerhouse was covered with the inevitable wisteria. But I didn't like the hornets which buzzed around and made their mud nests on the rails: they made a mean noise, and could sting.

We took turns working the separator by hand to extract the butterfat from the milk. Then both were put into large metal cans and placed at the farm gate where Dumpsy the carrier picked them up on his rounds of small farms, and took them to the railway siding. Once every few days some butterfat was kept aside and Gran or Mum churned it by hand until it was the right consistency to shape between two wooden butter-pats, and was ready for the table or for storing in the wet, hessian cool-safe.

Over the fifteen years of visits to Keysbrook, I absorbed the beauty, the sounds and smells, the feelings, of the bush. In the early years we would go for long walks with our mother. Bush knowledge from her own childhood became ours. She knew where to find many different wildflower species, and how they could become a resource of interest and activity. She also used to paint wildflowers onto fretworked wooden plant holders and trays. Sometimes on a bush walk we would make flower baskets. The pliable yet brittle spikes of the blackboy plant formed the spokes of the frame. We bound them with the sticky thread of the rainbow plant, and wove up the spokes, leaving some longer to make a handle. Then we'd fill these baskets with wildflowers and take them home for presents. We found the flowers of spider orchids, donkey orchids, bird orchids, enamel orchids, kangaroo paws, wattles and myrtles, and many more. Sometimes, when Dad was due to drive up on a Friday night, we wove from flowers and leaves a huge word WELCOME into the big wire gate.

Logging had stopped long ago, up in the hills above Keysbrook, where George Clark had worked, and the loggers' cottages had fallen into ruins. One day, Mum and Sis and I walked up there to lift some lily bulbs for Gran's garden. Some lonely wife had made an English garden in that wild place. As Mum lifted the long, withering lily leaves to find the place to dig, there, within touching distance was a huge, coiled, snake – an absolute whopper. I remember the fear, as we three fled, leaving pick and shovel and all thoughts of lily bulbs behind. It was an unusual thing for us – to feel fear in what we thought of as a friendly place, our bush, which we loved so much.

We lay on our tummies on the warm, flat, grey rocks, and watched tiny lizards darting around. We swam and caught jilgies (our word for yabbies) in the creeks, and fished for tadpoles in the dam. We kept them in jars and watched as their legs grew and they turned into frogs. Almost every day we saw gentle-faced, harmless kangaroos.

We also roamed the bush with the itinerant woodcutters. They came to fell jarrah trees for railway sleepers. First they would select a large tree with good straight grain, then make a scarf cut with broadaxes, taking turns at the hard chopping. Then two men would push-pull a huge cross-cut saw. We were well trained to stand back as the saw cut neared the wedge of the axe cut. The men would yell, 'TIM-BER,' and the giant tree would creak then gather speed and crash down with a great wallop. Then there was the strong, pungent smell of sap, the tree's lifeblood, and of eucalyptus from the crushed leaves and branches of the doomed tree. It made a labyrinth of branches on the bush floor where we could play for days or weeks. In those days it never occurred to us to worry about felling those majestic trees.

Christmas was always spent at Keysbrook and numbers swelled to perhaps twenty-five, until the house was bursting. A regular addition to the gatherings at Christmas, and sometimes for lengthy stays in between, was George Clark's old friend Mick Frawley. By now he was one of Western Australia's last surviving bullock drivers. He still had a colourful bullocky's vocabulary, learned from a lifetime of threatening the teams of beasts as they hauled their loads of great tree logs over rough bush tracks.

Christmas dinner preparations were intense – cake baking and icing, killing and plucking chooks. 'Don't miss his liver and lights,' Gran would remind us as we pulled out the warm innards. We gathered Christmas bush for decoration, and hung paper streamers. In the warm evenings we sometimes ate at a trestle table out under the huge fig trees, and everyone fell to yarning as we sat over the remnants of the long-finished meal.

Then the night, lying there with my sister, sometimes with

Mum in the middle of the big bed, sometimes top and tail if there were others staying. We listened for the call of the mopoke and pondered the mystery of what might be in the dark space under the hip of the iron roof above us. We looked at adult shapes through the thin cretonne curtains which hung on rods in the doorways. We fell asleep to the rise and fall of quiet voices and the dancing shadows from the kerosene lamps.

GROWING UP

◇

I was ten when the Second World War began. The sense of my father's foreboding as war seemed inevitable is still clear. We had driven down from Keysbrook that night and Dad rushed to the radio to hear prime minister Menzies announce that Australia was at war. In all those war years, we never missed a newscast. The family fell silent as soon as the fanfare, London's Big Ben striking the hour and the solemn announcement came on the radio: 'This is the BBC News.'

At first it was rather an interesting game at school, as my teacher moved coloured flags around a map of Europe and kept us in a state of patriotic fervour. I found most things Mr. Cook did fascinating; he was tall with blonde hair slicked back in the fashion of the day and china-blue eyes, and he was amusing – an eleven-year-old girl's dream. It was my first case of secret puppy-love. When the Japanese bombed Darwin we were prepared for air-raids, which included sticking black paper over all the windows, digging trenches in the heavy sand of the schoolyard and practising running to them in an orderly manner equipped with small, black rubber plugs. They were to put in our mouths when the bombs came, to prevent us biting our tongues from shock. Fortunately, bombs never fell on Perth.

By 1941 I was due to go to the city school but we were kept on in a make-do fashion in suburban school accommodation because of the war. The war news really depressed me now, as I heard the family talk and the radio news, and saw horror stories in the newspapers. I had a recurring nightmare about some sailors who were torpedoed in the Indian Ocean and had to struggle through oily seas to rafts, only to be attacked by sharks leaping at their buttocks and limbs as they drifted starving for days in hope of rescue. The day Dad went for his medical was just awful, as we feared he may have to go to the war, but he was rejected from military service because he was not suitably fit and instead was 'manpowered'. That meant he had to put his business on hold and work in the Munitions Department as an auditor.

We knitted socks and balaclavas for soldiers, sent food parcels overseas and generally worked hard in support of the war effort. We also knitted for ourselves, even dresses, since clothing – and some foods such as tea, butter and sugar – were rationed on a coupon system. We made blouses and underwear from reject parachute silk. The frugality which had been normal family practice became, in wartime, an art form.

Of course there was no television then and we were not a family of readers (except Sis, who stole time for this world of her own, chuckling or crying to herself in a way which made me a bit envious). Dad did get *National Geographic* magazines but I only looked at the pictures. After tea, our evening meal which was never served later than six o'clock, we spent the long evenings sitting around the radio, with wood fires in winter. On Sunday nights relatives who didn't have a wireless came for tea and, along with most of the rest of Australia, we'd listen to the Lux Radio Play. The girls and women always sewed and knitted as we listened. Dad often slipped out to 'do his books' on the kitchen table: auditing work for charity or for extra income. We were raised to be useful and no idleness was countenanced.

As the war dragged on and on, Mum and Sis and I continued with the work that women did on the home front. We made beds in Perth hostels for servicemen on leave and waited on tables in their canteens. Remembering how easy it was to set tables incorrectly or forget orders, I've had respect for good table service ever since. But our favourite war effort was ballroom dancing. Dances for servicemen were held in a hall with a fine floor and a piano was played, with a great swing, by another home-front volunteer. Mum and Dad encouraged us to ask the lonely men to our house and Sis, being the older sister, took the initiative. We had many meals and singsongs at home with other girls from the church and English sailors and submariners, or Aussie soldiers from the eastern states on leave. Our freedom seemed without limit.

For most of the war I was at school. In my last year of primary school when I was eleven, my teacher, the assistant headmaster Mr. Marshall, had been something of a mentor to me. He was a craggy-faced disciplinarian with a booming voice and a quick temper. When he caned bad boys it made me cringe. There were sixty-three children in the class, three of whom had what we would now unashamedly recognise as intellectual disabilities. Then, such children got no special help but were just lumped in with the majority and regarded as recalcitrant or pathetic – either way, a nuisance.

It is not surprising that I remember the exasperated behaviour of some teachers with horror. I have, for instance, detailed and emotional recall of a boy in an infants' class – the teacher was yelling at him to stand up, as he desperately tried to read but was stuck on the word 'the'. He dribbled and cried and battled against incontinence, bleating 'the, the, the', mimicking the teacher, without any comprehension, until she screamed at him to leave the room. The rest of us squirmed and held back tears and wished we weren't there. Witnessing canings in more senior classes was almost as bad; I could not cope with violence at all. At home even a banged door or a voice raised in anger was frowned on.

Mr. Marshall did not make pets of his students but I always felt that he liked me and would be pleased to see me develop my abilities. He took an interest in my drawing, though it didn't really show any boldness or creativity, and he would talk to me about my music and ask me to play for singing and marches at school assemblies. He encouraged me strongly to sit for the scholarship which would admit me to Perth Modern School, the one government secondary school for which enrolment was drawn entirely from scholarship winners or those who passed an entrance exam available at all the state's primary schools. Perth Modern offered special preparation for going on to university. But no one amongst my family and friends could really see the point. They expected that I would go to work until I married and lived happily ever after in the traditional role. One evening I overheard some neighbourhood women, gathered for a talk around a front gate at dusk, discussing my prowess at school and my opportunities to go on with my education. A phrase stuck in my mind: 'But she might grow away from us.' I didn't have the courage or independence to question that.

I wanted to broaden my experience but there was no one in my world who could guide me, at the age of eleven, to other possibilities. Except my dear Mr. Marshall, the teacher who tried. Perhaps if he had given me ideas of a career it would have focused my thinking, but his urging was in such general terms about just going on with study, perhaps to university, which seemed such a foreign world to me, that it left me confused. I didn't even know anyone who had aspired to, let alone attended, university.

As soon as the competitive element entered schoolwork when I was ten I always topped the class. At the age of twelve I went out as dux of one of the largest suburban schools, Mount Hawthorn Primary State School, to Perth Central Girls' School, which offered more of the same subjects plus shorthand, typing and bookkeeping. My friend, Joy from down the street, and I rode our pushbikes the three miles each way together, thus cementing our relationship as best friends for many years to come. I remember the three years spent there as just something I went through, all rather ordinary. I played piano for school assemblies or for anything else that came up, played some tennis but never competitively, had comfortable friends but no emotional ones (like some girls do in adolescence) and no boyfriends. When I was twelve a local boy rode his pushbike alongside me and said, 'I love you, that's what.' I was secretly pleased but in my confusion didn't answer him, only pedalled more furiously. I topped each class I was in, and was dux of the school in my final year. My prize was a gilt-embellished volume of Shakespeare's works – way beyond my reading aspirations – and much patting on the head from teachers and family.

Music was one thing in my life that was important to me and I put a lot into it. My mother commented that she never, over all the years of my childhood, needed to ask me to practice. Dad had bought a new piano – a Thürmer – and found a new piano teacher for Sis and me, Richard Bastian. He was different from anyone I had ever known, a gentle, cultivated man whose life was music – and concern for his family and how to pay the mortgage! He came to our house twice a week in his small motor car, taking the corners on two wheels – the only aspect of his behaviour which could pass as 'dashing', except that I think it was probably because he didn't know how to change gears, not being mechanically minded. Mr. Bastian demanded disciplined work and twice-yearly examinations from me, one with the Australian Music Board and one with the Trinity College of Music, London. On exam days, one in the spring and one in autumn, Mum would take me on the tram to Perth then on the trolley bus round the river to the university. It was a special occasion, a half day off school, and I would wear my best dress. Fifty years on, I can still see the dress and hat my tall, slim mother wore to most exams. It was pale blue, with navy-blue spots, cut straight and longish with a low-slung belt. The hat was navy-blue with a pale blue flower. She had these clothes from the time of her marriage. While I was with the examiners, A. J. Leckie for the Australian Music Board and Doctor Edgar Ford, out from Trinity College in his wing collar and spats, Mum would sit on a chair outside the room. On the way home I would give her a note-by-note description and tell her about the examiners' comments.

Then, when I was fifteen years old, my school days were over. Regret about this always nagged at me. Sometimes I would ride my bicycle around the campus of the University of Western Australia coveting, in some vague and uninformed way, the educational experience. I am embarrassed to recall how, later, I courted attention from a regular figure at a beach where we holidayed – he was very handsome, but he was also a university student, and that was desirable to me.

Sometimes it seemed the war would never end. I suffered from nightmares and prayed fervently that the goodies would win. I was sixteen when Japan's surrender meant the war was over. The news reached us at a dance for Pommy sailors; I was wearing a much-admired, green lacy-patterned dress I had knitted and a sailor had just told me I had 'wise eyes' as we danced the slow, rhythmic modern waltz – funny the things one remembers. There's no doubt that wartime had its glamorous side, and stirred the juices of young womanhood. Despite the innocence of the times, and the even greater innocence of Sis and me, I wonder how we got through the war years without mishap. But now it was over. Perth went as crazy as Perth could go. My sister and I joined in dancing and singing *Auld Lang Syne* in ever-changing circles of excited people in the streets. Strangers hugged and kissed.

After I left school, I began working as a shorthand-typist-bookkeeper with a small electrical engineering firm, where I stayed until 1953. Eleven years! Looking back I find it extraordinary that I stayed so long in such a job. But my life seemed already satisfactory. What more did I want? We were not taught to push, or to reach out, but rather to do our best wherever we were.

My job somehow suited my concept of the virtue of accepting modest situations. In fact, the premises were less than modest, they were positively sub-standard: old, dingy and with no decent facilities. Rats were a problem in the early years. That building would not pass today's workplace requirements by a mile. There were about fourteen staff members, all male skilled tradesmen and apprentices with the exception of myself and a senior office-girl. There were, however, freedoms and flexibilities that were possible in a firm that was run like a family. And we had fun. When the senior girl left to get married, the boss's cousin came as accountant. He was a man for whom I grew to have a deep affection. He'd fought with the AIF in the Crete campaign and then in Papua New Guinea, and suffered from the ravages of malaria and nervousness as a result of his terrible war experiences. Over our years of working together, I learned a great deal from our friendship. He was the first adult man I got to know on my own terms, who treated me as a colleague rather than a child.

During the war, the firm serviced corvettes at the naval base in Fremantle. There was a lot of overtime and some drama, especially when ships had to be turned around urgently. These ships of the British, American and Australian navies were in the Indian Ocean war zone. We all felt patriotic about our work. After the war some returned servicemen joined the staff. One of them haunted me. He had been a prisoner of the Japanese in Burma – a very tall, big-boned man whose ordeal had reduced him to just a few stone. I watched him slowly return to health and strength. My responsibilities in the firm grew, and although I don't regret the experience of those years, should I have reached out? Yes, of course I should have.

But my life was crowded with other interests and activities: church events and meetings, teaching, running the Girls' Club, playing the organ and my involvement in the activities of the state Congregational Youth Fellowship all took a lot of time. I trained to be a National Fitness leader and kept on in bursts with piano practice and music. When I passed my associate diploma (my 'letters' as they were referred to with due respect), Mum gave me a damask linen tablecloth and napkin set which she had paid off in sixpenny instalments collected by the insurance man who called at the back door each week. It was to save for my Glory Box. I played tennis on Saturday afternoons, drafted patterns and made my own clothes. I loved to go ballroom dancing. A bunch of us, boys and girls, went on long bike rides and picnics at weekends. Sometimes we would take the train up bush somewhere for long walks and barbecues. I was never, ever, bored and that has remained true all my life.

◆

An annual event in church life for teenagers was the Easter Camp. In those years they were held in a small guesthouse in the beautiful hills of Roleystone, about eighteen miles south-west of Perth. Walks in the hills, swimming in the creeks, tennis, and the general sense of the church family being on holidays was a new and wonderful experience for me.

It was at one of these camps that I first noticed Bob Hawke. I had been aware of him since we were nine years old when his mother had directed a Church play. I was Esther, dressed – I remember so vividly – in a long, pink satin gown trimmed with silver braid appropriate for a princess of the court, made by my mother for the occasion. Bob played a servant and the part involved carrying a tray of glasses. At rehearsals he would shake the tray, making the glasses rattle and drowning out the other players' words, to the utter distraction of his mother. He found it very satisfactory! Even then he could induce exasperation in his mother, but everyone understood that she really thought he was rather funny and that she enjoyed his pranks. I thought it all rather amusing.

In the Easter of 1948, when Bob and I were both eighteen, Ellie Hawke was a Camp Mother. The assembled teenagers were appalled to see her at breakfast on the first morning, quite openly selecting the best apple on the plate 'for Bob', who would arrive later. My reaction was to feel sorry for him having to deal with the ridicule this kind of treatment gave rise to among his peers behind his back. He was rather aloof during the few days of that camp, as if he regarded himself as different from everyone else, and he seemed to disregard the effect his aloofness produced. Many found his manner quite offensive, but not me. I accepted, even rather liked, that he was, in fact, different. After all, he was a son of the much-respected clergy and a university student. He was the only one amongst us who had won a scholarship. Now he was studying law, and he had a motorbike – very glamorous stuff!

My fascination with him was increased by a dramatic tragedy we all knew about, the death a decade before of the Hawke's only other child, Bob's older brother, John Neil. At the age of eighteen Neil caught encephalitis while swimming and died, after terrible suffering. He had been a good scholar throughout his school years and had been dux of the prestigious King's College in Adelaide. There was a nine-year age difference between the two boys and, as the family lived in the country while Neil was growing up, he went away to board at the school in Adelaide. No doubt there were special financial arrangements made for sons of the clergy. I was curious about this brother, remembered with almost reverence by his parents. I realised that Bob had hardly any opportunity to get to know him. Some of the Hawke family remember that Neil was the focus of Ellie's affections and hopes. Bob was his father's boy.

In 1947 Bob had been thrown from his motorbike and was on the critically-ill list at Perth Public Hospital for several days. After an operation for abdominal repairs and the removal of his spleen, it was clear he would survive and survive well. That he 'had been spared' was the religious interpretation. Bob had been close to death at exactly the same age at which his brother Neil had died, and it jolted him out of an offhand, playful approach to study into a determination to excel at university and equip himself for excellence in the rest of his life. All these things contributed to the feeling I had that here was someone very special.

I was also attracted to what I saw! I liked Bob's skin, tending to swarthy, his eyes were a good deep blue, his hair was luxuriously thick, dark brown and wavy. I always noticed hands, and I liked his hands very much – smallish, with the fine fingers I associated with an aesthete, but strong and taut in the way that he used them. Although he was five feet ten and a half inches tall, the impression was of a shorter man, perhaps because posture was not his strong point (I wondered whether it was due to the abdominal injury and surgery after his accident). I also liked the smell of him. He thought it was amusing when I wrote this in a letter to him once – that I looked forward to smelling him again – but for me it was a pleasing part of his close presence.

Our courtship began some time after that Easter camp. Bob had told his mother that he would like to take out one of the Mount Hawthorn girls and from a list of three names she suggested, he chose mine. There is a note in my diary, 'Mrs Hawke phoned me at Harrison's [our neighbour with a telephone]. Then Bob Hawke asked me out – we went to Araluen.' I went out with him that Sunday afternoon, riding pillion on his salvaged Panther motorbike. We launched headlong into what we both quickly recognised as a serious affair. Bob became demanding of my time in a way that surprised me. But I liked it and found it flattering, even though some of my own interests suffered, notably music lessons and practice. In fact, I was overwhelmed with what was happening to me.

When we began 'going together' it became our habit to go to one or the other of our families for tea on Sunday evenings and then on to church. The Hawkes lived in West Leederville near Lake Monger, a suburb a little up the status scale from Mount Hawthorn. Theirs was a solid, brick and tile house and Ellie Hawke took much pride in it. Although their limited finances meant it was modest, there was an air of comfort and gentility about it. One room, at the front of the house, served as a study for Clem Hawke, and Bob's bedroom was a closed-in section of the back verandah – a space just big enough to fit a single bed, a small wardrobe, a bookshelf and a side-table placed under the louvred window where he could study. He liked this room; it gave him a bit of separation from the rest of the house and his parents.

I already knew Bob's mother and father from the church and was aware that they were highly respected members of the community. They knew me too, of course, but meeting them as a possible future daughter-in-law was a different matter indeed. I felt a little overawed by the Hawke household when I began going there with Bob, partly because of my family's view of the clergy as somehow apart from ordinary people. Also, Uncle Albert, Clem Hawke's brother and an intimate of the family, was a senior minister in the state parliament, an institution beyond my ken. It was all rather new for me: was I getting a bit too uppity?

Ellie Hawke had a reputation for doing things properly and she would pursue any discussion vigorously. She was not a tall woman, but sturdy, with intense, focused eyes – they were kind eyes, too, china blue – and a way of walking that conveyed her sense of purpose. She had been president of the Women's Christian Temperance Union, which preached the evils of alcohol. Some people found her readiness to speak her mind uncomfortable, but she was overwhelmingly welcoming to me.

Edith Emily (née Lee), fondly called Ellie, was a woman

ahead of her time. A South-Australian-trained primary school teacher, she was frustrated at not being able to pursue further education because of the demands of marriage and family. She tried to redress this by beginning a part-time arts degree at the University of Western Australia in the 1950s, when she was in her fifties, but had to give it up when the workload became impossible. She was working full-time as a teacher as well as keeping boarders for extra money to help with Bob's university expenses. She also gave a lot of time to her duties in Clem's church and the pastoral work it involved.

I could see that Ellie and Bob were very much alike in temperament and character. She was a woman of formidable energy and application. Their minds worked the same way and they brought a similar intensity and thoroughness to whatever they did. Their vitality, love of games (bridge and croquet for Ellie) and the will to win were the same in each of them. But it was obvious to me that Bob was exploring the values of his own generation. I later came to realise that he was typical of a new generation of manse breakaways.

I was flattered by Ellie's attention, as she admired my womanly skills – music, sewing and homemaking. She also approved of my participation in sport. She had longed for a daughter and, as Clem, Bob and Albert were the only close family she had in Perth, she looked for friendship and confidences with other women. She was the first outside my own family who gave me a sense of how women can support each other – the solidarity of women. Perhaps above all, Ellie approved of the fact that I was in the Church Youth Fellowship with Bob. I was safe.

The Reverend Clem Hawke was a quietly spoken man who went about his ministry in a gentle, thoughtful way. He had none of the drive which characterised his wife. He was tall, lean and pale of visage. His strength was in his clarity of thinking and his philosophy. Yet in photographs, I saw that he had been a passionate-looking young man – passion which I believe was largely suppressed in the quiet and disciplined life of the cleric. He was always kindly and correct in his manner towards me but never, in those early days, made me feel anything but another parishioner. Albert Hawke was always courtly and jovial, almost affectionate, and more relaxed in his manner with me. He was a born politician, always 'working the crowd'.

The Hawke men had a way of behaving together – a sort of bonding ritual typical of many Australian men. They had a pattern of good-natured banter, mostly about sport and politics, always agreeing with each other in high good humour. It can be funny, even endearing, behaviour to witness. But it has a clubby feeling about it – it is a men's game, while women are the observers – and even Ellie was not one of the Hawke Men's Club. She would show quiet amusement sometimes, or even comment good naturedly, 'Oh, you boys!' More often she would withdraw and busy herself. She and I talked about our feelings of exclusion years later. She allowed herself to express some mild hurt, while apparently (but not convincingly to me) accepting the men's prerogative to behave that way. I found it ill-mannered but tolerated it, just as she did.

I remember, early on in our relationship, Bob and I arrived one Sunday evening to be greeted in the Hawkes' driveway by Clem and Uncle Albert. I think Bob had been playing cricket. On that Sunday they went to great lengths to make much of Bob, competing in their compliments, jostling, apparently, to see who could please him most. 'You beauty Bob, you killed 'em Bob.' They had eyes only for him. I knew at once it was a game I did not want to play.

My mother and father had accustomed me to an atmosphere of quiet acknowledgment and encouragement. It was only a different approach, but it made me baulk at the effusiveness of the Hawkes. I felt somehow mean at my own reaction, but thought, 'Why do they carry on like this?' I had never seen anything like it.

That was my first taste of unease at being outside a closed circle of congratulation reserved for men, something I saw more of in later years. But my family training in dealing with achievement stood me in good stead. When I badly needed encouragement and approval as a young wife and mother, I could survive without it, though I wished for it. Bob needs acknowledgment and is game enough to make it known, clearly and unashamedly, that he does. In the years when his career was forging ahead I praised his achievements often, but my manner was not demonstrative and I felt, perhaps mistakenly, that I was judged for not applauding him as much as others did. I admired him so very much in so many ways, and his jovial prompting of praise could be endearing. I have learned a lot since those days: even how to prompt a praising remark for myself if I really need it.

But all that was a long way in the future for me when I first sat around the Hawke dinner table listening to the lively talk of sport, politics or church affairs. There I missed the easy, personal exchanges about the work-a-day world, and the people in it, that I was used to at home and that kept us in touch with each other as individuals, knowing each other's work and friends. I would have liked a combination of the two – in both houses.

Despite the attractions of the Hawke family, I kept some distance, even from Ellie. Bob was on the course all spirited youth takes of establishing a life independent of parents, and my loyalty was unquestioningly with him.

My mother's family just before her brother George sailed to the First World War in 1917. Standing: Frank, Maud, George, Edith (my mother), Nell. Seated: Dot, George Clark, Laura Louise Clark (Beamer).

William Masterson, my father's father, as I remember him. He died in 1936 when I was seven.

My father, Jim Masterson, about the
time my parents were married

My mother, Edith Laura Clark, before
she married Dad

Coogee Street, 1925. Mum and Dad's house, before Dad painted the roof red, is on the
right – and the beginning of Mr. Kelly's hedge.

Me and Sis with my ma-ma doll and the furniture Dad made, and painted bright blue, for our cubby

Uncle Frank, with an armful, at Keysbrook:
Sis, cousin John (Dot's son) and me

Our second house in Coogee Street, built in 1939. Dad's Rugby car
and Uncle Sid's van are parked outside; our first house is behind them.

Sisters, 1941. I am twelve, wearing a dress made
by Mum; Sis is sixteen and wearing her first
shop-made dress.

Dad, Mum, Sis and me, in December 1944, during the war

Me, aged sixteen

Me, in 1947. Saturday afternoon tennis

At Easter Camp, 1949. The caption in my
photo album is 'My mate and I'.

Easter Camp, 1949

1950, at the Hawkes', where I was one of the family by now. The three girls were Ellie's boarders. Standing: Bob, me, Ellie, Shirley, Clem. Seated: Mary and Barbara with the young man who was the church organist.

Bob and me in January 1953, at the Congregational Youth Fellowship national conference at Morialta, South Australia

'HOW WILL HE SUPPORT MY DAUGHTER?'

◇

The years of our courtship were heady indeed. Our first big date was to attend the Law Ball at the university, a grand occasion involving a dinner suit for Bob and an evening dress for me. I wore an off-the-shoulder dress, white with rosebuds, that I had made to wear at my sister Edith's twenty-first birthday party. Bob brought me the then customary corsage of flowers and presented it to me sweetly. I was touched, even though I knew Ellie had made it and sent it.

The ball was my first introduction to Bob's university friends. I remember meeting Alan Barblett (now Deputy Chief Justice of the Family Court of Australia) and John Toohey (now a High Court judge) for the first time. When we meet now, we can talk of children and grandchildren.

I played tennis on Saturdays while Bob played cricket; we went to movies together (war films, musicals, mysteries and soppy love stories), and we went to the surf beaches to swim and walk and be alone in the sandhills. As our desire to be together increased we shared more of what we had done before separately. I would go to the Hawkes' for dinner and afterwards sit with him and his cat, Boof, while he studied. He would come to church where I was playing the organ.

Early in 1950, in the lounge room at Coogee Street, Bob asked me to marry him. It was something I had been expecting and waiting for yet when the time came I stalled, surprising myself as I asked him to let me think about it. For the next day or two it was never out of my mind. How much I wanted to marry him! Yet I was afraid that I would not be adequate. I knew life with him would not be ordinary. Years later, in a bitter exchange, Bob held me to blame for how hurtful it had been to him, and then I felt stupid for not having explained myself properly.

Throughout Bob's years at university there were many times when I had glimpses of his life there, but always as an outsider. I was not one of the blessed. One night when we were in my father's car saying goodnight – we had long, long 'good nights' and, like many young couples of our generation, the car was one of the few private places we had to share thoughts, and bodies – I confessed my feelings of inadequacy because I was not 'at uni'. 'But,' Bob said, 'if you were, I wouldn't marry you.' I was taken aback. I had thought marriage was about passion which transcended such considerations. It was an indication of his expectations of the role I would play in our partnership. I was not articulate enough to discuss it with him and, anyway, I felt our love was strong, and we didn't think in terms of roles in those days.

We spent time working together on church youth affairs and at university events, especially once Bob was president of the Students Representative Council. The SRC provided Bob with a forum for hitting his political straps. The cut and thrust, even though it was at an adolescent (in retrospect one might even say infantile!) level, was relished by the participants. For me, it was a first look at the political game. Bob and Terry (Jules) Zanetti, the editor of the student magazine *Pelican*, became a roistering duo in the heady pursuit of student politics of the left. For a period Bob was chairman of the Western Australian Congregational Youth Fellowship and I was the state secretary – the organisation was flourishing, the numbers up and the spirit high.

In 1952, we had a wondrous two weeks holidaying with family friends of the Hawkes, farmers on the York Peninsular in South Australia where Clem had served as a pastor. On another occasion we did a week's trip on the motorbike to the south-west of Western Australia, staying each night in a different town with friends or relatives. We fished and walked, ran over a snake on the road and one day had the excitement of having to speed dangerously over a corrugated gravel track because two crazy dogs were snapping at us – through a brushfire.

All this time Bob was studying while I was working. In church circles we were regarded, it has been said, as the Golden Couple. We felt a bit special ourselves – but that is true of most couples who are in love, making plans and looking forward eagerly through rose-coloured glasses to their glorious future. We *were* popular, though, and enjoyed it. Our families approved of our engagement, even if my father was a little wary about Bob. Dad had such a low-key manner himself that he had found it difficult to accept Bob's readiness to project himself – his flamboyance, as Dad saw it. My mother told me that she found Bob detached, unlike the young people she was used to having around the place, who were ready to enter into the life of our household. She said that if Bob had to wait for me to dress, or finish a task before we went out, he would pick up a newspaper and read. It made her, and me, uncomfortable. But the only time I heard my mother express real doubts about Bob, was when I told her I was planning to fly east to join him for a second holiday on the York Peninsular. She commented that it was time he settled down instead of doing all this running around. She knew that I would draw from my savings for the airfare and thought it indulgent on my part. I did, and I went.

One way and another Bob and I had some very good times. We were just bowling along on top of the world!

◆

When I reached young-womanhood, I knew very little about sex and reproduction. I had been later to menstruate than most classmates and was treated as an outsider by this special club of girls who felt womanhood and its implications dawning. Luckily, when I was thirteen our teacher, Miss Valerie Fitzell, gave us a sex-education lesson one afternoon in our all-girl class. This was not the done thing in 1941, and I had the feeling as she launched into this discussion instead of a scheduled lesson, that she was thinking, 'Damn it, I will.' Miss Fitzell was that kind of person and we girls adored her. She drew diagrams on the blackboard of male and female reproductive systems, of sperm swimming to the ovum, all a new discovery to me. I was excited by these revelations but still did not really understand what *happened*, or, more importantly, the physical and emotional complexity of relationships between men and women. My mother, in response to an awkward question from me later, began by asking, 'Well, do you know how a man's body is made?' I muttered yes, but didn't really know, as we'd never been around boys, and modesty prevailed at home.

When Bob and I began to go out together (we were eighteen) it was quickly clear that the physical attraction was very strong for both of us – the chemistry was right. It was inevitable that we would not simply keep company and hold hands for long.

I knew I needed more information. One day I went to the book section in a department store and blushed furiously as I bought a book about sex and marriage. In my ignorance and embarrassment, I chose badly. So knowledge was still meagre, and it was a case of experimentation, of trial and error. And we made a catastrophic error. While Bob was away in Melbourne as a delegate to a National Union of Australian University Students conference I became aware that I was pregnant.

In today's society an unwanted pregnancy is a dilemma but in 1952 it was something very difficult indeed to deal with. Even the word 'pregnant' came awkwardly to the tongue, and was usually described as being 'in the family way' or simply 'having a baby', or 'you know … fallen in' (terrible term!). The morals of the day dictated that abortion was wrong, full stop. Abortion was illegal, full stop. There were no sources of counselling or information that I knew about. I don't think I would have known then what counselling was. I felt alone and unable to talk to anyone. I was desperate for Bob's return to Perth.

I felt no guilt or moral shame. We were engaged and in love, committed to each other for ever. We had used contraceptives which proved unreliable. We were in robust good health and our sexual love was an integral part of our relationship. After all, hadn't God given us these wondrous bodies?

Why weren't we married? In 1951 Bob had applied for a Rhodes scholarship which would enable him to study at Oxford, an opportunity beyond his family's means if not their dreams. The prestige of a Rhodes stayed with its winners for life. When he did not win, the disappointment had been intense. Bob's whole focus, as well as his mother's and father's, had been set on it, so he planned to apply again in 1952. But Rhodes scholars in the 1950s were required to be male and single. Apparently to be female or to be distracted by females was not permissible! So, to marry at that time would have altered Bob's hoped-for course in life, and had a disastrous effect on us and his family.

During my childhood I had witnessed the social alienation suffered by a friend of my mother's who had borne a child out of wedlock. That her lover had been killed at the First World War did not soften the judgment of the community that she had sinned. I still admire my mother for her support of her friend: helping her protect her secret at work then throughout decades of struggle as she worked as a cleaner to support her child, with no assistance from the state or, by and large, from society. I saw all this as a wicked injustice, for she was a devoted and hard-working mother who gave her baby everything she could possibly manage. When I found myself pregnant and unmarried, attitudes had not changed. It seemed a straightforward decision to seek an abortion.

When he came home three weeks later Bob and I talked about it, prayed about it, made our decision, kept our secret and supported each other. I tried every old wives' remedy I had heard about, and there were many for this world-wide, age-old and not infrequent dilemma – including the most testing physical exertion and gin in a bath as hot as I could bear. A sign of my unworldliness was that I tipped the gin in the water, rather than drinking it! Nothing worked, so I braced myself and fronted up to three different doctors in turn to plead for help, only to be rebuffed by one after the other with a rigid moral lecture. I was humiliated. Time was running out. Meanwhile Bob was looking, through his university and sporting friends, for an illegal abortionist.

After several excruciating weeks of experiencing the changes in my body and my psyche and, almost worst of all, of deceiving my family for the first time in my life, off I went. I emptied my bank account and during my lunch hour walked two city blocks from the office to a mystery man. Goodbye innocence and modesty! Afterwards, I walked the two blocks back to work. The man had told me 'something should happen within three days' and gave me a telephone number to ring only if really necessary and then in absolute secrecy. I had no idea what he had done, and didn't even ask. Now I believe it was probably a saline solution injected into the uterus. My mind and my body were in a state of total confusion: it was without doubt the biggest trauma which had ever loomed in my pleasant and protected young life.

After completing that day and two more at work, I played hockey on the Saturday. I had only just joined the team and this was my first (and last!) game. That night I knew I was in trouble. The pain was severe, and Bob and I were worried. I made a phone call to the mystery man, who sounded alarmed but didn't offer any advice, except to wait. Secrecy was everything and somehow I concealed my anguish. I even went to work on the Monday. I had to leave the office, and aborted, alone and aghast.

I telephoned the mystery man again. He prescribed rest and taking care, proper nursing and getting away for a break. Bob borrowed a car and drove me to a quiet country resort where I stayed for a few days. Some of this time remains hazy, but I do remember keeping very much to myself, not mixing with the other few guests and being consumed by my miserable state. It was a lonely and agonising experience. Although I was completely secure in Bob's commitment to me and knew he shared responsibility for what had happened, in those days it was 'women's business' and, in the end, something I had to go through by myself. I never wavered from believing it was the only possible course we could have taken. From that time, however, I had fears that I might never be able to bear children successfully. I had a nagging fear of retribution, of unearthly punishment.

I admire beyond words the courage of people, mostly but certainly not exclusively women, who have worked against entrenched attitudes and laws in the area of birth control. The Brotherhood of St Laurence, where I worked in the seventies and eighties, were pioneers of family planning counselling in Victoria – in reponse to the needs of the people living in poverty with whom they worked. A great trail-blazer in New South Wales, Wendy McCarthy, has in recent years become a valued friend of mine.

◆

In November 1952, Bob won a Rhodes scholarship. A few weeks later he went to Travancore in India as the Congregational Church's representative at an international conference for young Christians. It was an experience that shook his faith, seeing the reality of India's poverty-stricken people alongside the protected idealism of the con-ference. His stirring report to the Congregational Church conference at Morialta, South Australia, on his return marked the beginning of the erosion of his belief in the church as a force for change, and the real beginning of his commitment to politics. I was already at the conference as a delegate from the Western Australian Congregational Youth Fellowship when he arrived late, having come directly from India. I was not surprised by his speech, as he had wrestled with a way to present his thoughts and discussed it with me beforehand. I was moved at his courage in questioning publicly what his parents had raised him and his brother to be – believing Christians. At the same time, although never doubting that we would go through life together, I remember a vague sense of foreboding. How would this change our partnership, which had been so church centred?

By then we had been companions for almost six years, and engaged for three years. He still provoked a range of reactions among my family and friends, from total approval to something approaching dislike. Some members of that safe, respectable community didn't know what to make of him. But I did! Our relationship soared in eager anticipation of our future together. We were very much in love – passionate and idealistic – and our intention was to be happy, have beautiful children, strive greatly and do good works as a partnership. We had both been cherished in the bosoms of families which had surrounded us with love, protected us from any hurt or danger and discouraged us from worldliness. But the nature of youth is to identify with its own generation.

Already I was vaguely disturbed by Bob's increasing use of alcohol in social situations, though he never drank at home. But my optimism persuaded me that with maturity, marriage and family, it would cease. I thought of him as just youthful, exuberant – wanting to try everything. And I knew that this manse boy had to slay his sense of being different from his peers, when he wanted to be one of the boys. I had absolute confidence in him.

In truth, I admired some kinds of outrageous behaviour. However, I was only courageous enough myself to adventure into territory that was unconventional, and possibly even unacceptable or risky, through Bob. He did adventure. He was, I have since thought, like Robert Burns, that sentimental rogue and great poet, 'a lad wi'out caution'. Bob's headlong approach to life would test me – almost beyond endurance. But our lives together opened up possibilities for change and growth in ways that I had never dreamed of.

Bob was to sail for England to take up his scholarship at Oxford in August 1953. In the months leading up to his departure, he and I drew from our savings so we could buy a small 1934 Austin car with soft-top and bucket seats. We shared everything, preparing to be partners for life – but looking back, I now approve of my father's insistence that the car be in joint names and not, as we had thoughtlessly assumed, in Bob's name. It interests me that Dad took that stance, given attitudes then about a woman's dependent status. I found it slightly irritating at the time but he was of course looking to my security. Dad was mindful of the fact that Bob still looked like being a long-time student, even though he was then earning a salary in a fill-in job until the scholarship allowance began. I think Dad still had a bit of 'How will he support my daughter?' in his mind.

His own life had been extremely disciplined, early on under the influence of his stern father, then later out of his own innate sense of order and responsibility. Bob's sporting and social activities, along with the vagaries and liberties of student life (or so it seemed to those who had not been full-time students) made Dad wonder about him ever settling down to wife and children.

Our plan was that Bob would arrive in Oxford for the beginning of the English academic year and I would join him about twelve months later. I have saved the letters he wrote to me after he arrived in Oxford and I am surprised when I look at them now at how detailed and frequent they were – sometimes written daily for three or four days in a row. In October he wrote asking me to join him earlier, and that letter is interesting for the insight it gives into the determined honesty of the young Bob and the pattern that we established early for my role in our partnership. It read in part:

> The great majority of blokes in College are bloody youthful and in the last few days John Evans and myself have palled up with a few of the senior chaps. They are interesting in their way and at times give one the feeling of how grand it must be to be free and enjoy all the delights which are available to the uninhibited Oxford undergraduate. I am reasonably sure that in the course of our relationship you have become aware of the fact that I am more than usually frank so I will say here and now that I have been assailed by the thought that young Robert could have a more delightful time if his sweetheart didn't come over to Oxford until the end of the academic year. I suppose this is only reasonably natural and I am not apologising for it but the other thoughts which come to mind are much more important and the ones which I really want to communicate to you. Invariably I come to my senses and remember what you mean to me, how much I need you, and how far superior are the qualities of our union to the merely passing delights of this other life of mine.
>
> In other words I am now telling you that you must come over here as soon as you possibly can – any other arrangement is completely out of the question if our love means anything at

all. I have been thrust into an environment which is full of opportunities for the satisfaction of my varied tastes, to which if I succumbed in their entireties, would only succeed in taking me away from you or at least making us more distant from one another. This may sound as if I am only telling you to come over here to help me get over my weaknesses – but that's not the case my dear as I have worked it out. This life has just made me realise as I have probably not had to realise it before that you have to make up your mind at some stage about relative values. And that is exactly what I am doing now. I have had a terrific amount of fun in life so far and have absolutely no cause for complaint – I have made a choice about the person with whom I want to spend the rest of my life and it is beginning to strike me more and more that it is silly to give up that companionship for other things which in perspective must turn out to be merely trivial.

I am not trying to tell you that when you arrive here there will not be times when I am tied up with activities that in their way will exclude you to a large extent – this would of course be rather ridiculous. But my darling you will be here and we will be able to see one another on many occasions and the doubtful pleasures which are now suggested to me will be replaced by those wide range of experiences which we will enjoy together … GET ON THAT SHIP DARLING FOR YOUR SAKE AND MINE.

I did, in November, and joined him in December of the same year.

My early departure meant hasty preparations, goodbyes and celebrations. My parents were quite remarkable, given family expectations of compliant daughters in the fifties. They didn't question any of my plans, but only gave me support. I booked myself on E deck in the bowels of the ship *Strathaird* in a multi-berth cabin and was seen off at Fremantle by fifty-four friends and relatives, whose names I still have listed in a memoir I kept of the occasion. Before the ship's first lifeboat drill was through, I was running for the side to lose my lunch. It was the first and only time in my life I have been physically ill from motion and I suspect that it was in part due to the fact that my emotions were running so strongly. I was making a dramatic break with all I had ever known. I was twenty-four years old and feeling a heady mixture of apprehension and anticipation. This was the beginning of a life of adventure.

HEADING OFF INTO THE FUTURE

◇

When I sailed for Oxford to join Bob in November 1953, the last thing on my mind was an interest in visiting a revered seat of learning. I was off to join the love of my life – as indeed he has remained, despite some turmoil.

The four-and-a-half-week voyage to England was a new world in itself, with deck sports every day and dancing every night. We made day-long stopovers at the ports of Colombo, Bombay, Aden and Marseilles, giving me my first brief glimpses of countries so unimaginably different from Australia. But I was impatient to reach my destination.

◆

Bob had got permission to board the *Strathaird* through the Western Australian agent-general in London, and he was first up the gangplank at Tilbury Docks. Our pleasure in seeing each other again was exquisite.

We set out to drive to Oxford and I got my first good look at England. I had that feeling many Australians have: the familiar names and places, especially in London, were a constant reminder of the historical ties between the two countries. And I could not believe how the cold actually hurt, arriving as I did in December directly from a Perth summer. I stood on the cobbles in Oxford in my light suede pumps, crying from the pain in my feet.

Bob was resident in University College as required by the conditions of his scholarship. Otherwise, I'm sure we would have got our own place immediately, although the prevailing attitude in the 1950s, certainly in the community we came from, was that men and women lived together only in marriage. But I found my own accommodation, a bed-sitter in a flat in North Oxford which I shared with an Australian couple. Bob and I planned to travel on the Continent in the summer, so I looked for a temporary job and found work as a stenographer in the diocesan office of the Church of England. It was in an ancient building next to Lewis Carroll's Old Sheep Shop, across the road from Christ Church College, near the Isis River – an historic and beautiful part of Oxford. My pedantic boss, Mr. Pink, was a campanologist. In other words, every weekend and sometimes in between, he was a bell-ringer. I found out that campanology is much more complicated than just pulling ropes – it's an art that requires practice and coordination.

Bob and I bought black pushbikes for a few shillings, the kind everyone rode – if you couldn't find your own you took another, as someone had probably taken yours, and round they went. We girls in the office all rode bikes to work, even in the worst winter weather. The office-girls were my introduction to the working-class in England. I quickly tuned into their particular sense of humour, as they gossiped about their personal lives and their attitudes to the middle and upper classes – not complimentary! But they unreservedly adored the Queen, and gave royalty unquestioning respect and devotion. Fresh from Australia, I thought it a bit odd: 'subservient', I told Bob disdainfully.

Before I arrived in Oxford, Bob had made friends with

Geoffrey Beck, the Minister of the North Oxford Congregational Church. Our friendship with Geoffrey and his wife Joy became important to both of us during our stay in England, and the friendship has lasted to this day. When Bob was permitted to live out of college he boarded with them for some months and I often minded their children. I learned much from Joy over the two years in Oxford; she was my first female mentor outside Perth and it was the first time I had been an intimate in another family's house, apart from the Hawkes'. I absorbed Joy Beck's thoughtful approach to family life and mothering, and I especially admired the relationship both parents had with their children. In fact, I was fascinated by everything the Becks did – how they cooked, how they talked over the newspapers in the morning. It wasn't like anything I'd seen. I loved the way the Becks included me and stood up for me, treating me as a person of just as much importance as Bob. Joy and Bob would spar with no holds barred, and in fun he mimicked her middle-class Pommy accent.

Before I left Perth I had sold the car and Bob bought a Fordson Ten van for our explorations of England and the Continent. We drove south from Oxford for trips around Dorset, Devon and Cornwall to test our camping skills. We were enchanted by those counties – the countryside, the ever-evident history and the people. We especially liked to listen to the farmers, who came into quaint village pubs in the evenings for their pint and to share the news about the cow that had calved or the sheep that was lost, or just to play darts and shove-halfpenny.

We visited the village of Loders in Dorset, and called in on Eddy Edrich, one of the lonely submariners who had gathered for singsongs at Coogee Street during the war. Eddy and Sally and their children lived in a modest terrace cottage, one of a row abutting a narrow, winding lane. At the top of the lane was the old manor house. For us Australians, it was like dropping back into history to see the deferential attitude of the villagers towards the current squire in the big house. He kept the feudal relationship alive and well by distributing gifts – perhaps a bottle of wine – to each village family at Christmas.

The only heating in Eddy and Sally's cottage was a coal

stove in the sitting-room. Food was prepared in an adjoining scullery and then the pots were carried into the sitting-room to cook. We were to have many hilarious times in that room, as the Edrichs became friends we often stayed with during our time in England. The sitting-room was also where we ate and there were two large, comfy chairs by the fire – one of which was usually occupied by their large Dalmatian dog, Solomon, while the cat Tiddles sat in the other when she was not out hunting, which she did with great purpose. (A tough cat, she even caught a badger once, but not without him landing some blows on her first.) One had to negotiate for a chair! Eddy brewed wines, using elderberries from the lanes or parsnips from the farms – in fact anything which would ferment to become drinkable – and some of his creations were very drinkable indeed. His 'winery' was in an outhouse, equipped with a collection of old-fashioned bedroom water-jugs and washbowls filled with various brews.

The house had no piped sewerage or water on tap. There was a hand-pump halfway up a steep hill at the back of the house and in the winter it was necessary to take some newspaper and matches up there to melt the ice before the water would flow. On one of our visits, Bob and I announced indulgently that we would love to have a bath. Well! The water from the pump up the hill was brought. A tin tub from the outhouse was fetched and large pans of water put on to heat. The tub was placed on the mat in front of the stove and everyone else retired while I had the first bath. Bob's turn was next, using the same water topped up a bit. It was obvious, from the feathers stuck around the greasy waterline, that the last time the tub had been used was for plucking chooks. We have a laugh every time we remember that very special bath.

Since leaving the navy, Eddy had become a policeman and looked the part in his Bobby's uniform and helmet. He had rounds to do, and had to phone the station from points along the way. Here our van came in handy. He and Bob would put his bicycle in the van and hurry off to the village pub for a drink and darts, or sometimes they went out rabbit shooting. When it was time for Eddy to report in, they would drive to the scheduled spot and take out the bike.

Bob would wait while Eddy cycled round the lane to the telephone. They worked out their routine carefully – mixing Eddy's duties on the beat with their recreation. After they had been hunting Bob didn't have much stomach for gutting the rabbits but Eddy insisted that what you shot you made ready for the oven. He delighted in mimicking Bob 'doing a rabbit', his face contorted with revulsion at the smell of the warm guts falling from the carcass, Solly the dog ready to swallow them.

Although, to our disappointment, we never saw Loders under snow, this village was like something out of a picturebook to us at Christmas time. Every cottage had a small Christmas tree sitting in its casement window, twinkling with coloured lights. At night it was like fairyland in that curving lane. And the smoke from every chimney would hang in the still, cold air.

But the snow fell for us not long after we began to live in Oxford, and we were entranced. I remember our very first experience of that hushed, white landscape in the garden of my digs. We looked out the window to see my landlord's black cat, Whoozit, walking slowly through the snow. All that could be seen of him was his tail, above the trenches his warm body made. The garden was woven with the patterns of his meanderings.

We had by then been down to the London sales and bought a rabbit-skin overcoat for me and good boots for both of us. We were like children, discovering with surprise how the milk-bottle tops rose on columns of icy milk. One morning as I made to step onto the approaching bus I found my boots had frozen to the pavement. When the common froze the warden's wife pronounced that we should learn to skate, taking a chair each to hold us steady on the ice and some apricot brandy for warmth and courage. It sounded a good idea at the time, and we went to watch, parking our car with the others to light the ice, but we never became skaters.

In the summer we set off on our grand tour. We planned it with extreme care, enlisting the help of the Automobile Association in London to make sure we didn't miss anything near our route. We wanted to DO Europe as best we could, with very little money. The van would be our home as well as our transport for the five weeks we were away. It was something of a contest amongst expatriates at Oxford to do the Continental tour for the least cost, and we thought we could make claim to the title. We drew up a route which took us in a clockwise direction through France, Belgium, Germany, Switzerland, Austria and Italy. Venice was our furthest point east, then we headed back through northern Italy, the Riviera and up through France to Paris.

On the camping trail we met people from all over the world and we eagerly grasped the experience of meeting those from cultures foreign to us. We communicated with them using phrase books, gestures and Bob's schoolboy French. We shared meals of black bread, cheese and fruit, and in each country treated ourselves to some local cooking at a modest cafe. We were educating ourselves, visiting historic sites and buildings, taking guided tours through galleries and gleaning what we could of the way other people thought and lived. I remember that we saw a lot of bomb damage from the war that had been over for nine years. I kept long, detailed diaries to send home to our families. In the last instalment I set out our living arrangements and our budget for the trip:

> What a wonderful, interesting holiday it was. Our gear was:- two sleeping bags, laid (with the front seat folded down) on the old mattress which is always in the van; two travelling rugs – my cushions by day and for use at night if extra cold; 1 suitcase of clothes, stood on end on the driver's seat at night; my hat-case of towels etc. – on my folded seat at night to bring it level with the mattress; 1 large wooden case of food – on the floor in front at night; 1 small wooden box for the stove and bottles of paraffin, petrol, soap, water – on the other side of the floor at night; iron wash-up dish full of cooking things and utensils – middle front at night; coathangers for jackets hanging from roof bars – hung around the windows for curtains at night; spare coathangers on which to hang washing to dry, soon dry with wind from the windows whilst travelling. Quite comfortable, clean and adequate, could have lived like it for weeks.

Costs were:-

£21	ourselves and van across the Channel and back
4	A.A. charges
8	insurance
3	French visas
74	travellers' cheques (half of this for petrol)
£110	

Back in Oxford, I found a job at the Institute of Statistics. Their office was in an ancient nunnery on the damp, foggy flats by the Isis River where – it was held – the ghosts of nuns walked. Alongside the Old Nunnery was a string of lawn tennis courts and in the summer I played there most days from knock-off at six o'clock until about nine in the long, light evenings. I began in the typing pool but was soon working for two of the Institute's economists, Tommy (later Lord) Balogh and Dudley Seers. They were doing a feasibility study on the possible integration of Malta with the United Kingdom. Balogh was the senior of the two, a Hungarian, a don at Balliol College and somewhat eccentric. Some people found him exasperating and others, like me, saw him as interesting, likeable and amusing. He was in correspondence with Harold Wilson, then leader of the Labour opposition in Britain, Richard Crossman, who was to publish *The Crossman Diaries*, the key book on the political life of that era, and Dom Mintoff, the prime minister of Malta. This was my first taste of being on the working end of politics. I found it intriguing.

During our two summers in Oxford, Bob played cricket. He was twelfth man in the Oxford XI captained by Colin Cowdrey and also played inter-college games, with the Authentics and with North Oxford. In 1954, when Bob toured England with the Oxford side, he was thrilled to get the chance to play on the hallowed turf of Lords. When he misfielded on the slope, Bob was amused to hear a Pommy accent call, 'Get a bag, you mug.' There was always plenty of cricket to be played, even twilight matches in the high summer. I had not grown up around cricket and this mysterious ritual, so much a part of Bob's life, was relatively new to me, but I was learning. At weekends we went to matches in the Cotswolds. The village greens brought to life childhood images of 'dear old England' – as my Gran used to say. While the men played, I would explore, and sometimes read the headstones in village cemeteries, creating fantasies about the lives marked there. When Paul Grice, an endearingly scruffy Balliol philosophy don with wispy, silvery hair, was one of the team, he and I would walk circuits round the edge of the playing field as we talked. I was delighted to find in him a rare ally on the subjects of ghosts and flying saucers. He quoted *Hamlet* to me, 'There are more things in heaven and earth, Horatio, than are dreamt of in your philosophy.' A far more elegant way than mine of questioning the sceptic's need for proof! My attitude had made me the object of mild ridicule so I found comfort in Paul. Both teams would have cold lunch at trestles in the village pub. After the game we would all return for the odd pint of ale, darts and the inevitable post-mortem of the match. I must say I always enjoy cricket stories – the endless store of reminiscences which surround this game an English aristocrat said the British invented to give them some idea of eternity! The humour and the mateship are captivating. At that time it was almost exclusively a man's game but I am pleased to see that cricket for women is now more popular and that Australian women are particularly good at it. As prime minister's wife, I was patron of the Australian Women's Cricket team when they were world champions.

◆

Although Bob and I were taking every opportunity to enjoy ourselves, we worked hard too. In 1955, our last year in England, Bob won a scholarship which sent him off to a four-week course in American industrial law and labour relations at the Institute of American Studies in Salzburg. We drove down to London, but were drastically delayed on the way by a traffic pile-up, and he only just caught the train. Afterwards, I climbed into the van where we had parked it outside Victoria Station, studied the map carefully and set out for the Strand. One 'No Entry' sign after another took me round and round Whitehall until the Bobby on duty got to know me. This was my first experience of driving in London and I felt quite ridiculous, especially in our tiny van, low on the road, like a small beetle among the double-decker buses.

I got used to Bob going off alone to pursue his interests and have never felt any resentment; there was usually plenty happening for me too. At this happy and carefree stage of our lives we exchanged letters while he was away and I remember him commenting on a love letter from me that he really liked, and asking for more. While he was gone I discovered Damon Runyon's stories and read them in the bath, laughing away to myself. When Bob came home, I introduced him to them and we laughed at them together.

During his first year in Oxford, Bob had sat his exams for the last subject he needed to complete a Bachelor of Arts (Economics), his second degree from the University of Western Australia. At the end of the second year, in December 1955, he was to submit his thesis on the history of wage-fixing in Australia for his Bachelor of Letters from Oxford. It was entitled 'An Appraisal of the Role of the Australian Commonwealth Court of Conciliation and Arbitration with Special Reference to the Development of the Concept of the Basic Wage' and I typed it for him. We had planned to spend our last English Christmas in Dorset but when the whole village of Loders was smitten with measles we couldn't take the risk. Bob couldn't afford to miss his final oral exam which was due just a few days later. When I asked how he had gone at the *viva voce* he was quite relaxed and said, 'Those Pommy blokes told me I knew more about it than they did.' But, as he said, this was not surprising, since his was the first research on the subject – and anyway it was 'Down Under'. He got his third degree, B.Litt.(Oxon), and we sailed for home.

Those two years had been time out for us, distinct from our past or our future, salad days with no responsibilities in the community or any family life. We made friends, went to the theatre, travelled and energetically plunged into the Oxford experience. It was a time that provided us with a resource of shared happiness to draw on for the rest of our lives. Perhaps, looking back, we missed a crucial opportunity to develop a maturity in our relationship that would have helped us through more difficult times.

◆

We sailed from England in January 1956 towards the next phase of our lives. The journey was unremarkable; the most exciting event was a storm in the Bay of Biscay. The decks of the pitching ship became hills and we learned to walk up and down them with the same swaying gait as the crew. We danced most evenings, sunned ourselves and played games on the sports deck. We had a day in the port of Naples where we engaged a rather roguish guide to show us this great Italian city, with its romance and squalor.

Our families were on Fremantle wharf to greet us, waiting patiently under a sweltering sun while we went through endless delays in landing procedures. It was so good to see them again!

Our wedding was planned for three weeks hence. It was all go, go, go, seeing friends to share our experiences and catch up on theirs, completing arrangements for the wedding, and for me the making of my wedding dress. My sister Edith, who was to be my matron of honour, had already made her dress. We were married in Trinity Church, Perth – it was a sultry day, one hundred and four degrees Fahrenheit, and was brewing up to a great storm, but we took no omen from that. We had been so busy with reunions with friends and family that I needed a quiet morning, with teabags on my eyelids, to be a clear-eyed bride. The marriage ceremony was performed jointly by Bob's father and our friend from the church community, the Reverend Johnny Bryant. The wedding itself was something of a reunion of family and friends. Terry Zanetti was master of ceremonies, Alan Barblett was best man and John Toohey proposed the toast, invoking a six-year statute of limitations to make jokes about our extraordinarily long engagement. Alan, John and Bob had been Modern School friends, but by now both Alan and John had established their families well ahead of us.

We borrowed the Hawkes' small Willys sedan and, after a night at Perth's famous Palace Hotel, drove southwards to Caves House at Yallingup, a well-known honeymoon spot. For four lovely days we swam and fished and explored that very beautiful part of Western Australia's coast and bush. We also spent many hours working together in the landscaped garden that sloped down towards the sea. Bob dictated to me as I sat with a much-travelled portable typewriter on my knee, producing the four ABC radio talks he was doing to pay for our holiday.

A few days after that trip south we left Perth again. Our train tickets to Canberra were one-way. Bob was one of the first batch of scholarship holders to the Australian National University. He was to join the law faculty for two years to work for a doctorate on wage fixing in Australia, under the supervision of Professor Geoffrey Sawer.

◆

Our living quarters were on campus in University House, a brand-new, well-appointed block of serviced flats, with common rooms and a dining hall where everyone had their meals. There was plenty of company – all the resident students were graduates about our own age. Bob got on with his work and was happy in this very small law school. I soon found a job at the Indian High Commission in the centre of Canberra, a brisk, fifteen-minute walk away, mostly across open land. I felt the all-over cold on those walks, as the wind swept down from the Snowy Mountains, more than I ever had in England. My job was as a receptionist and secretary and, until he returned to India, I worked for the peppery head of mission, General Kariappa, who was quite unlike the other gentle and communicative Indian staff.

Before long, to our great delight, I became pregnant. This meant that we had to move out of University House – children had no place in that quiet, studious environment. So, in mid-winter, we moved into the university flats in Masson Street, to another community, this time of young marrieds and their families.

Canberra is a planned city but in 1956 much of that plan was yet to be implemented and it was a scattered, semi-rural town. It was the seat of the federal parliament, and public servants predominated. The new university provided another cluster.

Canberra had a rawness about it, and had not yet found its character. Most people knew each other's salaries and business and personal affairs. Gossip ran like brushfire. The town had a higher than average suicide rate. I felt it was rather like shipboard life – most Canberrans were just sailing through to somewhere else. Canberra was very easy to live in because of its new facilities, though there was only minimal public transport. Childcare centres, baby clinics, schools and sports grounds incorporated in its plan made it a privileged community compared to the rest of Australia. From time to time it was necessary to escape to the real world, usually Sydney, in case one lost one's view of how other people lived. Canberra was a place filled with young, single people or married couples without the broader family links which bring cohesion and character to a community. There were apparently no elderly, disabled or disadvantaged citizens. There was no lake at that time, and Commonwealth Bridge, the main link between the city centre and Capital Hill, was a two-lane plank and pitch structure. Each day I made the long walk from the suburb of Turner into Civic to work, good exercise in a pregnancy.

We had made friends with another scholar, Dave White, and his wife Marge, and she had become pregnant at around the same time as me. Marge and I became closer as we anticipated and planned our approaching motherhood. I was considering a home-birth, knowing how Joy Beck in Oxford had been so pleased with her four home-births with a midwife in attendance. In England, a home-birth scheme had been set up during the war, freeing up hospital beds and giving women and their families an alternative to the rigid institutional procedures. I could not, however, find support for my plan. As it turned out, Marge and I were very pleased with Dr. Blackall, a woman who met all of our hopes and expectations. We found out everything we could about pregnancy and childbirth. Like many things, the only way to really learn is to experience it, but there was a lot we could do to feel responsible – we did exercises and paid special attention to our diets. At Marge's suggestion we sent to America for Adele Davis's book, unobtainable in Australia. Davis was something of a trail-blazer in writing about shopping and cooking for healthy family eating. In my first attempt at baking her wholemeal bread, I must have got the yeast proportions wrong. When I opened the small electric oven with great anticipation, the two tins of dough had become one large square shell the shape of the oven. It had a very thin, hard crust with the two bread tins and the oven racks baked into it. The whole centre was just air! We drank Tiger's Milk, a concoction full of nutrition, ate brains and fish as well as meat, and of course lots of grains, fruits and vegetables. Many of Davis's ideas are outmoded now but she helped to set me on the lifelong path of respect for the importance of what we consume.

We bought a small, almost derelict car which became known as the Steam Engine, a reference to its leaky radiator and consequent overheating. It had no self-starter and to get going, we had to push it then jump in and start in gear. As my pregnancy progressed, on shopping trips I always made sure I parked near some workmen so they could do the pushing and save me from the jumping in! It got so that when they saw me coming, they dropped tools, ready to help me.

There was a neighbourly atmosphere in the Masson Street flats. We had gardening plots, and the four flats in our block had a contest to see who could grow the most and best tomatoes. I had read somewhere that the trenching of vegetable and fish matter nourished the soil, so Bob and I collected tubs of fish cleanings from the fish shop and the chop-offs from the greengrocers. Bob dug them into the soil before we planted our crop. It happened that a heatwave followed, and one morning we found the ground was heaving with maggots from the rotten fish. We wondered what we should do, whether we had started some kind of plague, but the maggots were a one-day wonder. Anyway, our tomatoes were large and plentiful, and I believe we won the contest. We enjoyed that garden. I remember one day when Bob eagerly touched an almost-ripe cantaloupe. His face was a picture of dismay when its stalk broke and I laughed to see him, like a small boy, holding it back in position, willing it to finish ripening.

Bob found friends in Canberra who shared his liking for conviviality and left-wing politics. Professor Fin Crisp of Canberra University College, was one, a Labor man who had written a well-regarded book on the Australian constitution. Another was Ron

Heiser, a senior lecturer in economics at Canberra University College, and I became friendly with his wife, Deretta. He was a man of high intelligence, lively wit and great energy, but an inveterate drinker who ranged from being thoughtful and cleverly articulate to being irresponsible and aggressive. Often this was humorous indeed, as his irreverence towards stuffy attitudes and sacred cows could be scintillating.

And there was Professor Manning Clark, the historian, who had made his mark as a writer and observer of the Australian experience. Manning, a softly-spoken, quiet-living man, warmed to Bob, who was by now notching up a reputation for his exuberance and drinking prowess. His remark that Bob was a fine roisterer, was looked on as a badge of honour among Bob's companions. Manning observed that there were five sons-of-the manse at the new university, all of them rather rebellious. While I admired – even envied at times – Bob's gregarious ways, I had to admit to myself that they were causing me some anxiety.

I felt wonderful throughout my pregnancy. I stopped working a week or two before the baby was due and on 19 January 1957 our daughter, Susan Edith, was born. I had read Grantly Dick-Read's book *Natural Childbirth* which taught me how to become involved in the birth, rather than relying on the medical staff to do everything for me. The exercises and breathing I had learned were indeed helpful, if only because they kept me busy. I had read that I would feel as if I were about to split in half in the second stage of labour: can't say I wasn't warned! Then before long she was born. I felt blessed to have delivered this most beautiful, perfectly formed baby girl. For five years, since my first, frightening pregnancy, I'd had waves of fear that this perhaps could never be. The relief was indescribable.

We were high with excitement. While still holding this wet and messy precious bundle in the labour ward, I was demanding a telephone to tell our families in Perth. Bob was ecstatic – his thoughts of wanting a boy-child first vanished as he looked at her. It pleased me enormously that she bore an unmistakable resemblance to him.

♦

In the course of his research Bob was making trips to Melbourne – the industrial headquarters of the country, one might say, as the Australian Council of Trade Unions and the Industrial Court were based there. While studying basic wage cases he had established contacts with people working in union affairs and had involved himself increasingly. He worked with Dick Eggleston, the Queen's Counsel hired by the ACTU to argue its case before the Court.

In Canberra, we were enjoying our expanded family and a sociable life with friends, mostly at modest picnics or parties. There were always endless discussions about the meaning of life – particularly of course in political contexts. Our life was interesting and pleasant, except for the occasional ripple caused by alcohol-inspired revelling. The most notable of these led to Bob being told his services as student representative on the University Council were no longer required. He had jumped into the ornamental lily pond at University House late one night and upset a visiting bishop and, of course, the warden, with his loud, bawdy remarks.

While Bob was at ANU, his Uncle Albert suggested that Bob stand for an ALP seat in Western Australia. We thought about it briefly and decided against it. From the safe haven of 1992 I can say with relief that it was the right decision. His career experience has been more richly varied than would have been possible there. Also, for our personal lives and our marriage in particular, it has been much better that we didn't live and work in close proximity to the connections of childhood – families and neighbourhood – it let us sort it all out ourselves, at a distance.

Bob's ability and energy while working in Melbourne with the ACTU had impressed them, and they offered him a job as their research officer. It immediately appealed to him. This was his chance to get to the meat of the matter rather than looking at his subject through academic theory. It was the next logical step in his career, and the offer made the acquisition of the doctorate seem of secondary importance.

FAMILY LIFE

◇

We drove down from Canberra to Melbourne in March 1958, with
our baby and our cat, in a Ford Zephyr which we were buying with
a loan from my father. We stayed with cousins and were early on
the road every day, running hard to find somewhere to live. Bob had
negotiated an advance on his salary from the ACTU for a deposit
on a house, and real estate advertisements had given us great ideas
about the place we would buy. Reality soon took over. We decided
that we wanted to be near the sea, and began looking in suburbs
near the city on Port Phillip Bay. What that amounted to, really,
was going suburb by suburb round the Bay until we saw something
modest enough to suit our deposit. Within five days, we had found
a double-fronted, two-bedroom, weatherboard house in Keats
Street, Sandringham, freshly painted, on a large block of land with
established trees and a garden which would be great for children
to play in. Bob and the vendor reached an agreement at four
thousand pounds, to prevent it going to auction the following

weekend, but the vendor's wife was wiser and persuaded her husband to wait.

We went to the auction that Saturday but I had to retreat beyond hearing distance because Susan, by now sixteen months old, was in my arms and crying, probably with the cold. I missed out on the tussle as Bob and another determined buyer bid each other up until the price was four hundred pounds more than our offer. We bought it anyway. The difference was a lot of money to us but we had found a home and we moved in practically straight away. One of the first things we did was to explore the beaches only a few minutes' walk away. We laughed to see little Sue playing excitedly in the sea, fully-clothed and waist deep. The fact that it was May and the water was very cold did not overcome her pleasure. The sea was a new thing to this landlocked-Canberra baby.

Then a period began for me of simply coping. I was more alone than I had ever been in my life. For the first time I experienced isolation, as I managed a small child and established a new household. Bob undertook, as he always has, unquestioningly and generously the role of financial provider. But he was never really a home-body. He took our car to work except when I really needed it. Then I would drive him to the station and pick him up again at night when he phoned. On one occasion he arrived at our station, the end of the line, fast asleep. He was taken right back to the other end of the line, on the other side of the city, where the train was then put to bed for the night! He had to stumble back along the track in the dark and find an expensive taxi ride home.

When we arrived in Melbourne, I was pregnant with our second child. Pregnancy is said to be a good time for nestmaking and I set about trying to furnish the house and make it liveable. On one side of the central passage were two bedrooms, on the other a sitting-room and a dining-room. At the back of the house, behind each other at one side, were a tiny kitchen, a laundry with a gas copper and washtroughs, and a small bathroom with a bath, a gas water heater and a minuscule, corner handbasin. The other side of this back section was enclosed with flywire and canvas blinds above a dado-height wall. This room faced the northern, sunny side – a great plus – and looked over the large back garden with an expanse of lawn and trees that we loved. In the middle of this garden was an old woodshed, covered with a tumble of vines.

The house did have disadvantages. There was no hot-water service and no washing machine, a convenience I'd got used to in Canberra, and no heating except an open fireplace. The toilet was outside, up the garden path. Coping with a toddler and a pregnancy, I resorted to chamber pots as the weather became bitterly cold.

I bought a new mattress and put it on the floor. I papered apple crates and stacked them for bedroom storage, using a length of conduit between two stacks for hanging clothes. A cretonne curtain protected them from dust and made it look vaguely like a piece of furniture. We found a wooden table and chairs in the 'Used Furniture' columns in the newspaper and then I began the rounds of auction rooms, travelling by train with Susan in a stroller. This was my somewhat unpleasant introduction to big-city bustle. I found the walking, the crowds and the impersonality of the auction places daunting but I did buy some very cheap chairs, which I covered with headcloth, and a cupboard to hold our turntable, records and radio. Another acquisition was an old carved, wooden chair upholstered in leatherette, which I painted red. Bob called it his throne, until one night the bottom fell out of it and the dust of ages filled the room!

My first expeditions in Melbourne and Sandringham didn't boost my confidence one bit. On our first evening in the new house I walked to the corner store with Susan in the pram and found it already closed. Peering through the window, I could see the owner inside, so I knocked to plead for essentials. I must have looked harum-scarum with my unkempt hair, my shivering, cold look and no doubt frantic expression, and the overall impression would not have been enhanced by my army-disposals duffle coat. The wary fellow thought I was an intruder up to no good and became very agitated, until I finally persuaded him to open the door a chink. I bought what we needed and fled home feeling foolish. And my first trip to the auctions ended with *my* having to get an expensive taxi home: I had caught the wrong train which landed me at the end of a spur line instead of the Sandringham line. I felt incompetent. It seemed that most things I did, I bungled. The Golden Couple days seemed a long way in the past.

◆

Bob was plunging into a career, his first outside academic life, at the age of twenty-seven. He had been at school of some sort or another, except for vacation jobs and some months as a trainee with an oil company while he was waiting to sail for Oxford, for twenty-one years. His appointment to the ACTU as research officer and advocate in the Industrial Court was the first of its kind in the unions' history and met with mixed reactions. A Queen's Counsel and his assistant had always handled their court work until Bob took over, and top jobs in the trade unions had usually been filled from within their own ranks by tradesmen and blue-collar workers. Although Bob had the political commitment and credentials for the job, he was derisively dubbed 'Egghead' by some and regarded with suspicion.

So he was in the position of having to overcome the fact that he was different. He was not One Of Them. He set out to establish his credentials as an advocate and to prepare for an assault on the wage cases coming up in 1959. Another way of proving himself was to be one of the boys. The watering hole of the Trades Hall workers and the ACTU members was the Lygon Hotel (later renamed the John Curtin), next door to Bob's workplace. The one-upmanship of pub culture, urged along by the 'my shout' tradition, led to heavy sessions. By now Bob was a regular drinker, and patterns which put great strains on our home life became entrenched. His working and playing were providing another world for him, and did not leave much time or energy for his family.

He genuinely enjoyed the companionship and the talk – the unending adventure of swapping ideas in a new, different and challenging milieu. He threw himself into it all with his usual gusto. It must have seemed very dull to come home to a somewhat spartan house, a tired and pregnant wife, and a baby already asleep.

At first we had spent most evenings together. I always

stacked the dishes until morning so that we could relax together and play records. One of the few couples we had met in the neighbourhood, relations of a friend from Perth, had a television set. This was still a novelty in 1958 and we sometimes visited them for supper and to watch the show that was the rage of Melbourne, Graham Kennedy's 'In Melbourne Tonight'. But these domestic evenings seemed tame to both of us after our carefree past, and Bob's time at home became more unpredictable. Before long I was seeing very little of him.

All our time together, until now, had been spent in the relatively tight-knit communities of Perth, Oxford and Canberra, where friends were always close at hand and dropping in was a regular feature of daily life. But here, with Bob leaving for work early each morning, working hard and gregariously winning his way in Lygon Street, I began to give up any thought of us having evening meals together. I felt terribly lonely and the idea of fleeing Melbourne sometimes tempted me.

But there I was, with a job to do, and there I stayed. I was a busy housewife and took pride in slowly getting the home going. One Saturday afternoon I was in the back garden building a cupboard frame and doors to fit under the kitchen sink when I struck a snag and went inside to ask for Bob's help. He was immersed in his reading, and obviously couldn't imagine what on earth I was up to! I went on as best I could, and after the weekend visited Cartwright's hardware shop for advice. I was to beat a path to that place over the years – it was my university of carpentry and plumbing. I had grown up amongst people who were homemakers and I imagined that everyone 'made house' once they had one. In Sandringham, I began to realise that if I wanted domestic comfort and a homely atmosphere it was up to me to do the hands-on part of it. Our times of being quiet and communicative together were lessening with the demands of home and children on me, and of his away-from-home life on Bob.

So these were the years in which I felt increasingly the sadness of being left behind. I began to make some tentative friendships with neighbours and the local shopkeepers and looked forward to the birth of our second baby. My main joy was Susan. I treated her as my best friend and talked with her even before she could understand the words. Occasionally I would take her with me when I went to the Arbitration Court to listen to Bob's advocacy. One day, during a break, Bob went to Justice Gallagher's rooms and there was little Susan, sitting on his desk being fed juicy grapes by His Honour. But once, when she was a toddler and I was not coping well, I hit her, then was overcome with remorse and guilt. For the next half hour or so we sat together on the wooden, back step as I tried to convey to her that I was sorry. I felt that she did understand me. I have almost never smacked the children since. I would remind myself of Joy Beck's belief that being a bully created bullies – the ugly survival of the biggest and burliest.

◆

In February 1959, in a severe heatwave, I called the doctor late at night. She confirmed that a six-weeks premature birth was imminent. Had the steep walk back from the beach the day before, pushing the stroller, hastened the event? Or was it that I'd been so long on my feet slicing apricots and stirring chutney I was making from the neighbour's fruit? Bob was immersed in preparation for the basic wage case and under pressure – he had no assistance and the workload was mind-boggling. He came home when the doctor spoke to him on the telephone. He had hoped I could go home to Mum to have the baby, but it was all too clear to me that now was not the time to go flying across the continent. He took Susan to a neighbour to be cared for, and drove me to hospital.

When he came to the labour ward on his way to work next morning, I heard his voice in the corridor and called to him to come and meet his very new son. He was overcome with a combination of emotion at the birth of his son, and exhaustion. That summer several babies died in Melbourne from a staphylococcal infection. This risk and the heatwave conditions made us fear for our baby. He weighed just over five pounds, and when he became heavily jaundiced I had to leave him behind in hospital for several days. Bob made the 'milk run' with my expressed milk each morning until we were able to bring the baby home to be one of the family. We named him

Stephen. Later I could take Stephen in his basket to the Court. Once, when Bob paused, to give a point impact, the sound of an infant yawn coming from the basket turned the serious effect intended into smiles all round.

Marge White, my good friend from Canberra, had moved to Melbourne and, although we lived many suburbs apart, our friendship resumed and deepened. It became our habit to drive to each other's houses in turn for a whole day. The children played and we talked incessantly – about absolutely everything. Bob always joked that we would bust any verbometer. Marge had a university degree and had trained and worked as a pre-school teacher. I found her a source of wisdom and information and she gave another dimension to my experience as a young mother. Above all, she was a principled and energetic companion.

My life was busy. By this time we had acquired an exuberant German Shepherd pup, Tessie, whom we loved greatly though she caused a deal of havoc. Bill Mansfield, who was Ron Heiser's brother-in-law, a scientist and bachelor, used to call in to walk the dog, put the bins out and generally help out. Bill became a thread in our lives. This was before he found his future wife, Ensa, and he loved the homeliness of dog and babies. He treated domestic tasks as a natural part of life and enjoyed tennis with Bob each Sunday.

Over those first few years Bob involved himself in some improvements to the house. He and Doug Poulter were painting the living-room one Saturday and were in such a hurry to get off to the football that they painted *around* the piano! He built a barbecue, Bill Mansfield and he built a side fence and a carport, and with Wally Curran of the Meatworkers' Union he concreted the driveway. This was progress indeed. The amusing part of the driveway enterprise began when our neighbour, a builder, leaned over the fence and asked me if we were about to rebuild the house. The nature strip was covered, for the whole width of the block and down to the gutter, with piles of bluemetal and sand, and the entire front verandah was stacked with bags of cement. Bob had cubed his measurements instead of squaring them! As the great driveway task was tackled we had lots of laughs and yarn-telling – although I was not so amused by the ever-slowing rates of work as the grog flowed, or when the heavens opened and rain pelted onto the new, unset concrete. Parts of our driveway took on a permanently stippled effect. Bob was also helper to Ted Innes of the Electrical Trades Union when they installed Marge's discarded briquette heater in our house. Bob's role was to keep Ted entertained while he worked, by telling jokes and talking union politics in between handing him the spanner.

Bob's working life was overwhelming, and his commitment to the political process in Australia was total. Already he had been offered another job with a very much higher salary and perks, but he turned it down to stay where he could work for the principles he believed in. He wanted to make a contribution towards changing Australian society, influenced by his parents' religious belief in service to others and by his strong links to the ideals of the Australian Labor Party – the party his Uncle Albert led in Western Australia, where he was premier from 1953 to 1959. I understood his motivation and shared it. It was the dream we had dreamed of our lives together. But the differences in the jobs we were doing now were so stark that each of us was to miss out hugely in the following years: he on close involvement in family life and I on the interesting aspects of public and political life. Each of us would have to experience those things vicariously, mostly through the other. The pattern of doing things separately eventually tested the family greatly.

Our sexual pleasure in each other also began to change. With our new responsibilities, we couldn't sustain the buoyant 'playmates' relationship we had joyously begun at eighteen. This was the fifties, and we were typical in the way we let married life set our roles for us. It was just the way things happened – he building a career and she in her reproductive phase. We were putting all our energy in different directions, and had very little left over for supporting or enjoying each other. And yet it was Bob's drinking which was the demon in a situation which might otherwise have been satisfactory. I was afraid of an unplanned pregnancy. His successes for the ACTU in the 1959 basic wage case and margins case had broken new ground and had won over most of the early critics of his appointment – unionists now claimed him proudly as their own.

People saw him and he saw himself as a power in political life, and power is an aphrodisiac, both for the powerful one and for those attracted by it. I was unsure of his fidelity and began to question my trust in him, and that is a debilitating thing. I felt that if I openly expressed my doubt, I might have to face the fact that it was justified. I chose to remain silent about my insecurity. But that didn't make it go away and for years it gnawed away at me. My concern was not just for our own relationship, but also for the children.

Despite our difficulties, I always cared deeply about Bob and worried about the stress he was under. I also knew he cared about me and that he was quick to tell his mates I was a wonderful mother. In the eleven years, from when he became advocate in 1958 to when he moved on to the presidency of the ACTU in 1969, Bob revolutionised the wage fixing processes in Australia, and was regarded as the best advocate the Court had seen. He fought whatever tough battles were necessary and, as the job burgeoned, the ACTU appointed Ralph Willis as his research assistant. Bob had good relations with his opponents, the employers, and with the government's representatives. They usually gathered in the pub together as each case concluded. He and Jim Robinson, the Queen's Counsel who represented the employers, formed a good friendship. We would dine with Jim and Ruth in each other's homes, laughing together, but in court they could be 'cutting out each other's kidneys.' Jim called Bob 'the adversary *par excellence.*' During these years Bob suffered from an allergic reaction to something we could not identify. I remember him going off early one morning to an important court appearance during his first basic wage case with his arms covered in red weals and his top lip grotesquely swollen. I looked up at him from our mattress-on-the-floor bed and thought, 'I don't know how you are going to get through the day.' But he did … and the next, and the next!

In the early days of his advocacy, Bob struck up a relationship with Justice Alf Foster who lived nearby. They would yarn together on Sunday mornings. Dick (to become Sir Richard) Kirby, head of the Conciliation and Arbitration Commission, later became a friend too, partly through a shared interest in horse racing. Those of us who were in the know, would be amused when Dick's tipstaff would place a note on the bar table for Bob as though it referred to an important arbitration matter, when in fact it was the result of a race Dick had heard when he replaced his hearing aid with an earplug from his transistor.

◆

In September 1959 my father died suddenly from a heart attack. I was shocked. I had never faced the fact of my parents' mortality and Dad was only sixty-one. He and my mother had been looking forward to building a beach house and enjoying his retirement. I was distressed at being so distant from my mourning family in Perth. I thought of flying over but quickly dismissed the idea. We couldn't really afford the fare and anyway I felt that my life was in such disorder that I would be no use over there. I was struggling to wean seven-month-old Stephen as my milk supply failed – due, at least in part, I felt, to my emotional resistance to the unsatisfactory way we were living our lives. I grieved quietly and alone.

I was filled with regret that I had not given Dad anything like the attention and devotion he had shown me. Perhaps it was because I hadn't seen him as an exciting figure. I remembered my irritation with his uncompromising straightness. Dad did not court popularity and I hadn't had the wisdom to acknowledge his positive, loving attributes while he was alive. After his death we became aware of just how generous he had been, with his time and money, both to members of the extended family and through his activities as a Freemason to others in need. My mother was stricken. Their partnership had been a traditional one and she was utterly dependent upon him as a good friend and companion, as well as financially and in the management of their lives. I remembered how they always treated each other with affection and consideration, and how they so often walked to the shops on a Friday night or along the beach, chatting away, arms linked. I thought about the great holidays our little family of four had spent together and the idyllic childhood my parents had given Edith and me. My mother now had some difficult decisions to make. It was decided that my sister, her husband and their two young sons would live with Mum in the family home.

From then on, until our children were grown up, Mum would come to Melbourne on the train once every couple of years to stay with us for a few months. This was of course a great help to me. Bob really liked Mum. He joked that he always got his underpants ironed and his buttons sewn on when she was there. And the children built a loving relationship with her, which they all still value.

◆

In 1960, Bob and I drove to the Snowy Mountains to have a look at that extraordinary engineering achievement, the Snowy Mountains Hydro-electric Scheme. We met unionists and saw their work sites. It was good for us to take a break, together and in wonderful countryside. During our week there, Bob met Bruce McKissack, politically an extreme leftist. He, his wife and their four children were ostracised in their country-town community because of his open and active beliefs – such was the hysteria about communism in those years. The two men hit it off immediately. Bob loved to debate political ideas with both his friends and opponents, not letting differences in ideology interfere with the value of the exchange. Bob and Bruce's mateship led to a warm connection between our families and we would visit them in Gippsland for picnics, fishing and bushwalking. It was great to be in the bush with Bruce – he knew it and loved it so well. He was an environmentalist before the term was coined. Later their youngest daughter, Jill, boarded with us for two years when she came to work in Melbourne.

In November 1960, I was well-advanced in my third pregnancy. I was still hard at work on our home improvements, and on rainy days or when the babies were sleeping I set about painting the woodwork inside the house white. I also bought a gas stove in the auction rooms for seven pounds to replace the very small and ancient one in the house. I had it in pieces on the back lawn and was using stripper to remove the greasy accumulations of the years, when early labour began. Much to the amusement of the nursing staff at the hospital where I delivered Rosslyn (four weeks prematurely), my hands looked like a labourer's and my hair and skin bore signs of the paint job. They dubbed me 'Whitey'. Now we had three children born within four years.

Rosslyn proved to be a friendly and contented baby, an absolute joy, and she slipped easily into what had now become a group. She had a pert and self-contained way, and caught the attention of those who saw her. Once when Bob was feeling really down, he commented as he watched her, 'She will save me, that one.' Stephen had been an affectionate baby, very easy to manage except for his determined resistance to weaning, and had become a resourceful potterer, able to amuse himself for lengthy periods. He had a long concentration span and unending curiosity – in his own young way he was always asking, 'Why is it so?' of things he saw around him. Sue had already impressed us with her logical way of working things out which, as parents tend to do, we saw as exceptional. We were very happy with our little brood.

In the blackberry season of 1963 we were in the Gippsland bush gathering berries with Bruce and Ruby McKissack when Stephen was overcome by an allergic reaction. He had suffered from allergies before, but never as severely as this and we were very alarmed. He had been on medication that wasn't doing anything and I was at a loss about what to do next. By great good luck the doctor in that country town was a young man who had trained with a specialist at the Royal Children's Hospital in Melbourne. He strongly recommended that we consult this man, and it was a breakthrough. I have been grateful ever since to Dr. John Colebatch for the thoroughness of his diagnosis and treatment.

I had to keep Stephen resting, at first for twenty hours out of each twenty-four. That tested us both, as he was just three years old. Steve and I went through the whole gamut of books, records, playdough, drawing, cutting-out and whatever else I could think of to keep him happy. He'd missed the kindergarten intake, but he began when a place became available in mid-year. This extraordinary bit of luck brought me a great friend. There was one other little boy, called Murray, beginning that day and, because we were the two new mothers, his mother, Yvonne Edmonds, and I sat together on the kindergarten bus that took the children to visit a goat farm. From that day we pooled transport and child minding. Our friendship deepened, and we have shared probably the most difficult times of our lives as well as the most celebratory. Yvonne is a fun-loving, warm and resourceful woman. She more than balanced what I saw as my dreariness, and brought lightness and humour to our friendship. And she was a gifted and remarkably compassionate nurse – which saved me a lot of worry from time to time.

◆

In 1963 I had my fourth child, a boy. I went into labour about seven weeks prematurely, began to haemorrhage and had to have an emergency caesarean and blood transfusions. A curious thing happened to me during the surgery. I saw myself, just head and shoulders, in the top left-hand corner of the theatre, dressed in a white hospital gown, looking down at me as I lay on the operating table. The self that I saw up there looked very gentle, softer and prettier than I thought of myself. But that me was looking down at a cluster of people in white, busy around me, and saying more and more desperately, 'But where is the baby, I can't see the baby.' This experience was very vivid, indeed the memory still is, but I couldn't talk about it at the time to anyone, and only much later to one particular friend. Years later I read a book about close encounters with death. Some of the 'out of the body' experiences recorded there were uncannily similar to my own.

While I was recovering, our baby boy was transferred to a city hospital for special treatment in a humidicrib and I was moved out of the maternity ward to a general ward. I had suggested that he be named Robert James, for Bob, partly because I felt he might be our last child and also because I felt it might lift Bob's spirits, which seemed to me to be in a kind of malaise – a vague, indefinable thing which saddened me.

But young Robert James, born on 1 August 1963, struggled for his little life for only four days, and I never saw him or held him. That was the practice adopted in those days. There seemed to be a conspiracy at the hospital that I should not believe I had borne and lost a son. Bob described him to me – how well formed he was and what a strong little body he had. As I lay in the ward, I imagined how he looked, and how he was experiencing his battle for life. The pregnancy had been a placenta praevia, undiagnosed, and he had been starved of oxygen by the heavy haemorrhaging for too long. His lungs never had a chance to do their job. Everything continued to go wrong. The patient sharing my room was in severe pain, and the drip the doctor had prescribed for me was administered incorrectly. It was bitterly cold weather and when the children were brought to see me they looked all shivery and bewildered and sad. I couldn't cuddle them properly because I was so sore.

I discharged myself earlier than advised and planned to stay with Marge until I was strong enough to care for Bob and the children again. Sue, Stephen and Rosslyn were swept up by friends and neighbours. I went home to get some things and found evidence of Bob's distress and the house in a big mess because the cat had been accidentally locked in. The winter's day was so cold it felt cruel.

That whole episode was a horror which stayed with me and would not go away. I went through agonies of guilt and blame and frustration. My doctor understood my grief, drew diagrams to explain the condition, and reminded me, 'But we saved you'. In my despairing and unreasoning state, that was meaningless, even though I had three healthy surviving children.

For a long period my feelings were driven by my emotions rather than by reason. It bothered me to be around other young babies and I felt painful jealousy of a woman I saw almost daily at the local state school. She had been pregnant at the same time as me and had produced a healthy baby. I was so filled with envy when I saw her with her child that I didn't like myself very much.

I fought against the idea that Robert James had never existed. To this day, when we are asked how many children we have, I reply, 'three', but I always think to myself, 'four'. In my grief I wanted to talk about him, and yet I never, or rarely, did. I became angry with Bob for leaving him out, not realising that Bob had never assuaged his own grief, and we didn't know how to talk about it.

In the year in which I turned sixty, the inner sadness and anger I still carried were stirred yet again by a conversation about a family who had lost a child. We were discussing parallels between this family and ours when I mentioned that we had lost a child too. I listened to the story of how this other family had known their child before it died, how it had been a real person whom they had loved. I thought about how my baby was already a person for me too, whom I very much loved, hoped and dreamed for. He and I had been denied the opportunity even to know each other, and that seemed to me an equal or an even greater loss.

Our youngest daughter, Rosslyn, was always very sensitive about the loss of Robert. I think she had felt that for her, the youngest of three siblings, this baby would have been a special companion, or her partner. And, I suppose, as she was just three years old when he died, that she was very aware of the feeling of tragedy pervading the family, without completely understanding it. On Mothers' Day in my sixty-first year she and I were having a picnic lunch in a Canberra park with her children, and scanning the newspapers. She found a review of a book by Margaret Nicol called *Loss of a Baby, Understanding Maternal Grief* and said she would buy it for me the next day. I had to be in Sydney the next day and couldn't wait. I bought it myself and began to read. It triggered floods of tears and then a most extraordinary sense of relief. I have wondered countless times since Robert's death how each of our lives, and our family life, would have differed had he lived, for our baby was severely brain damaged by his ordeal and would have needed very special care and sacrifice.

My experience makes that dilemma which faces doctors and families real for me – whether to sustain, by extraordinarily complex and costly means, the lives of those who have suffered severe physical or mental damage? And how does one evaluate the severity, or the grounds for hope? The suffering I witnessed during work I undertook as the prime minister's wife never failed to stir the most confusing and sympathetic feelings in me. Whenever I saw damaged children in hospitals or institutions, and the anguish of their parents, I thought of Robert, and tears were close.

AFTER ALL, A PARTNERSHIP

◇

Thinking back to the time of the death of our baby, I am dismayed by my self-absorption. I was so shattered by the shock, the physical assault of surgery and the debilitating grief, that I had nothing to spare for Bob. Worse, I recall that one night when he visited me in hospital I abused him terribly about the mess our marriage was in, blaming him roundly, saying that it was all his fault – which of course it wasn't. I was groggy and dazed with medication but, even so, I remember it with a sharp pang of guilt. Was I so reeling from the hurt that I could not share our common grief? In our culture it isn't easy for men to grieve. He and his mates, who thought they were supporting him, drank themselves into stupors, and Bob's binge extracted its cost.

One Saturday afternoon, very soon after I'd come home from recuperating at Marge's, Bob asked me to go to a football match with him at the Melbourne Cricket Ground. It was the last thing I felt like doing, but he was so insistent he wanted my company that I agreed to go. On the way there, he collapsed. He seemed paralysed down one side and was disoriented and very distressed. So I got us into a taxi and headed for casualty at the Royal Melbourne Hospital. Bob was gasping in a frightened and frightening way, speaking to me as if he thought he was dying. What would I do, if … ? There was no doubt that I loved this man; my only thoughts were to help him and will him to survive. The importance of the mistakes we were making disappeared alongside the main game, this partnership.

He was discharged from hospital that night with instructions to consult our family doctor the next day. When I telephoned, our doctor described the hospital's report to me. He was shocked at the amount of alcohol they had found in Bob's system. The casualty doctor had compared his brain to a computer which toxicity had sent berserk. He had indeed been in danger.

◆

A federal election had been called for 30 November 1963. Bob was still on medication and taking things cautiously when he was persuaded to run as a candidate for the Labor Party in the seat of Corio. Labor had lost the previous election by one seat and the Party thought that with the right candidate it might be possible to pick up Corio. The polls forecast that the November election would be very close, so there was considerable pressure on Bob. We both felt he should give it a go, even though an election campaign could not have come at a worse time for us. Neither of us was very strong, physically or emotionally, just six weeks after losing our baby.

We rented a house on the sea front in Portarlington near Geelong, the major city in the electorate, and went to live there for six weeks of campaigning. Susan went to the local primary school, Stephen to the kindergarten and Rosslyn had her third birthday while we were there. The hyperactive business of a campaign loomed as a daunting task for me, but I wanted to be there. It was the first time I had been so closely involved with Bob's political aspirations. I attended meetings but did no door-knocking; my main task was to get the home running and keep it running.

The intense camaraderie fostered by the campaign allowed us to get to know some of the local people quickly. I remember a fisherman nicknamed 'Oigle' who took us out in his boat at dawn one morning to catch our breakfast. There we were sitting, Bob and Oigle and I and the three children, when a cargo ship loomed, approaching the port by the channel where we were fishing. Terror best describes our state as the ship drew closer at an alarming rate. Oigle could not start his motor with the piece of rope he wound and pulled to get a kick start. He tried and tried, and fortunately we are living to tell how he got it going just in time and our small boat careered out of the way.

Jack Payne was another of the fishermen we got to know, and his wife taught Sue at the little local primary school. Living there made me feel how wonderful it would be to live right on the sea. I loved to watch the continuously changing colours and moods of sea and sky, spread in a great picture across our windows. I felt I was part of a community, seeing the fishermen and their boats going out each morning then coming in again when the fishing day was done. I would wonder whether the catch had been a good one.

The house we had rented took on the atmosphere of a motel as helpers came from all directions – personal friends and Labor party workers. On the night before the vote there were people sleeping everywhere, even on the floor in the passageways. Bob's ACTU research assistant, Ralph Willis, elected to sleep in his car to avoid John Hayes' (the ACTU accountant) snoring, but was driven inside by the mosquitoes. Keith Edmonds, my friend Yvonne's husband, kept us amused with his ingenuous good humour. Breakfast time was hilarious, as everyone related their experiences of the night before, then headed off to their allotted polling booths. We were all excited.

That evening at the party headquarters some members were ready to break out the champagne, but George Poyser, the campaign manager, warned that votes were not in from the outlying booths. Many rural voters in Corio were staunch Catholics and the Democratic Labor Party, the breakaway Catholic labour party, had run a scare campaign, warning of the horrors of communism and the ALP's guilt by association. This was a legacy of the devastating split in the fifties within the ALP and the trade union movement, which caused such bitterness.

Sure enough, the result was not as good as we had hoped. Although Bob picked up a three per cent swing against a national swing of three per cent away from the ALP, he did not win the seat. The Labor Party was to be in opposition for another nine years until Gough Whitlam led it to victory in 1972. We were both disappointed at the time but over the years we have been thankful for a loss that set Bob's career in politics on a more constructive path – just as we have been glad that we decided not to return to Western Australia. My own belief is that if he had won, and been confined to sitting on the opposition benches for all that time, it's London to a brick that our marriage would have collapsed under such strain. There is a heavy attrition rate in political marriages!

So Bob went on with his work at the ACTU and I went on with home and children. I clung to my ideal vision of how our life should be together, the family experience I wanted our children to have. And yet I had chosen to break out of the comfortable patterns of my own childhood. The excitement that life with Bob offered was part of the magnetism he held for me. I had never thought, for a moment, of marrying one of the safe young men of my home town and it never occurred to me that I might find fulfilment without a husband. I had reached out, with and through Bob, and I had to remind myself: this was my own choice and it had always carried risks, as indeed any marriage does. I wanted it all – the values and experiences of my past as well as the changes I had sought.

When our youngest, Ros, reached kindergarten age, I felt that I might try something of my own. Perhaps in some way I was remembering what had happened to my talented mother, how her life had left her with part of herself unexpressed. I saw a correspondence course advertised and wrote off for details of the fees and the text books I would need. But when I confided in Bob he told me I was being unrealistic; that I had plenty to do already. This was enough to stop my tentative step towards the academic study that I longed for.

Bob thought a new environment would lift our spirits and

The day I left the West to join Bob in Oxford.
Ellie, Clem, me, Mum and Dad on the deck of the
Strathaird

Bob and me in a friend's Oxford flat the night after I arrived; the beginning of a round of introductions to his new friends

Bob in the garden at my digs, Woodstock Road, Oxford, wearing the jumper I knitted him and playing in our first snow

In the lanes near the village of Loders, Dorset. Eddy and Sally Edrich's children Bill and, holding my hand, young Hazel Edith, named for me and my sister

Bob, me and Solomon, with our proud possession the Fordson Ten van

3rd March, 1956, our wedding day. Back: Clem, Ellie, Mum and Dad. Front: Alan Barblett, Bob, me and my sister, now Edith Baker

Kissing me off to my new life: Dad, me, Mum, Bob and Uncle Albert Hawke

Bob the mechanic, fixing the Steam Engine outside our university flat at 12 Masson Street, Canberra

Bob, our baby Susan, our kitten Niffy (Magnificat) and me just home from hospital in January 1957

Our first home in Melbourne, in Keats Street, Sandringham. The paling fence, the carport and the driveway bear witness to weekends of work, and some play, by Bob and his friends.

Rosslyn and Bob, 1961

Daddy's been out on the Bay catching our tea. Stephen, Bob, Susan, Rosslyn in 1961

Stephen, Rosslyn and Susan in the Keats Street garden, winter 1962

THE AUSTRALIAN LABOR PARTY

proudly presents

Its Social Service Programme and Its Candidate for Corio

R. J. (Bob) HAWKE,

B.A., LL.B., B.Litt.

BOB HAWKE AND HIS FAMILY

Money Spent

on Social Welfare

is an Investment

in

Australia's Future

A VOTE FOR BOB HAWKE IS A VOTE FOR FAMILY SECURITY

- CHILD ENDOWMENT more than doubled.
  1st child, 11/-; 2nd child, 19/-; all subsequent children, 22/-.
- MATERNITY ALLOWANCE doubled.
  £30 for first child, rising to £35 for 4th and additional children.
- AGED PENSIONS
  Married Pensioners will receive an immediate rise of 10/-.
- HOSPITALISATION
  Free Public Medical Service based on public hospitals.
- PHARMACEUTICAL BENEFITS
  Abolition of 5/- prescription charge and increased Free Drug List.
- REPATRIATION
  Free medical attention for all First World War veterans.
  The acceptance of cancer as a war disability.

BOB HAWKE is STANDING for You — GIVE HIM A SEAT

ON SATURDAY, NOVEMBER 30th, VOTE THUS—

1	**HAWKE, R. J. L.**
2	MAHONEY, J. J.
3	OPPERMAN, H. F.

MERCER PRINT, GEELONG   Authorised by Cr. W. R. Johns, 70 Keera Street, Geelong West

Election poster, Corio 1963

suggested that we should move to a new house. The one we really wanted was way beyond our means – we thought. It was not far from where we were, a much bigger house, with a tennis court. To our surprise, our bank manager had confidence in Bob's prospects and encouraged us to buy it. The house was on offer at a lower price than we'd expected since the land could be subdivided, by cutting off the tennis court block. We were offered a year's option on the separated block. We took it!

In July 1964, while all this was being negotiated, Bob was asked to go to Western Australia to do a wage case. We put tenants in our old house, packed the station wagon and took the children and the dog, Flash, with us. It was a trip back to the place where we had been so happy, and an overdue visit to our families. For the several weeks of our stay, we lived with Bob's parents and Susan and Stephen attended his old school, West Leederville Primary. Rosslyn went, sometimes, to an old-style kindergarten with the Bennett sisters, spinsters typical of their time.

When we returned to Melbourne, we went straight to our new house. Yvonne had seen to the arrangements for moving our possessions. The feeling of space was exhilarating; there were four bedrooms plus a huge playroom. The garden was just the kind of garden we loved – not in the least formal, and with lots of established trees.

Just before our option on the tennis court block was to expire, a friend phoned Bob to point out a possible libel in a Sydney paper. An article had referred to Bob as a communist, an assertion which would damage his standing in most of the trade union movement and in the Labor Party. The upshot was a settlement which enabled us to safeguard the sunshine that streamed through our windows, and we had a tennis court for ourselves and the children.

The surface of the court was coal-ash and tar, a harsh, black substance with cracks and crumbling patches but it was playable. It made a safe area for the kids too, where they could ride bikes and play football, hopscotch or skippy. In summer we would set up a matting wicket and Steve's friends came to spend hours playing cricket. There Bob bowled endlessly to Stephen: it was the main thing they enjoyed together. I began to play mid-week women's competition tennis on the urging of Mick Sweetnam, a real character who had worked with some top players in his day and now coached children. Hordes (it seemed) of kids came to our court once or twice a week after school for their lessons, and Mick would give me a run to sharpen my game. Through the children's school I met Barbara and Chris Rogers, who were keen tennis players, and we started a Sunday morning tennis foursome which we enjoyed for many years. Barbara became another of my close women friends. That tennis court was a source of great pleasure and many friendships during our twenty years in the house. For many years we repaired the cracks and holes with warmed roof-pitch, until we upgraded it in the seventies to a synthetic surface with night lighting.

Life went along through the sixties in an economically secure way. I took another boarder, when Jill McKissack moved on, and Barbara Rogers sold me her tiny car. This gave me the mobility to go to matriculation English classes at the local technical college, one night a week. The children were good at their schoolwork and developed their networks of playmates and friendships. I have talked with our children, who now all have children of their own, about how Bob's career in public life affected them and how they felt during their years of growing up. I used to call on the saying 'What's lost on the roundabouts is made up on the swings'. Apparently that is how they saw it too. Although public prying into our privacy was something they could have done without, they were well aware that Bob's work brought interesting people and events into their own lives. They say there was never any doubt that they were loved. They could see that home and children were the overwhelming focus of my life, and there were many good times we all shared as a family. But the unhappiness the children saw and heard when Bob and I argued was hard to bear. At these times, like most children who hear their parents arguing, they just wanted it 'to be all right'. It bothered me terribly that our kids witnessed the hurt Bob and I could inflict on each other. They loathed the waiting, the times he didn't turn up, the yelling late at night or in the mornings. I remembered how in my childhood there was none of this, not even a stamped foot, and I winced at the way we sometimes behaved.

By now Bob and I had ceased to be churchgoers. Religious faith had become increasingly difficult to sustain, and eventually we became agnostic. Bob's loss of belief began in India in 1952; for me the process had begun later and been reluctant. But as I saw and experienced the world outside the cocoon of my childhood, I agonised more and more about why some of us should be given access to the love of God through the church, while others would never know it. It didn't make sense. I became confused, then agnostic.

◆

In 1965 Bob began working on a wage claim for the public servants of Papua New Guinea. The ACTU was lending his services for the task and he went there to prepare the case he would argue with the assistance of the local Public Service Union. He travelled around the country taking evidence and arranging witnesses. As the case came together and the time set for the court hearing by the Commissioner drew near, Bob arranged for the children and me to join him for about three months. Ralph Willis, whose later parliamentary career was to include a period as a senior minister in the Hawke Government, was a bachelor then and he stayed in our house in Melbourne when the children and I left for New Guinea. He looked after the dog, the cat, the budgie, the pet mice and the silkworms, on this and other occasions.

It was a long day's journey of three flights, each plane smaller than the last. Bob met us at the Port Moresby airport and took us to settle in to the public servant's house we were to live in, high on the severe slopes which rise from the township. The next day, Sunday, there was to be a big 'journos' picnic on Fisherman's Island, about sixteen miles off Moresby. I was a bit intimidated by this prospect. I'd never really felt at home with the clubby mode of journalists *en masse*. Then, to make matters worse, Bob decided he needed to do more work on the case and couldn't go with us. He arranged for the children and me to go on ahead and said he would join us by small boat later. The trip was to be made in a traditional New Guinean boat called a lakatoy, which is constructed from two huge, hollowed-out logs set wide apart, surmounted by a platform.

So there I was, surrounded by strangers, having been whisked out of mid-winter Melbourne into the tropical sun which was threatening to burn the kids' skin to bits. When I saw the cartons of beer being loaded in quantities appropriate to a journalists' day-long picnic, I gritted my teeth and said to myself, 'here goes'. As often happens, the dreaded occasion was in fact a wonderful day on this barren and deserted beach. There were shade umbrellas to protect us and a jewel-like sea to swim in. My doubts about the company of journalists were set aside when David White, then writing for the *Sydney Morning Herald*, thoughtfully befriended me. By the time Bob and another journalist, Don Hogg, joined us by speedboat during the afternoon, I was thoroughly at ease.

On the way home we had to contend with very strong winds, which made the sea rise and roughen. The logs were taking a lot of water and for a while it was all rather hair-raising – most of the men supposedly in charge had put away a fair bit of ale that day. But the drama rallied them and somehow things got organised. The towels, bags and picnic gear were put in a large circle on the platform deck with the children inside it to keep them confined and on board. In the middle sat Don Hogg, singing songs to entertain and divert us all, especially the children. We laboured back to Port Moresby over what seemed a very long sixteen miles of water.

Betting on horse races broadcast from Australia was a popular recreation in Port Moresby. Don Hogg, who lived down at the water's edge behind the famous Koki Market, held open house on Saturday afternoons for the punters. It surprised me how Bob took to this pastime – he had always been irritated by racing broadcasts on the radio when they interrupted cricket or football commentaries.

The children went to school at the small Eila Beach government primary school, just across the road from the beach. With them away for most of the day, and since a 'houseboy' went with the place, I really had no work to do. One day I took a book from the shelf, Boris Pasternak's *Doctor Zhivago*, and I began to read in a way

I never had before. Nothing was waiting to be done, I did not have to feel I was being indolent. I remember how much I relished reading that book, which so vividly unfolds the history and politics of the Bolshevik revolution, and how I enjoyed entering into the lives of its characters. From that day I felt different about reading, though I have never been able to shake off completely the Coogee Street feeling that reading for pleasure comes only after all the work is done.

Once the court hearing began, I went to watch the proceedings each day. I enjoyed listening to the evidence, as the witnesses were examined and the shape of the case gradually developed. I equally enjoyed seeing Bob's energetic advocacy , though I did wonder whether he would survive in one piece, as he repeatedly flung his hands in the air to emphasise a point, narrowly missing the whirring fan above. He was really putting all he had into achieving an increase in pay for the New Guinean workers who received much less than expatriates. For this they loved him, and we were warmly welcomed as a family, never lacking company or hospitality.

It was a matter of amusement to all, but especially to an assisting lawyer who had become our friend, Paul Munro, that when a matter before the Commissioner had to go to the Supreme Court, Bob could not conduct it. He had never applied to be admitted to the Bar, not wanting to practise as a lawyer. As they walked into the court with pecking order reversed, Paul saw the joke in having Bob as his sidekick, carrying the cases of documents.

I would pick up the children from school each day at three o'clock and take them over the road to a swimming pool. Most expatriates used a whites' pool specially set aside for them but I preferred the one where all the local kids swam on their way home from school. They would wander along, peel off down to their knickers and frolic like young water-nymphs. It was great for our kids to be with them. Susan's hair was long, blonde and straight and the New Guinean children would touch it, intrigued. In turn, our children would feel their wiry, fuzzy black hair, so different from their own. Rosslyn remembers these children teaching her to swim. And cricket on the beach is another memorable image – Stephen, with his tanned skin, his short crew-cut hair and his lithe little body, mingled into the black boys' game in the nicest possible way. I loved watching them all play together with such innocence and abandon.

We were invited into the villages and homes of the New Guineans in a friendly, unofficial way. One especially lovely evening we went to the village of Konedobu, built on stilts out over the water, where the women showed me their basket weaving, we ate kai-kai together and our kids curled up with theirs to sleep on woven mats, while we talked on. And there was the ready-made group of companions among the public servants and journalists from Australia. The night before we left New Guinea we had a party in our house for everyone involved in the case – which, after all the effort and commitment put into it resulted in some disappointingly small improvements for the New Guinean public servants. There was lots of guitar playing and singing and we sang *We Shall Overcome* with the glow of feeling which comes from working together for something worthwhile. And spontaneously, thrillingly, the local New Guineans began to beat their drums, to sing and dance in their traditional way.

There was a famous dog which lived somewhere on that Moresby hillside, famous because whenever he heard a party, he went. He came to our party, and so did another dog, and after the euphoria of the singing and companionship the party temporarily turned into chaos when the two of them got into a savage fight over the chicken scraps in the kitchen. Bob, with a mixture of derring-do and grog in his veins, struck a karate blow on the skull of the larger, boxer dog. Don Hogg also leapt into the fray. The fight was stopped but they both sustained injury (the men, not the dogs). Early next morning we had to search for Bob's glasses and call in a doctor to bind a small broken bone in his hand. When we went to the airport to leave for Australia, there was Hoggie, not to be outdone, with a heavily bandaged shin.

◆

I did a lot of painting, gardening and sewing at the new house in Sandringham – homemaking all over again, and always with a frugal approach. The garden was my delight. I couldn't say how many kettles I boiled dry or saucepans I ruined because I went to the letter box or to shift a sprinkler, only to catch sight of weeds that needed pulling, a branch that needed tying or vegetables that were ready to be gathered … and I would be lost to everything but the garden.

By now Bob had been with the ACTU for almost a decade and he was looking towards the presidency. Albert Monk, the man who had asked Bob to become research officer in 1958, was nearing retirement. In political matters Albert played his cards close to his chest, and was a taciturn man. His wife Frankie was the antithesis – full of fun and friendship. But on rare occasions Albert would open up about his early years around the Trades Hall, the sombre, monolithic and historic headquarters of the labour movement in Victoria. Bob and I listened, fascinated, to his tales of ballot-box skulduggery and such. The long-serving secretary of the ACTU was Harold Souter. Harold had been kind to us when we first came to Melbourne. He had negotiated the advance on Bob's salary for our deposit on a house and he'd helped us with our scanty furnishings by giving us a carpet square. Over the years the contrast between Harold's and Bob's personalities and between their different political power bases had led to some friction. The two were rivals for the presidency of the ACTU when Albert Monk retired and the battle lines were clearly drawn.

Delegates from all over Australia were involved in the presidential campaigns. In 1969, all 749 of them assembled in the Paddington Town Hall in Sydney for the conference at which the decision was to be made. A close vote was predicted and tension in the ranks was considerable. For the first time I actually paid a housekeeper to be with the children for a few days, and I bought a new dress for the occasion. I knew many of the delegates from union functions and through their involvement in the ALP. The two contenders made speeches before the vote. I could feel a particular stir of interest in the hall when Bob outlined his policies for access to good and higher education opportunities for the children of working-class men and women.

When Bob won there was jubilation amongst his supporters. And I thought, 'Great, another win, here we go, next phase.' That night we had dinner with those who had worked so hard to support him with endless lobbying - 'tying up the numbers' as it was called. There were Ray Geitzelt of the Miscellaneous Workers' Union and his wife Violet, Charlie Fitzgibbon of the Waterside Workers' and Nancy, Freddie Petersen of the Clothing Trades Unions and Heather. Twenty years later, all six of them came to the Lodge for our joint sixtieth birthday party.

After Bob took office as president, all the delegates would come to our house for an informal dinner when they descended on Melbourne at the time of each Federal Executive meeting. Often when Bob was away they would take me for a night out. One evening we went to the Windsor Hotel and while we were sitting talking I kicked off my shoes. Time to leave and they were nowhere to be found – until I spotted them parked neatly on a high window-sill: a message from the Boot Trades Unions that I should not be wearing foreign-made shoes. And if I wore one of the cotton kaftans imported from Asia which were so popular then, the Clothing Trades Union reps would look askance.

Bob was already travelling overseas to International Labour Organisation meetings each year, and there was a lot of interstate travel as well. In 1970 he was appointed to the governing body of the ILO which met every three months in Geneva, so his time away from Melbourne was considerable. His first long trip away from home had been in 1962, when the children were small and we lived in Keats Street – he went to Canada for the Duke of Edinburgh's Conference for representatives from Commonwealth countries. That was a long, study trip of about three months and I had missed him very much. By the time of the extended ILO trips, I still missed him but I also looked forward to things I could do while he was away: tasks, visits to and from friends – nothing dramatic, but the difference was knowing I could make plans and keep to them. I knew too well that the unpredictability of life with Bob could lead to disappointment as well as excitement. I had become much better at coping with the disappointments and maximising the excitement.

Now that he was President of the ACTU, Bob would go to Adelaide for the traditional Labour Day march and the sporting events which were still celebrated there with great enthusiasm. The first time he did this, he announced in his all-embracing way that the whole family would go, and we would stay at Mick and Mary Young's place. Mick had been intensely involved in the Australian Workers' Union and the Labor Party since his shearing days, so Bob and he knew each other well. The visit was an instant success. Our kids and theirs teamed up, Mary and I really liked each other and Bob and Mick shared an immense gusto for the politicking and the bonhomie. We marched through the streets, went to the Club, the lunch, the sports, the barbecue, the dinner dance – not a moment was wasted of this annual long weekend. Bob and Mick got a bit wild sometimes, and Mick had a tendency to sing the rousing hymns of his Irish heritage in the VERY early hours! And we developed a great combined rendition of the Welsh tune *Cymn Rhonda*.

We went for Labour Day weekend I think every year for the ten that Bob was president and made many Adelaide friends. I found it striking what a difference the size of Adelaide made to relationships between families there. Melbourne was so big and sprawling that it was an effort to pursue friendships with families from the unions and the Party. In Adelaide they could see each other more easily, the women and children all knew and supported each other, and – it followed – supported the men: for the roles were very much divided according to gender in those years. I could see the very clear community advantages of keeping cities to human proportions.

In this same year, 1969, Susan won a scholarship to a private church grammar school. We had agonised about the children's schooling. Sandringham East Primary School had been very good, but the local high school was still struggling to upgrade its programs and the lack of satisfaction expressed by parents was not encouraging. Our dilemma was whether to stay with the state system, which we supported ideologically, or go private. It was a problem we discussed with our colleagues, notably Clyde Holding, then leader of the state Labor opposition, and Don Dunstan, the Labor premier of South Australia. They argued that as politicians they would continue to work towards equal standards and opportunities for all children but in the meantime, as parents would seek out the best they could for their own children. We went the same way. We researched our options diligently before making the choice, but we will never know whether the children would have had a better experience had we chosen differently.

In the late sixties, my concern about Bob's health was growing and I found it helpful to talk with our family doctor, Brian Woodward. Together we tried to persuade Bob to stop giving himself such a hard time. Every so often, sometimes with only a few months respite, he would go down with a sinus attack or flu or a bad back, or simply collapse from exhaustion. It was disturbing, and very unsettling for the children. It got so that I could usually spot an attack coming on. Once when I was anxious, Brian carried us all off for a weekend with his family at his farm near Yarram in South Gippsland. Brian was astute enough to keep us all busy and we spent the whole of Saturday clambering over hills and wading through streams to get the cattle in for branding. We had fun, fresh air, exercise and good tucker, but more importantly we did it as a family and with friends. That weekend was the first of many relaxing times at Yarram. Brian bought another piece of land which had a small fibro cottage on it, and we made it modestly livable so that we could visit whenever we wanted. There were some very happy times when we would build a big fire by the creek for the evening and the two families would join in a barbecue, telling stories, singing to a guitar and generally luxuriating in the pleasure of being there.

One Christmas Bob bought a two-stroke motorbike for the kids to ride there. He rode it down from Melbourne, one steaming hot day, with the kids taking turns to ride pillion while I drove the other two in the car. We all enjoyed that little bike: it was useful as a runabout but its main function was for leisure. Once I went for a wonderful, solitary ride to the mountains and was enjoying the sense of space and freedom whizzing along the Grand Ridge Road when, splutter … splutter, I had run out of petrol!

Another happy Yarram memory for me is of the time when Stephen was preparing for his HSC exams and I took him there for a quiet weekend of study. There were such torrential rains that the swollen creek made leaving the farm impossible, and our weekend became a few days. But we had the firewood in and dry so our enforced isolation was cosy. Our only chore was to don raincoats and gumboots and plod around the soggy paddocks each day checking that the new calves were with their mothers. When the skies cleared, the sun burst through onto the freshly washed, glistening bush, and the birds were celebrating. It was one of those very special moments.

◆

In 1971, Bob took a strong position against apartheid on behalf of the union movement. The ACTU had taken an anti-apartheid stance since 1963 and its policy was in line with an international position on South Africa, endorsed by the International Confederation of Free Trade Unions. A South African rugby union team, the Springboks, was to tour Australia in 1971, after their government had vetoed the inclusion of two non-white players. Bob called for international sporting sanctions, and for the Australian government to stop the tour. The row that followed, between those for and against racism and the intervention of politics into sport, polarised attitudes throughout Australia and led to vitriolic and frightening abuse of Bob and our family – even Ellie received threatening phonecalls. The ACTU imposed bans on the Springboks' tour, the conservative McMahon Government took the opportunity to raise the old cry, 'Who's running this country, the government or the Unions,' and the union movement split over the issue. Protests at the rugby matches led to unprecedented violence between passionate anti-apartheid demonstrators and police unused to dealing with such outbursts.

Black paint was tipped on my car in the driveway one night. Ros was ridiculed, and hurt, when the kids in her class at school, making papier-mâché, looked for pictures of her father in the papers, tore them and pushed them into the glue, taunting her all the while. I was horrified that these nine- and ten-year-olds were taking up the cause of racial intolerance, even though they probably didn't understand what they were doing. The police insisted we had security at the house. I unreservedly agreed with Bob's position on apartheid, but I was furious at the way the divisions between Australians on the subject were translating into some kind of persecution of his family – it was just another way of getting at Hawke. I made – and still make – no apology for closing ranks against any intrusive journalists who sought to further inflame the effect of those events on our children. I believed the less said by me to the media, the better.

During the run-up to the federal election campaign of 1969, Senator Sam Cohen, the first Jewish Labor senator in Australia, had collapsed and died while he was campaigning in Adelaide. It was a great shock. The Jewish community wanted a memorial to him that would also be a dynamic contribution to society. A fund was established to send an ALP member or trade unionist to visit Israel who would then, on their return home, deliver the Sam Cohen Memorial Lecture. Bob was invited to make the first visit, in 1971, and the consequences were to have a profound effect on him. It happened that not long before the invitation Susan had begun to show an interest in Israel and the Palestinian question, so Bob arranged for her to accompany him and see for herself the problems of the embattled state. When Bob and Susan arrived in Perth on their way to Israel there were nasty protests from unions who opposed Bob's stand on the Springboks' tour, and as their flight took off, there was a bomb threat. The plane had to jettison fuel and return to the airport.

They travelled around Israel with the guidance and companionship of a driver and an officer from Histadrut, the equivalent of our Australian Council of Trade Unions. Susan had the extraordinary experience of being with Bob for a meeting with prime minister Golda Meir in her office, where she spoke, in tears, of the agony of committing the youth of her armed forces to the horrors of the 1967 war. Then Susan went off on her own to spend two weeks on a kibbutz in the north, at Kfarblum, where she worked with other teenagers and lived in their quarters, while Bob went on to an ILO meeting in Geneva. But, during talks in Tel Aviv, a plan was developed for Bob to meet with Alexander Shelepin, the Russian trade union leader, to discuss the plight of Soviet Jews.

Susan's overseas trip was extended when Bob collected her from the kibbutz after his Geneva talks and they went on to Moscow for the first of Bob's attempts to do something for the refuseniks – Jews who wished to leave the USSR but were denied exit.

When they arrived back in Australia, Bob delivered the Sam Cohen Memorial Lecture in which, while recognising the rights of the Palestinians, he strongly expressed his belief in Israel's right to exist within secure and internationally-recognised borders. This identified him even more closely with the Jewish community – something that did not sit altogether easily with many of his colleagues on the left of Australian politics.

◆

Young people came to our home constantly, drawn by friendship with our kids, the space, the tennis court and now a swimming pool. I felt that knowing my children's friends and opening our house to them was important for me and for them. My own parents had encouraged Edith and me to bring our friends home when we were in our teens, although in our younger years the family house was off-limits for play. The Coogee Street culture had been that kids played on the road, in the backyards or on the verandahs.

The freedoms of this new generation brought difficulties. The kids questioned everything. The solid social mores and the moral codes that were preached, if not practised, when I was growing up, had vanished. My children and their friends were better educated, certainly more outspoken than I was – in many ways they were stronger, more experienced and wiser about worldly things. I welcomed this opening up, this release from the rigidity and repression that had been imposed on my parents' generation and, to a lesser degree, my own. But there was an absence of structure in the lives of these youngsters of the sixties and seventies, a discipline that would have helped them sort through the barrage of dilemmas that faced them. Life was much more complicated than it had been for us. We went to school, went to work, married and raised families in a pattern that was rarely questioned. Roles were clear, choices and distractions relatively few. In 1974, when Susan was sixteen, I withered when she cried out accusingly to me, 'What have you and Dad given us to believe in ... except the Labor Party? And look at the [expletive deleted] mess *that's* in?'

IT'S TIME

◇

For Australians like us who cared so much about getting a federal Labor government into office, 1972 was a big year. The election was set for December. Under the leadership of Gough Whitlam, with Mick Young as Federal Secretary, the Party was confident that it was indeed time for change. During the year, the Party began to rouse itself to levels of energy and excitement which had been missing during the long, hard years in opposition. The slogan 'It's Time', and the song that went with it, reflected the national mood exactly and provided an effective focus for the campaign.

I went electioneering with Bob and Geoff Gleghorn, his media assistant. Campaigning in those days was not as focused on television as it is now, twenty years later. We would fly or drive to various electorates to support candidates, helping to consolidate the Labor vote and hopefully win some over to the cause. Bob did interviews with local papers and radio stations, we walked the streets to meet people, attended fund-raising dinners, visited regional schools and institutions, and in general helped people get to know Party policies and their candidate. That was the last campaign in which I saw Bob speak from the back of a tray truck in the time-honoured way, and on one occasion I was up there with him. Those days have gone.

An incident which affected the results not one whit, but which caused some laughs, happened at the Newcastle Workers' Club. The podium was a platform built to raise the speakers a couple of steps, large enough to accommodate a microphone and half a dozen plastic chairs. As a speaker left the microphone, I edged my chair back just a little to let him past, but that was enough to tip my chair backwards off the platform and there I was with my feet in the air! Bob's introductory remark was 'Well, that's a hard act to follow.'

One day after campaigning in Sydney we missed the scheduled flight north for an evening function. A four-seater charter plane was quickly organised and I was afraid I would be airsick, flying in the searing cross-wind. But we flew so low over the eastern beaches, and the westering sun catching the rolling surf was so breathtakingly beautiful, that I enjoyed every moment. That night proceedings had begun in the packed local hall when there was a security problem and the hall had to be cleared. More delay, then the evening's program was resumed. It was a long, exhausting day and back at the motel Bob showered then flopped on his back, naked, spreadeagled across the bed. Geoff, in his dry-humoured way, turned to me and said, 'Well, Haze, when he's spent as a political force, we can exhibit him.'

We travelled interstate and to remote places. We could feel the shifting of allegiances around the country and the meetings where Gough spoke, with his much-loved wife Margaret beside him, were groundswells of optimistic and adoring support. Crowds around the country took up the chant, 'We Want Gough'. He was offering a breakthrough of hope. The Party's proposed reforms to Australian society promised to move things on after twenty-three years of conservative government. Since the first election for the House of Representatives in 1901, Labor governments had been in office for little more than seventeen years.

On 9 December 1972, the ALP swept into power after the

long drought. Bob and I and the children were at the tally room in Melbourne and went on to Party headquarters to share the delight. You can imagine how happy Labor members and supporters were that more than two decades of tiresome, debilitating opposition had given way to the reality of government. The politically committed – particularly, I think, since they represented a party which undertook to further the aspirations of the working classes – felt a surge of expectation, of what was now possible. Exhausted workers and party apparatchiks, spouses, children and hangers-on all crushed into the Party headquarters in Melbourne to share the glow. As the night wore on and morning approached, the sparkle was becoming sentimental and the children and I headed for home. Bob stayed on: he was never one to leave a party before it finally petered out.

In January 1973, after the strain and excitement of the campaign, we took the family on a cruise in the Pacific with Mick and Mary Young and their children. John Ducker, an ACTU Executive member, his wife, Val, and their boys came too. It was a good holiday, with only one anxious moment when Bob and Mick made a drama of seeing how fine they could cut their return to the ship after a day of hospitality in Fiji. They leapt onto the gangplank as it was being removed. Together, those two were like kids seeing how naughty they could be. When the ship reached Sydney we visited Gough and Margaret at Kirribilli House, the prime minister's Sydney residence, and the celebratory visit was an affirmation that Labor really was IN.

◆

My mother came to stay with us for almost six months that year. I am sure she was shocked by the way we lived. It was so different from her own experience of family life and the way she and Dad raised Edith and me. Our lives were not church-centred now and our activities and friendships were mainly built around the Labor Party. By now I had a network of good neighbourhood friends who Mum liked, but I know she was upset by the drinking she saw. She had never kept liquor in the cupboards at home, probably remembering the bitterness caused by her father's drinking habits. She never, ever, in all her visits, made any criticisms or passed any judgments. She just fitted in, being helpful and quiet, as she always was. Although she was now seventy-six years old, one would never have guessed it, to see her digging the garden and doing whatever other tasks needed to be done.

And by now I was a smoker, which Mum found difficult to accept. I had never smoked in my life until the mid-sixties. It was foolish to begin, but at the time it was very voguish for women to smoke and most of my friends did. Besides, it allowed me to feel a little more worldly and a little bit defiant of Bob. I came to enjoy the companionship of lighting up with friends and the lift the nicotine gave me. I didn't become a very heavy smoker but it was too often a reaction to anxiety and I became dependent upon it.

In the middle of the year Mum looked after the children while I went overseas with Bob. After seeing union officials in Singapore and Tehran, we went to Israel. I stayed there for six days while Bob went on to more union meetings in Geneva. The Histadrut provided me with a generous-spirited Israeli-born driver who had fought in the Six Day War, loved his country, knew it well and was full of anecdotes. For four days Arieh and I travelled around this tiny country, while he explained all about the people, the places and their history. When there was a gap between points of interest he would announce, 'Hazzell, you have a forty-kilometre sleep now', which I would proceed to do on the back seat of the car, gathering energy for the next bit of the marathon. I began to see why Bob and Sue had responded so eagerly to the Israelis, their inventiveness and the passion they bring to building a productive country from the stony desert. They joke that: 'When Moses came from the Red Sea he turned the wrong way', since the rich oilfields are on the other side of the Jordan River.

◆

At home in Sandringham, I sometimes thought Bob was trying to destroy himself. He was now federal president of the ALP, as well as president of the ACTU and sat on many bodies and government committees as a representative of the union movement. It can be easily understood that his time at home was negligible. It was almost impossible for me to get any input from him on family matters and they were becoming more and more difficult for me to manage alone.

I had intended to raise our family in much the same way as Mum and Dad had raised Edith and me, but I became increasingly confused by the challenges of the 'Age of Aquarius'. In the early seventies our children were on the threshold of their teens – a difficult enough stage at the best of times. Now, as I saw it, the three main things that made their lives different from mine at that age were television, the contraceptive pill and their social experimentation with drugs that were new to me. In my youth it was alcohol and tobacco that young people tried – but both were the preserve of males. These new developments produced striking changes in behaviour even among my own peers, but more so among the young. I was aware that marijuana was available in the schools and parks, and that curiosity about sex and drugs was openly expressed. Young people were pressured with accusations of being 'square', or worse, if they didn't go along with the crowd. I read all I could get hold of, especially about marijuana – 'dope' or 'pot' as the kids called it. They countered adult worries with the argument that 'dope' made them peaceful, better than being a 'juice freak' – a reference to the aggression they saw alcohol causing in the older generation. I was not convinced by marijuana's harmless image. My real fear, bordering on a state of chronic panic, was that it could be a bridge to the use of the dreaded heroin. I was determined to use persuasion and what discipline I could, without losing communication and trust with our children, to keep them safe.

I wouldn't want to live those times again, they were so difficult. Bob was freeing up his own life, partly, perhaps, in defiance of the constraints he had experienced as a manse boy: he drank 'the evil alcohol' and he 'womanised'. Alcohol could plunge him into deep despair or make him aggressive. I was the one on the spot. When he did respond to my pleas, he was good and strong, but there was no continuity. I longed for his support in day-to-day interaction with the children but, because it was not available, we would often address the difficult issues together only when they had blown out to crisis proportions. I felt inadequate in the face of the responsibilty I was bearing and resentful about his lack of involvement. Our family was typical of many around us.

As I feel my way back into the years when I needed to adapt to responsibilities of family which almost consumed me, and the adjustments necessary in our marriage, I fear that it may, to the reader, appear too glum. Certainly I had low moments and so did Bob, but together and separately there were many positive aspects and events in our lives which offered new experiences and new friendships, opening up our view of the world. And even in our somewhat abnormal lifestyle there was a thread of the normal everyday pleasures. We always had friends in the neighbourhood – mostly through our children – and an easy drop-in culture for cuppas or a drink. Impromptu, shared meals and outings were very much a part of the way we were with our children, as they liked it when their friends were included. Bob's specialty in the kitchen was 'Muck', his name for a dish his mother used to make on Sunday nights, and he made it his own creation now. Basically it was a tin of spaghetti in tomato sauce, with chopped onion and tomato and anything else he could find and eggs to bind it as he stirred it in the pot. Then he piled it all on top of hot toast with lots of grated cheese. It was very good! I always had something in the freezer and I also had friendly relations with the local small shopkeepers – so I could rustle up a meal. Bob's spontaneity tested the system at times: once when he asked the touring English Test Cricket team home at short notice, the local butcher opened up on Sunday morning and brought me the meat for a barbecue. Our friends Doug and Carmel Poulter sometimes called in during their courting days, and Carmel would say she had never seen anyone create a meal so quickly from apparently nowhere.

As President of the ACTU, Bob was much sought after by the media. Public relations were an important aspect of his work and he had many journalist friends who he asked home. Sometimes I felt uncomfortable, and thought they saw me as awkward and unworldly – but among the media circus I found another special friend. She was Vera Wasowski, a few years younger than me, a post-war immigrant from Poland who had an air of sophistication and glamour about her as well as a refreshing earthiness. She was sensitive to my unease and befriended me. When Vera came to Australia in 1958 she found a job with the Australian Broadcasting Commission as a make-up lady. She had an M.A. in Literature and a degree in journalism from Warsaw University and by the time I met her the ABC employed her as a researcher on current affairs programs. She loved the arts and we began to go to concerts and films together. We visited at each other's houses where we would cook and philosophise endlessly, in our amateurish way, about the meaning of life. We read books and discussed them together. Vera was married, counted many men and women amongst her friends, and was very much aware of the value of women to each other – the 'sisterhood' as we had come to call our female networks. She was always good company and some of her friends and ABC colleagues became friends of mine.

Vera was a realist, and knew how prevailing attitudes, particularly in the television industry, meant that a woman's physical appearance affected her opportunities for success. A woman who was not conventionally attractive or, worse, who was old, was less acceptable. In the course of her work, Vera had met a cosmetic surgeon and become interested in the idea of having a face-lift. She reminded me that I was showing wear and tear, with sagging eyes, and enlisted me to join her in finding out more about it. Coincidentally, my friend Doctor Brian Woodward was the anaesthetist for Vera's cosmetic surgeon. When Bob and I and the kids were at Yarram helping to get the hay in, Brian and I sat in a paddock on some bales and talked it over. He strongly encouraged and reassured me. Vera and I would toss the idea around from time to time and I slowly got used to it as a future possibility.

◆

In 1974 Bob went to a conference in Belgrade and arranged for the children and me to meet him there, then motor south through Yugoslavia for a two-week holiday in Greece. The sun shone and the sea sparkled. We visited Delphi and the ancient outdoor theatre at Epidaurus. We walked the streets of Athens, and visited the

Parthenon, the Plaka, and the cafes. We spent five glorious days on a yacht, fishing, swimming, relaxing, and touring the islands. It was a wonderful holiday.

News reached us while we were away, that Gough Whitlam had appointed Lance Barnard, his deputy, to an ambassadorship. In Athens, Bob knew immediately that the posting would prove to be a serious, wounding blow to the Labor government. He spent hours on the telephone, answering calls from the media in Australia and talking to Labor officials, cursing roundly! The direct result of Lance Barnard's departure was a disastrous by-election, losing his seat in Tasmania.

Later that year my doctor recommended a hysterectomy and I was in hospital when the federal election was held on 18 May 1974. Paul Munro, our friend from New Guinea days, and his dear wife Jane sketched a cartoon of me prostrate in bed, captioned 'Hazel, lying down in protest against labour' - the two kinds of labour which had perhaps caused me most effort in my life, the reproductive and the political! It was a couple of days before the result of the election was clear. Labor limped home. Pressures increased.

Things were not going well for Rosslyn, and I made an appointment for an interview at an alternative school that I thought might suit her better. I insisted that Bob come. Stephen wanted to come, too, because he was unhappy at Melbourne Grammar, the elite school where he was on a full scholarship. Woodleigh, the alternative school, was in the bush, an hour by train and bus from our house. The children there were given more freedom but more responsibility. Rosslyn and Stephen began there in the second term of 1975. Sue was already at University.

Many years later, Steve wrote a piece for *The Independent Monthly* about Melbourne Grammar and the way it shaped his ideas in his teenage years. It read, in part:

I won a scholarship to Melbourne Grammar. I still don't know whether this was a fateful move, or just another path towards the same conclusion. To what extent are attitudes and values mould-ed by the social environment, or in my case by a violent reaction against this environment? Is it thanks to Melbourne Grammar that I have spent most of my adult life in the corner of Australia furthest distant, geographically and in almost every other sense, from the South Yarra milieu of my secondary school years?

My apologies to those who were the exception that proved the rule, but you would be struggling to find a more arrogant, self-satisfied, self-seeking congregation of teenagers than the Melbourne Grammar boys. Even the other private schools, with the possible exception of Geelong Grammar, were looked upon as inherently inferior. We were the crème de la crème.

The longer I was there, the less comfortable I felt, and the more questioning I became.

Fourth year, when I was fifteen, was the critical one. It was at this point, according to the immutable social traditions, that the Melbourne Grammar boys began going to 'socials' with the girls from Merton Hall and other suitably proper schools.

There was nothing genteel about the process. The talk in the back rows of the class on Mondays about the 'scrubbers' and the 'goers' and the various uses to which vaseline could be put, was worlds away from the gentlemanly style the masters and the hierarchy liked to promote.

I found it all offensive – an extension of the arrogance I was coming to dislike so much – and fascinating. Not being a participant, I drifted apart. You are either one of the boys or you aren't.

By fifth year I loathed Melbourne Grammar and all it stood for. There was a very small number of my contemporaries who were, to varying degrees, similarly left-leaning, or at least malcontent. We found a haven, almost by accident, in a small dark room on the top floor of one of the newer buildings that overlooked the main oval.

This was the newsboard office. The newsboard was a noticeboard for official notices, and a rarely used forum for students to write articles about whatever took their fancy.

It was supposed to be run by a committee headed by a prefect, but the newsboard committee was pretty informal, and seemed to have slipped outside the system. So a few of us adopted this room, and brought in a kettle and coffee and teabags and tried to make it our own. One of us knew a dealer, and I was furtively introduced to grass, and very occasionally, hash, in the rotundas of the Botanic Gardens after school. We thought ourselves to be very radical, and by Melbourne Grammar standards we were …

I had had enough of my soccer coach and Melbourne Grammar. I typed out a two-page article … accusing the coach and the captain of racism, and pinned it up on the noticeboard.

Within an hour I was in the headmaster's office. The allegations against the coach were simply unacceptable; the question of their accuracy or otherwise was not even discussed. As for the captain, I was told such actions were not condoned, but he was a very fine chap who was an important figure in the school.

I was censored. The offending paragraphs were to be removed. I went to the noticeboard, and folded back the last section of the final page and the top of the second, which contained specific allegations, and left a general attack on racism in the school. But I let it be known where readers should look …

It all seems very schoolboyish in retrospect, but I must admit to feeling rather proud of myself at the time. I felt I had put on record my loathing and contempt, and declared myself a rebel.

I went up to Melbourne Grammar when Stephen was in trouble over his piece on the noticeboard. There was to be an open day at the school and his words were an embarrassment. I defended him strongly, partly by saying that boys not much older than him could be sent, by law, to the Vietnam War yet here were not permitted even to voice controversial thoughts. It was clear that, although Stephen caused them discomfort, they did not want to lose such an academically successful student. He had only two of the annual three terms at Woodleigh for his last school year, and missed most of one of them through glandular fever. But he passed his Higher School Certificate very comfortably.

◆

I was smoking more now, and drinking. It had become a routine for me to have a drink before dinner, the time of day when the loneliness got to me and I was feeling apprehensive about what the evening might bring. How silly to drink alone, though at the time it seemed a comfort. I had always been a half-hearted drinker even though the circles in which we moved practically demanded it – to be a 'wowser' was to be beyond the pale, socially. Recently I recalled those times with my friend Wendy McCarthy. She cried 'It was that cheap cask-wine!' An idea which immediately rang bells for me. We recalled how it was the done thing to keep a cask always in the fridge for drop-ins. It became part of the housewives' culture, and showed up in the way our days and nights would end; and even in our skin, and our weight. I had hung on doggedly to my Responsible Mother and Wife role and remained cautious. But everything around me was changing. I was angry and confused and, I have to admit, afraid of the complications in my life. One Saturday night we went to a friend's house for a fund-raising barbecue for the local conservation group, of which the children were a part, and that night I got really DRUNK, for the first time. It is so hard for me to commit that to paper, even now. It was a good party which the young people and their parents, including me, had worked hard to organise. It was just walking distance from our home. The children were mildly amused and put me to bed. But Bob was not amused.

By now I was in trouble. Perceptive friends realised that if my life were less isolated, I would cope better. I knew this too. I had passed my nightschool English course and had gone on, in 1969, to do another matriculation subject, politics, through the Council for Adult Education. I had been looking for a job, in a tentative way, without success. A dinner was arranged with David Scott, director of the Brotherhood of St Laurence, a prestigious, church-based charitable organisation, where it might be possible for me to do some voluntary work. It was a pretty disastrous introduction. Bob and I both got drunk. I took a taxi home and Bob did not come home at all that night. But I discussed things with David and was eased into voluntary work for half a day each week. Here I was known just as Hazel Masterson, and I began to relax and feel comfortable. Eventually the word got around but by then I was accepted for myself, without the sometimes dubious attention that the Hawke name attracted.

I began on a support work program at the Family Centre for Low Income People. This centre had been set up in 1972, with some funding from the Whitlam Government, in an attempt to do something about the long-term, endemic poverty afflicting clients of the Brotherhood of St Laurence. Sixty families who bore the many-layered disadvantages of chronic poverty were chosen, and agreed to become members.

The project was housed in a former nunnery behind the offices of the Brotherhood in Fitzroy, an old, inner suburb of Melbourne. It was the brainchild of Concetta Benn, who had written her Masters thesis on the subject of how people remain powerless to change their circumstances while they are on a generational treadmill of deprivation. Support workers and the provision of a minimum wage would assist the families towards achieving more order and less conflict in their lives, and create a breathing space in which they could identify their needs, establish goals and work towards them. In the second three-year phase of the project, when it was renamed the Action and Resource Centre for Low-income People, I attended a three-day camp in the country where the families redefined and adopted their goals:

power over information
power over relationships
power over resources
power over decision-making.

Thinking these principles through, it becomes clear that the dynamics within a life, and the possibilities for a life, can be transformed.

I increased my hours at the centre, learning all the time from the support workers and the families. And as I watched and worked and learned there, the possibilities for application in my own life-development did not escape me. The program was full of pragmatism and courage and I felt privileged to be part of it. I had never fully understood, as I feel most people probably don't understand, the consequences of chronic poverty, the depth, breadth and complexity of the obstacles that must be overcome by people in such circumstances. 'Chronic: lasting a long time, lingering, inveterate,' according to my dictionary – here it was, and here in this place was the challenge to break the cycle. Of course, there were upsets galore at the Centre. The lives of the people were precarious and disaster prone, extremes of behaviour were displayed and much work was done on the resolution of conflict.

After my years at the Centre, I moved to the Brotherhood headquarters and worked a four-day week in the library for a while until I went full-time to the Social Issues and Research Department to be secretary to its director, Connie Benn. This brought me into contact with a broader scope of the Brotherhood's work. It was a period of increasing concentration on social justice strategies; on developing projects which were, like the Action and Resource Centre, not just bandaid charity, but serious attempts to bring about change in the lives of their clientele and also in the broader society.

I had lots of new ideas to think about, came into contact with different attitudes, made lasting friends and enjoyed their company and talk enormously. I discovered the pleasures, which Bob had known for so long, of evenings after work at the pub, where the wine flowed with the argument and drinking was happily accepted as part of the companionship. I enjoyed the company of men and women and had no hang-ups about going to the theatre or out to dinner with a man – just as I would with a woman. But at no time did I even contemplate an emotional or sexual relationship with another man. It was clear that I was Bob's life partner and that was sacrosanct. I loved working for Connie, and it all provided good ballast and balance which I needed.

At home, life was not plain sailing. I was torn between welcoming the changes that were taking place in social attitudes and feeling very insecure in my own family role because of these changes. In 1975 Anne Summers published her book *Damned Whores and God's Police*. It clarified my understanding of the way our society is constructed. In writing about the colonisation of women and the stereotypes it produces, she described God's Police as those 'who do not resist their female socialisation ... [they] seek a male protector and remain faithful to his will while raising children within the prescribed family institution.' The Damned Whores, on the other hand, might 'fulfil the colonial imperative of producing offspring but because they have done so outside the prescribed institution ... they and their children are usually subjected to some form of social disapproval.'

'With women divided as they are', Summers writes, 'men can have it both ways. They are able to have both a wife and a mistress.' These are minuscule snippets from a book of nearly five hundred pages but reading the whole gave me explanations which in a curious way helped me. I didn't much like falling into the category of God's Police even though I had no desire to be a Damned Whore. This type-casting of women was, and perhaps still is, condoned by political and church organisations, a consequence of their origins as exclusively male domains – and their continuing domination by men. The self-interest is clear: if they wish, men may pursue more variation in their relationships than women, constrained as we have been by economics and our biology. It is clear to me now that when Bob wrote for me to join him in Oxford urgently back in 1954 and I so eagerly and unreservedly responded, that it was, on his part, an honest and open request for me to protect him from his own natural, worldly desires; and that I felt honoured and gratified that he had chosen me to fill that role ... to be one of God's Police.

◆

Life was not comfortable, either, for the federal Labor government, for which we had such hopes. Would it remain in office long enough for its refreshing reforms to become entrenched? One reform especially dear to me was the universal health care scheme. I knew how crucial it was to low-income families. Although it was not yet finely tuned, there was no doubt in my mind that it was a most necessary and civilised innovation. It was also one which the conservative parties opposed. Their policy was to dismantle it, though seventeen years later I am pleased to say that Australia still has a universal health scheme. But in 1975, the Whitlam Labor Government was lurching towards failure less than three years after coming to power. That story is not for this book but I was in a position to observe some of the personalities and events in what was looming for us as a political tragedy. The telephone at our house kept me aware of how events were moving, and Bob's involvement in them. For journalists, overseas callers or colleagues wanting to discuss political emergencies, the time of day or night was no impediment. Bob would phone at any hour too, and often talked to me about politics and union affairs. It was of endless interest to me and I felt the privilege of following momentous events from the inside. During 1974 and 1975 these events were taking their toll on Bob. His life was on overwhelm and his drinking at its most harmful. There was a drawn-out series of political nightmares which in the end brought down the Whitlam Government.

On the afternoon of 11 November 1975, I had just driven home from the artist Louis Kahan's place. He had asked me to see his almost-completed portrait of Bob, which was to be hung in the federal offices of the Labor Party in Canberra. Susan was at home and took a telephone call. I heard her scream at the news. At the request of the leader of the Opposition, Malcolm Fraser, and after a stand-off over the Opposition's blocking of bills and denial of supply in the parliament, the governor-general, Sir John Kerr, had declared the Whitlam Government unable to govern. The Opposition had become the government. It was a sickening blow. As I drove into the city with a bag packed for Bob to go to Canberra, my mind flashed back to the day Bob, on that busy telephone in our kitchen at Sandringham, had been appalled when Gough told him he had appointed John Kerr as governor-general. Bob's anger, and the invective he had used to tell Gough exactly what he thought of the decision, had been extreme.

◆

In 1976, Bob and I went to Israel for a ceremony to dedicate a forest to him in acknowledgment of his active support for the country. Clem and Ellie Hawke came with us. It was a very special journey for them not only because of the honour to their son but also because of the identification they felt with the historic, Biblical places. They visited the Garden of Gethsemane, the Holy Sepulchre in Bethlehem and the Mount of Olives. In their ageing years, this trip drew together the two most significant and constant threads in their lives: their religion and their son Bob.

◆

Our drinking, Bob's indecision and my unhappiness about our marriage were serious. Probably the most difficult thing of all, which I couldn't really do much about, was the insidious pressure from people around Bob who had their own personal or political agendas to pursue through him. It was all eating us both away, separately and maritally and as parents.

In 1977, at a dinner for the Queen at Parliament House in Canberra, Bob and I were seated at the same table as the writer Tom Keneally. Bob had a few drinks under his belt and took on a prominent newspaper proprietor at the table in a ribald manner. But, more seriously, he was in fact concerned by the media's hostility towards the trade union movement and was proposing they should somehow get together to reach a better understanding. Tom now remarks that this was consistent with what Bob did when he later became prime minister: the summit, consensus. Bob also asked Tom that night to write a book that would reconcile his children's generation to his own, and dedicate it to him. Tom replied that he couldn't write such a book and remembers that I said, 'Maybe if you were home for more than one day a month you would not need a book.' But Tom did write a book about Antarctica which he dedicated to Bob. He wrote, 'To Hazel, the Consort *par excellence*' in the copy he sent to me.

◆

By 1977 Stephen was the only one of the children still living at home. In March, I urged Bob to spend time with him – maybe they could go on a fishing trip, do something in which they would find companionship. There was no easy or regular interaction between them, and I felt like a messenger telling him about the children and them about him. As they approached adulthood and independence, I felt a sense of loss about it for him, for them, for all of us as a family.

Steve finished school that year. He enjoyed learning, but he was quite firm that he would not go on to university. He said to me one day, 'There are other things to learn and other ways to learn them.' He soon went to Tasmania, where he lived in the bush in an abandoned shepherd's hut for peppercorn rental, and worked with people interested in protecting the environment. Conservation was emerging as a political issue at this time, particularly among young people looking to right the wrongs they saw around them. They were critical, disappointed with much of what they saw, but there was a refreshing optimism and challenge in some of the protest action that was taking place.

After a little while, I went and stayed there with Steve for three days and could see how he was enjoying it. It was so bitterly cold that in the mornings we would break the film of ice on the dam to get water for making porridge. I took my sturdy walking boots and each day we drove to a different place and took long walks in the beautiful Tasmanian bush. Later that year, Bob and I were in Tasmania and spent an evening in the hut with Stephen by a glow-ing log fire, discussing the pros and cons of the uses of uranium and nuclear power. In those days the public debate on the issue was quite divisive. Bob and Stephen tried, but were unable to get close on the issue.

◆

Meanwhile, Vera and I were nearing a decision on cosmetic surgery and finally took the plunge in 1977. We submitted ourselves to the knife, feeling – well – almost confident. We had decided to keep the matter light-hearted and went prepared with music to listen to, books to read and Mickey Mouse masks to wear when visitors came. A day later the bandages were removed, to reveal swelling and bruising and stitching which made it seem unbelievable that our faces would ever be recognisable again. But we trusted Leo, our sur-geon, and had each other to keep our spirits high. We convalesced together at our house. Vera's husband, Jan, brought us a bottle of champagne to celebrate, and flowers and food supplies daily. We cooked really nice meals for ourselves, played our favourite music, pottered in the garden and rested a lot. When we began to venture out we wore dark glasses, had haircuts and got used to being looked at with the slightly perplexed expressions of people wondering … it was as if we were the same, only different! We just pretended we didn't notice their unstated curiosity. Only two weeks later, Bob wanted me to go with him to a dinner, at the home of his mate Colin Cunningham and his wife Gloria, where the guests were mostly jockeys. I braced myself and, if anyone looked inquisitive, I told them I had sore eyes. Which I did. When our faces settled down after a few weeks we felt pleased with the result.

◆

Bob was invited to go to China in the Australian spring of 1978 in his capacity as leader of the trade union movement. We were excited by the invitation. China was still relatively closed to outsiders and was undergoing considerable upheaval in the post-Mao Tse Tung era. I took leave from my job and went with him. What an extraordinary trip it was.

Friendliness, good humour and courtesy were the order of the day as we were shown their systems of agriculture and industry, their communes and Street Committees. I was made welcome at all of Bob's discussions with officials and committees, so with their approval – in fact they were delighted – I took shorthand notes of the proceedings. When we were in Shanghai, I sat at a bench in the Post Office to type a lot of it up on an ancient, hired machine that sounded more like a chaffcutter than a typewriter. We found apparent openness in our hosts, yet there were some questions which met with that polite evasion which Westerners are not very good at dealing with and call inscrutable. The big, black, Russian-made cars we used were fitted with curtains which I pulled back to see the sights but, every time we left the car, they had been drawn closed by the driver on our return. Denouncing the Gang of Four was routine and obligatory; we lost count of the number of times we heard the same speech. But we saw projects which displayed the organisational skills of the Chinese – and what they were achieving predominantly through people-power rather than modern technology, was breathtaking. The feasts we shared were memorable and ranged from grand banquets to dipping into communal pots in factory canteens. Our guide and interpreter, Mr. Wang, had learned English in Africa and was an excellent guide and companion. On occasions we invited him to eat with us, but he always kept a professional distance and declined politely. That is, until his tour of duty was completed and we were on a train to our exit point from China. Bob had dozed off, and I invited Mr. Wang to play Patience with me, as he had shown interest when I played it alone. He was just delighted to learn, and would ask in the most charming way, 'And now, can I open this little fellow,' as he checked which card he could turn up. He had relaxed and, when Bob woke, we chatted about his family and his living conditions in a way which added another dimension to our China experience.

◆

In late 1978, Bob stepped down from his five-year presidency of the ALP. The Federal Executive organised an informal drinks party in Canberra to mark the occasion. The Federal Secretary, David Combe, phoned me at the Brotherhood during the day to say I must be there, so I asked permission to leave work, drove home to pack, then to the airport and flew to Canberra. It was a tense and difficult occasion for me. I was not in a mood to hear the testimonials to Bob, though I knew only too well the extent and value of his services to the Party, and it was my Party too. I am not proud of feeling some resentment by then of its pull on his time and energy, away from the family. My confidence was low and I felt socially inept in the company of the Party members. I drowned my sorrows, making matters worse, and next day suffered a crippling and humiliating hangover. Rosslyn had come and, although it was lovely to see her, I was filled with concern for her: at this stage she was living interstate with some other young people and I was worried about the world they inhabited. I daresay she was concerned for me, as well. I just couldn't cope with it all as we picnicked next day with the Combe family, trying to pretend limply that all would be well. Even now, as I recall that day, I re-experience the wretchedness and despair I felt over what appeared to be the disintegration of my family and my life.

◆

On Australia Day, 1979, Bob was to receive the Companion of the Order of Australia. It was at a time when he was withdrawn and his life was overwhelming him. I arranged for his father to go to the ceremony in my stead, as the only accompanying guest. Clem was thrilled, even more so when he was invited by the governor-general, Sir Zelman Cowan, to offer the grace before dinner. He overflowed with pride and pleasure.

TURNING POINTS

◇

Early in 1979 I consulted a lawyer to find out what my options and rights were if Bob and I hit rock bottom. I didn't want to leave the marriage even though it was in a fragile state. One thing, however, was clear to me. I did not intend to be one of those middle-aged women whose husbands discard them when they have served their purpose. This was the era when older people were referred to as 'the Olds' or 'Wrinklies', and youth was idolised. 'Geriatric' was often a term of denigration.

It is so easy for women to be left behind in their experience of the world outside the family, and lose the interest of their more urbane husbands. It is perhaps not surprising that when men leave marriages it is usually for younger women. It seems that at times this can be reason enough, that it gives middle-aged men the feeling of regaining their youth and virility – another chance. A lot of couples I knew in those years were separating like this, and I saw many sad, humiliated women who had to rebuild their lives alone, most of them at financial disadvantage, without the skills to find work, and sometimes with children still to be cared for. Perhaps what hurt them most, if it happened, was seeing their ex-husbands enthralled with a new, young family and giving them the devoted fathering his first family had not enjoyed because of the treadmill a man can be on while building his career. Years later a man in the public eye admitted this with clarity and poignancy when he told me wistfully, 'I didn't see my first children, they passed me by ... I wasn't looking.' I wanted to save my marriage for myself, but I was ferocious in my determination that our children had a right to their father.

In earlier years I was intent on protecting our marriage and being completely loyal to Bob in all circumstances, but I was changing and times were changing. People were becoming more open. Women, especially, were able to support each other, both by comparing experiences and in practical ways. Even small things – sharing the care of children, being company for each other, developing interests together – could become important to women who had been totally home-centred. By now I was really hurting, and felt glad that I was freer to accept, or even to seek, understanding. I found I was not alone, and slowly we women found each other.

Melbourne had not been an easy city to settle in when we came in 1958. There was an initial welcome, but somehow everyone was already busy with friends and family. Years later I realised most of the intimate and lasting friendships I had made were with women who, like me, were from elsewhere – immigrants to Melbourne, looking for each other, and that we had all experienced the same thing – we had been outsiders. Now, women's networks took on a new dimension. I discovered that goldmine.

Bob did not know about my visit to the lawyer. By an extraordinary coincidence, when I got home that evening, he was lying on the kitchen sofa – ill, in a reflective mood and resolute that he would give up drinking totally and forever. I had made considerable efforts to understand the use and effects of alcohol. I read widely and had spoken with medical practitioners and psychologists. Many of Bob's friends had talked with me about their concern for him; notably Lionel Revelman, George Rockey and Col

Cunningham. We were searching for ways to help but, of course, no one could resolve the problem except Bob himself. In the early years of our family life I had been judgemental, but not now: I had long ceased feeling that it was character weakness, indulgence or irresponsibility which drove his drinking. I had seen his dark despair, his remorse, the times when he had felt defeated and seen his life spin out-of-control – conditions no one would willingly submit to again and again. I was no help. Since I had been working, I knew the after-work pleasures of the pub with my own friends. I knew too how easy it was to drink too much – and I had experienced excruciating remorse over my own behaviour. Two factors which concealed the extent of Bob's problem were that he did not suffer the usual headachy hangovers, and he had an extraordinary ability to bounce back to fulfil his work commitments, with the kind of intellectual and physical application not normally possible after such an intake of alcohol. His resilience repeatedly amazed medicos, his colleagues and me.

That same evening I told him I had been to the lawyer and why. Even while I was talking, I felt some hope that this might be a breakthrough, for I believed his constant drinking was the source of most of our troubles. The difficulties we both had – to understand and to be understood by the other – were overwhelmingly caused by our lack of opportunity to really talk about what was happening to us. Drinking excluded that kind of communication between us; so his intention to stop certainly had my full support. The next night we went out to a dinner, 'on the wagon'.

While we were there Bob received a phonecall to say that his mother was seriously ill, and perhaps would not recover. Would he go to her? Ellie was failing, with pneumonia – this was nature's way of taking her. He asked me to go with him, so I did. By the time we got to Perth, the doctors had done what they are trained to do. She had rallied and we were able to have a little, limited conversation with her. She lived for several months more in intensive care, an almost unconscious, tragic figure. Perhaps we found it even more difficult to accept because of the contrast with her vital and powerful life. Ellie was only once more in communication with her son, when he visited her in June that year – an intimate exchange which he still treasures. Beyond my expression of sympathy, we didn't talk about it much. But I could see it was difficult for Bob. I knew his affectionate, matey relationship with his father had in certain ways marginalised Ellie. She once said to me, 'Bob would never let me touch him when he was little, when he was sick and needed some medicine … all those things … it was Clemmie he wanted.' But, as an adult, Bob was aware how much he owed her. He never hesitated to acknowledge that it was Ellie who had expected so much of him and who had relentlessly urged him on. She had convinced him that he must try for the scholarship to Perth Modern School and she had sat with him, in her teacher role, coaching and encouraging. Winning that scholarship had been, in a sense, the gateway to the rest of his life.

◆

Back in Melbourne I kept on with my work and the friendships that sustained me. I never liked to be far from a telephone, though, so the children could contact me. They were no longer at home but they were still young and vulnerable. No matter where the kids were or what they needed, the door was open, and they and their friends were welcome. I made sure they knew that we would support and help them.

One of the most important things in families, both for children and spouses, is never to close off possibilities – particularly, never to make demands or threats. There may always be room for change for the better if the lines of communication are left open. It is still a matter of great comfort to me that over those difficult years I always had a confiding and open relationship with the children and many of their friends, and they took me seriously, as a friend.

Early in 1979 another instance of networking among women proved to be of inestimable value to me. It was Susan who suggested that I should consult a psychologist she had found helpful and who had become a friend. Her name was Donna. She worked out of a community clinic and I liked her immediately. When I spoke to her about my lack of confidence in dealing with my life, she responded with wonderful freshness, and optimism when it was appropriate. She had listening skills such as I had never come across, and always thought carefully about how to manage the tactics and strategies of a situation. There was no grinding over the past, or wallowing in it, but an intelligent, canny understanding, and a 'where do we go from here' approach. She didn't ever advise me what to do, but helped me deal with my exhausting inability to sleep and my drinking. Then she supported me while I came to decisions in my own circuitous way. Her value was of pure gold for me, as I dealt with some unsteadying blows. Bob was thinking through his political and personal future and I wondered whether he was ever going to be able to control his drinking – he had quickly fallen off the wagon.

We had reached our lowest ebb. Both of us, at times in our trauma, took extreme positions. I had developed the confidence to know that the children and I would manage and could take the risk of putting everything on the line. Each of us asked the other to leave. We both stayed.

Letters were one of the things I found hard to handle. Some were meant to hurt me and others had good intentions, but I would have preferred never to have received any of them. I had been getting painful letters for years, including some from women who felt they had a claim on Bob. But now, when speculation and gossip about Bob's personal life and my unhappiness began to get around, I was receiving more unsettling mail. Most was from strangers – tell-tales – and some was anonymous. A few letters were composed of cut-out newspaper type. Some said I was weak for not opting out of the marriage.

But I was steadily working through my own thoughts and feelings. One thing I clung to, which may seem crazy to others, was that Bob was so much like his mother. To many, including me at times, Ellie seemed abrasive and judgemental as she pushed obsessively towards her goals in life, but in her late fifties she mellowed beautifully – somehow she let herself relax and become more accessible. Her undoubted wisdom and intelligence became less threatening. She was softer, more easily lovable. And Bob was already fifty! But a more rational, sustaining part of my hope for us was the closeness we'd established at the beginning. We'd had such unforgettable years together when we were younger. I had known the young, loving Bob. I was not going to dissociate myself from that man. Nor was I going to walk away from my whole adult life-time's thirty-three-year input to a partnership, marriage and family, only to carry with me the sense of failure that I knew would engulf me.

◆

In May 1979 Bob was asked by Isi Leibler, president of the Exec-utive Council of Australian Jewry, to go to Moscow to plead again for the release of Soviet Jews. Isi knew the trip would be stressful and felt that I should go with Bob as support. We flew to Israel, then on to Moscow with a mission which called for strong nerves and quick thinking.

We were met at the airport by a group of stolid-looking, dark-suited men and taken in a large, black, curtained car to the Hotel Sputnik (where Bob ran the tap while he talked with me in case we were bugged), then straight on down to dinner in the base-ment. We had been seated at the dinner table for a few minutes when I was asked to go back upstairs with two men to check the luggage. Off I went, but the lift got stuck. There I was, marooned between floors with two fellows from the KGB, neither of whom spoke English – not a good feeling. Eventually the lift got going and we found that the luggage was in our rooms all right – but one case had been opened and presumably searched. I was appalled and rather intimidated by this introduction to Moscow.

Back at the dinner table, glasses were raised astonishingly frequently for obligatory toasts of straight vodka. The Australian ambassador, Murray Bouchier, who was seated on my right, noticed my hesitation. He muttered to me from behind his bushy mous-tache to hold the vodka in my mouth and release it into the glass of water set before me, and to keep taking some rye bread along with my meal and the toasts. I was determined that throughout our stay in Moscow one of us would remain entirely sober.

For the next few days there was a constant round of meet-ings and discussions about the exit of Jews from the USSR and a wide range of foreign affairs matters. We developed a guarded cordiality with the two KGB officers who accompanied us everywhere, except on some evenings. Then, on three occasions and using transport provided by the Australian embassy, we visited gatherings of refuseniks at the flat where one of the families lived. Those evenings were sombre because of the oppression these remarkable people had experienced over many years and yet electric with a daring hope that the time of their release from the Soviet Union might be hastened by Bob's efforts. We heard of the accusations against them by the state. The authorities claimed, for instance, that Victor Prestin was in possession of State secrets through his work. He was an accomplished scientist whose research had long been superseded in the years that he had been forced to stay in the USSR and work as a lift driver. We met the wife of Professor Alexander Lerner who was incarcerated in Siberia for years, experiencing horrifically severe conditions.

During our last two days in Moscow, I was urged by our two KGB attendants to go to Leningrad as their guest for a sight-seeing tour. Much as I would have loved visiting that great city, its buildings and its artworks, the idea of leaving the USSR at the earliest possible moment had far greater appeal. I also thought it was important to accompany Bob to Rome, where he was to meet and report to Isi Leibler and an international gathering of Jewish leaders.

The evening before we were to leave Moscow we were taken to a nightclub, to sit at tables eating and drinking and being entertained. Well into the evening, quite suddenly there was a move on – the men were taking Bob somewhere, exactly where was not clear to me. But it was clear that I was not included. Given that it had been a night of flowing hospitality, and bearing in mind that an Australian Foreign Affairs official had been placed in a compromising situation some weeks previously, I was distinctly uneasy – but impotent to do anything. After Bob left I had to stay at the night club for a while and then I was taken back to our hotel. Bob was returned some time later, not in very good nick, but with justifiably high hopes for the success of his mission.

Officials were in our apartment early the next morning, and

some accompanied us to the airport, still discussing the details of their agreement about the release of the refuseniks. Bob was exhausted from the emotional strain of the visit – and the vodka.

The Rome meetings were conducted in an atmosphere of guarded optimism but at later talks in Geneva it became clear that the USSR had no intention of changing its policy. Bob was devastated. He felt totally betrayed.

I had decided not to accompany Bob to Geneva as he would be constantly busy with ILO meetings that were closed to non-delegates. Instead, I went to Inverness in the north of Scotland, to spend two weeks in the Findhorn community. I had read about this peaceful place, which encouraged personal and community development integrated with work in its gardens. I was looking forward to some peace and isolation. I would be away from everything! And everyone! I went on the sleeper train to Inverness and made my way by bus to Findhorn. I stayed in a complex of ancient, stone buildings set in gardens brimming with tulips and forget-me-nots. Have you ever seen a swathe of white tulips blooming in a carpet of that special forget-me-not blue? The vegetable gardens were lovingly tended and supplied enough produce for the whole community. There were days of warming sunshine and long, quiet evenings of misty twilight. It was nourishment to my spirit. I did rostered duties along with everyone else each morning, including work in the vegetable and herb gardens, the laundry, the kitchen, the dining hall, some cleaning and working on a productive craft. There were lectures, yoga, music and discussion. When there was time we took long walks in the Scottish woods. The guests included people from all round the world and I made friendships which felt as though they would last forever.

After Findhorn I had some time in London. Justine Rettick, a friend and neighbour from Sandringham who was a retired opera singer, got me a much-coveted ticket to the opera at Glyndebourne in the south of England. The theatre is small and intimate, a place where singers like to launch their careers, although some of the greats still sing there. I dressed myself up and boarded the special train which carries guests to this unique place. Everyone was in evening dress and a carnival atmosphere prevailed.

I was fortunate indeed that on this, the only night I was able to go, *Fidelio* was being performed. A recording of that opera had been our favourite listening at home for the previous few months. Then, at Findhorn, I was thrilled to hear the music in the vaulted, stained-glass-windowed dining hall one sunny day as I set tables for lunch. And now, at Glyndebourne, here was *Fidelio* again! The performance began at six o'clock. During the long interval, while that late summer evening was still light, members of the audience strolled into the exquisite garden by the river to break out champagne and their lavish picnic hampers to the mingled sound of conversation and the tapping of croquet mallets on balls. I soaked up the atmosphere, taking pleasure in it even though I was alone.

I found that travelling by myself had its compensations and people would make friendly gestures. A musician in a dinner-suit asked me during the interval if I would accompany him for a drink after the opera. This was a new situation for me and my slightly reckless acceptance of the invitation no doubt had something to do with being anonymous abroad. It was probably also a part of opening myself to a world outside my marriage, so I could better test what it meant to me. I got back to London in the early daylight hours after an enjoyable but harmless diversion. That day Bob and I spoke on the telephone. His spirits were very low and he asked me to cut short my next stopover in Amsterdam, to join him in Geneva.

Still, Bob's request allowed me two days in Amsterdam. I stayed with a young university friend of Susan's who was there on a working holiday. She lent me her bicycle and I felt courageous cycling around the city alone, seeing the sights including Rembrandt's house and the Van Gogh museum. One evening we went to a women's pub – a very lively place down by the fishermen's wharves, and a logical setting for an enterprise owned and run by women. The women on the seafront were strong, with a sense of sisterhood which came from having to raise their families and find support in each other while their menfolk worked out at sea.

I flew on to Geneva but by the time I arrived Bob had withdrawn into himself again. As I touched him he felt wooden, and I was saddened. This was indeed an unhappy man. I learned later that his depression, triggered by his failure to help the Soviet Jews, had bordered on being suicidal – although he didn't then share the depth of his despair with me. He had to return to Australia the next day but asked me to stay on after him to represent him at an official function. So I did stay, spending some time with his Australian friends and making the acquaintance of some of his Geneva colleagues – something, I observed to myself, I would not have had the confidence to do in earlier years.

◆

The ALP national conference was held in Adelaide in July. In earlier years I had often observed at Party conferences but now I found them far from enjoyable and avoided them like the plague. Vera would not see my fiftieth birthday unacknowledged and hastily put together a small party at her home on the Friday of that week. Bob returned from Adelaide, and photos of us taken during a post-conference media interview at home the next morning show us both with hollow smiles and puffy eyes.

On and on this awful year lurched. One morning, as he was leaving the bedroom, Bob paused in the doorway, leaning, hesitating, and said, 'Two women want to marry me – say they love me. In fact one says she doesn't just love me, but is IN love with me.' He looked puzzled, mildly amused, then went on, 'Whatever that means.' Despite the hurt produced by this missile, I felt sorry for him and found it enervating to be unable to help in any way someone I loved. I felt futile and irrelevant.

Susan had her twenty-first birthday overseas, on a break from her university studies. Stephen was working in the Kimberley. Rosslyn was living in Queensland with some other young people. She was eighteen years old and I worried a great deal about her. She had left school at fifteen, too early. Thankfully, she wrote to us or phoned reasonably frequently. I felt that even her upbringing had been foreshortened when she left home, partly due to want of a nurturing atmosphere. How grateful I was for my work and friends at the Brotherhood of St Laurence. They kept me on a reasonably even keel and better able to cope with whatever had to be dealt with.

In August Bob settled himself in to work at home, writing every day at the desk in the sitting-room bay window where the sun streamed in, the healing sun. He was preparing the Boyer Lectures – a prestigious, annual series of six, thirty-minute lectures commissioned by the Australian Broadcasting Commission. At this time there were fears that Bob might have a brain tumour and he underwent a series of tests which proved all clear, but the situation caused a flurry of concern to himself and those he told about it. Perhaps the pain he felt was due to the unbearable pressure of his lifestyle, as he seemed to be on the path to self-destruction. It was good to see him begin to enjoy the relative calm of preparing the talks. Such calm was short-lived, however, as the ACTU National Congress was due to be held in Melbourne in the second week of September.

During that week we were deeply saddened and yet relieved to hear that Ellie's suffering had finished. Even after her long illness it was eerie, unsettling, to accept the ending of this extraordinary woman's life. With the news of his mother's death Bob immediately asked his father to come and live with us. It was not the time to pursue the matter, but I was quietly furious. To me it was another example of the old expectations which locked women into a role as the givers of care no matter what other considerations there might be. At that time, Bob had not resolved, or conclusively discussed with me his thoughts about whether our marriage would survive or the direction of his political career. Yet he assumed that I would care for his father, though he himself was rarely home. I would have to give up any notion of study or of work if we were to look after Clem, an old man with a penchant for immovable domestic routines and with very definite views, many of which were Bob-centred. I knew that such an arrangement would put nightmarish limitations on me. The children understood my feelings and shared my reaction. As I write this, more than a decade later, there has been a lot of research and discussion about the effect on women of the burden of ageing parents. Women no sooner find the pressures of raising a family easing than they are once more left with the responsibility of providing care. Good, essential work, but not properly valued or supported by society generally. I understood Bob's spontaneous invitation to his father, but it irritated me that I felt guilty and mean at my apprehension about the effect it might have on me and on what was left of our family life and marriage. I let the matter rest for the time being. As it turned out Clem planned to live in Adelaide, near his brother Albert.

Connie Benn and I went to hear Bob's opening address at the Congress on the Monday morning and agreed that, understandably, he was not at his best. Later that day Bob and I flew to Perth for Ellie's funeral. Family grievings are not easy times. After he had kissed his mother goodbye in her coffin, Bob repeatedly said how very cold she was. It was as if the reality of death somehow produced the physical shock he needed to release some of his pent-up feelings, his grief and sorrow and perhaps some guilt. He returned to Melbourne and the Congress later the same day, while I stayed on in Perth to be with Clem, attending to what had to be done. For me these few days brought some unexpected comfort. Clem and I pottered about, making and sharing our meals together and chatting in the most companionable way we ever had. One day he stood leaning in the kitchen doorway and I was aware of him watching me set the table for lunch. Out of the blue, he stuttered, 'This whatsername … what is she about?' I steadied myself for a moment then decided to be frank: 'She wants to marry him. And perhaps he wants to marry her.' He came across the few steps between us and, for the first time ever, embraced and held me tight. It was the only time I had ever known him to make a spontaneous gesture of close physical affection, and it moved me greatly. Having indulged in this unaccustomed expression of his emotions, he retreated the few steps to the doorway and spoke for some minutes in a reflective way – as if to himself, yet including me. He quoted the Bible, Shakespeare and, if I remember rightly, Milton. He had retreated to what he felt safe with – the crafted words of others who expressed his own beliefs about trust, values: 'What is right in the eyes of God and Man,' he said. I remember none of it verbatim now, but those few minutes were something of an emotional blockbuster for me, and left me with a special feeling of being acknowledged and valued, in his eyes.

The other comfort came from our son Stephen, who had

come south for the funeral. Before he left Perth, he and I took a long walk together in the bushland on the steep slopes of Mount Eliza rising from the banks of the Swan River. In a letter to me later he recalled our walk and our talking together in a way which gave me a sweet, quiet pleasure.

At the end of the week I flew back from Perth on the 'red-eye' flight which leaves at midnight and arrives in Melbourne at five in the morning. As I walked along the corridors of the Southern Cross Hotel to join Bob in his room, I saw, at every door, the newspaper's front-page photograph of my husband's anguished and desperate face staring out, his mouth a gaping hole. In the still, sleeping hotel my every step was like a repetitive drum beat in my gut. The front page banner read 'HAWKE LASHES OUT', with the sub-heading, 'Unions reject leader for first time'. The story below then described Bob's position on uranium mining. His last ACTU Congress as president had not been an easy one, certainly more stressful than the public realised.

During the next week Bob recorded the Boyer Lectures and I fitted in two conversations with my wise guru and friend, Donna. On the evening of Friday 21 September, I drove home from work in blazing heat – one of Melbourne's climatic aberrations at the equinox. As I came along Beach Road to Sandringham, I encountered the smoke of a brushfire that was threatening the local croquet club and the foreshore bush. It was hot and horrible. At home I kicked off my shoes and drank lots of cold water, feeling I needed just to sit quietly for a while. Then I received a phone call to say Bob was at a friend's house in a bad way and I was needed. I pulled on my shoes and drove back for twenty minutes to where he had wilted under the combined pressures of alcohol and anxiety. He had a speech to make that evening but had been overcome by the imperative to decide his personal and political intentions. The only time I ever resorted to such a measure, I asked for a fruit juice, slipped two sleeping pills into it, then took it to him in the bed. He did not get to the function he was to attend, thanks be. Later, I drove him home.

The next day Bob told us of his decision to enter federal

parliament, and the following day I accompanied him to a press conference at his office to announce it. On 14 October he was pre-selected to run for the seat of Wills.

◆

This is my story, not my husband's. But Bob has been the major single influence on the course and tenor of my life since I was eighteen. My adult experience has been indivisible from his, as it has also been from my family, my children and friends, as well as the places I have lived and the multitude of events I have absorbed. And now, with his pre-selection to contest a seat in the federal parliament, another major shift was upon me, the effects of which I could not possibly forecast.

There are only two significant entries in my diary for the rest of 1979. The first is that I wrote to Melbourne's leading newspaper, the *Age*. There had been an increasing concern about media intrusion into the lives of the families of politicians. It became something of an issue in the press, and I wrote in support of a family experiencing this. I could well relate to their distress; I had been fighting battles with journalists for years in an effort to retain some privacy in our family life. This is what I wrote in November 1979 and it is probably more revealing about my personal situation than I thought at the time:

I would like to register my utter revulsion at press and media coverage given to the recent court case in respect of the son of one of our well-known politicians.

Wives particularly and families generally of public figures have a dilemma with which I am very familiar, and as a result of the line I have taken (excepting when I have been trapped) I am not number one with working journalists or at times with my husband. Our children, however, have a healthy cynicism about being used in this way.

My main argument is that any politician or public figure must be assessed on his job performance, and that whether his wife and family are glamorous and interesting or have two heads and are naughty should be irrelevant.

One feels mean refusing interviews because it is the job of media men and women to collect them, it is their bread and butter. But these stories should be non-stories – and often are.

If the story is to get a personal slant on the man, to make him 'more human' my view is that it is just sticky-nose stuff; and almost without exception it would be true to say that men or women would never achieve prominence without the support and love of an understanding family.

But why need it be spelled out publicly? It is difficult enough when one member of the family becomes public property.

It is argued that one could speak out on issues from a ready-made platform – more effective because you live with someone famous. My answer to that is that on issues in which I am interested I can always think of someone who is more informed and more competent to do it and they should have the opportunity – otherwise it gets back to curiosity about him and us, not primarily about the issue itself.

Media managers heavy their staff to pursue this 'family colour' because it sells. Some news-gatherers are embarrassed by the invasions of privacy they are required to make because it offends their sense of decency, and just occasionally they jack up. Newspapers and media generally will only cease to thrive on this kind of story when decent citizens, enough of them, stop consuming it.

There is also a responsibility on the part of the public figures and their families. There are many times when it would be pleasant and ego-boosting to let nice little stories run, which would perhaps lift and soften the public image of your front-runner.

But I insist that no public figure who is good enough needs it. The electorate which makes this demand avoids its responsibility of properly assessing the worth and performance of that figure on the contribution he makes, or does not adequately make, in his particular area of public affairs.

The other diary entry read 'Bob's 50th birthday'. There was a big party at our home one Sunday afternoon to celebrate the occasion.

But without doubt the main event for me in the closing weeks of this year was that I had applied, and been accepted, to do a two-year, full-time course of study at the Caulfield Institute of Technology for a Diploma of Welfare Studies. I had been encouraged by Connie Benn, and made the application, only to be baulked because I was fifty years old, the upper age limit for the course. Connie, my referee, pointed out that this was yet another 'ism' in the age of 'isms' – ageism. For mature-age students in that discipline, however, application points could be given for 'life experience' and that, along with my matriculation subjects and the interview, brought me up to the required level. My first tertiary education was to begin at my half-century mark.

STANDING TOGETHER

◇

On 3 March 1980, I began the diploma course of Welfare Studies at the Caulfield Institute of Technology. Every little thing made me nervous: finding the right lecture theatres and tutorial rooms in unfamiliar buildings, feeling awkward that I was a mature-age student amongst youngsters fresh from final-year high school, and hearing the frequent exclamations at my name – 'not BOB Hawke's wife!' I had been slowly learning to establish a separate me. Working at the Brotherhood had given me a whole new circle of friends who were my own – men and women to laugh and talk and work and be myself with. But many people were still curious about Bob, the public figure, and therefore curious about his wife. I knew that at Caulfield I had to be careful about opinions I expressed in discussion, especially in the subjects of politics, psychology and welfare practice.

Before the course started, I had thought out strategies for participating without catering to the sticky-beaks with their interest in my personal life and political connections. Part of the welfare practice subject involved learning to communicate in a professional context: how to avoid letting personal feelings intrude into the interaction between welfare workers and those we worked with. Empathy alone is not enough in offering professional, constructive support. I became good at staying once removed.

At the Brotherhood of St Laurence I had made friends with Sue Spence, a woman some eighteen years younger than me. We met as fellow workers at the Action and Resource Centre and then began to share our cut lunches in the parks of Fitzroy. Sometimes we joined other colleagues from the Brotherhood for drinks after work. And so another of my important friendships with women was cemented. As it happened, neither of us knew that we had applied for and been accepted into the same course at Caulfield. But this coincidence made studying immeasurably more enjoyable for me. Sue was a constant companion while I was getting used to student life. She lived on my route to college and it became a habit for us to travel and study together. It is good to have a study friend, but Sue was also an immensely valuable confidante.

The detachment I was learning in my welfare practice classes served me well on the home front. Everyone in the family was involved in something controversial, or at least different. Susan was active in student politics at Monash University, spending more time on causes than her studies. Also, around this time, she was involved in a car accident. Rosslyn was living an alternative lifestyle – and it was truly that. She didn't much like the pressured life we lived and the tensions it created at home. She was looking for another way with like-minded young people in communes in Queensland, the sunny and beautiful north. But I was still deeply concerned at the use of marijuana, or worse, in such communities. Stephen was working with Aborigines in the north-west of Western Australia and had phoned me early one morning to tell me of police charges against him before I would read it in the newspapers. Bob was still unresolved about his personal life. It never rains but it pours!

I found relief from all this in talk with Sue Spence, some good tennis every Saturday afternoon at home with a regular foursome of girlfriends organised by my friend Barbara Rogers, and occasional Saturday morning shopping at the market or outings to theatre with Vera. Bob's friend George Rockey phoned me sometimes, or we would meet in the city, and offer each other support while we hoped and willed that Bob would sort out his affairs. And from time to time I would talk to Donna.

Meanwhile my friend Sue and I were giving our attention to the course. I particularly liked the politics subject I did in the first semester. We took psychology and sociology, which I also enjoyed, as first-year Arts degree subjects, supported by classes at Welfare House where we did role playing and experiential group work (which we joked about as group grope). Our psychology lecturer, Michael Singer, was derisive about the 'touchy-feelies' but Sue and I found his style refreshing and referred to him as 'The Brat'. Nevertheless, the group work did let us get to know ourselves in unexpected ways, once the initial inhibitions evaporated. We talked about needs and values, and learned about the principles and techniques of welfare and social work.

In lectures I had to develop note-taking skills, and found that the business of handwriting was difficult for me. Sometimes I couldn't read my own notes later. For the last twenty years or so, my writing had been limited to shopping lists, accounts, cheques and the occasional letter to my mother. I remembered Mum once commenting mildly, 'I like it when you type your letters, dear.' Obviously they were much more legible. Essays filled me with dread at first. To have to commit myself to paper and be assessed on my thinking and ability made me feel vulnerable. The mystique of education had certainly got to me, and I was afraid of showing my work to strangers. It was, though, another form of self-examination. After a while the mystique went. I wondered whether there was, after all, a conspiracy among academics to make the rest of us think it harder than it is. A ghost which had haunted me since I left school at the age of fifteen was at last fading.

Now my appointments diary was littered with lecture and tutorial reminders and due-dates for essays. Then in May 1980, Blanche d'Alpuget, who was writing a biography of Bob, came to our house to talk with me about the book. This was not easy for me and, as well, the visit meant precious time away from my first big essay assignment. I was not in favour of the biography. Although Bob had authorised the book, it had been embarked upon without my approval even though it would clearly need to refer to myself, the children and Bob's personal life. But now it was happening and I would cooperate. I must say that I have since been glad the book was written. It broached areas of Bob's life, drunkenness and marital problems, which could have been used against him later by the sensationalist press. When he entered parliamentary politics, voters had an understanding of the man they were considering for election. The biography also released me from feeling I needed to protect the marriage totally from public scrutiny.

◆

At the end of May 1980, Bob resolved not to drink ever again. He had stopped drinking before, but it was a bit like me stopping smoking – we were always starting again. The difference is between keeping on stopping, and having really stopped! He had, however, realised that there was no alternative to complete abstinence, that he could not risk even 'just a glass'. Crucially, he had gathered the motivation and strength of purpose to make it stick this time. I decided to react with my practised detachment to the change. It was important that I did not adopt the role of a co-conscience: that would have been an intrusion on his own journey. If I expressed praise it would seem patronising. I stood aside, as if to say, 'I knew you could, I knew you would, one day.' I summoned the tolerance to cope with recurring patterns of behaviour ingrained during the drinking years – the anger, the yelling and the criticism. This period is referred to as the 'dry drunk' stage, and as he worked his way through it he became just nicer and nicer. This was the Big One dealt with: I knew that other difficulties would now wither away.

Before I began the Welfare Studies course, I had established a bed-sitter in the home of a friend where I could stay and study when I needed to: it would be hard enough to create patterns of study and reading even without the possible disruptions at home.

But here I was, not even through the first semester, and there was no longer any need for it.

◆

Meanwhile, Stephen's involvement in the Kimberley was developing. When he left Tasmania and went to Darwin, he wanted to work as a journalist and wrote occasional reports on Aboriginal affairs for *Nation Review* under the name Steve Masterson. His interest in indigenous peoples had formed in his teenage years during a splurge of reading, mostly about the American Indians. Perhaps our time in New Guinea and the apartheid issue in the early seventies had touched him. He had always been independent and hadn't asked for any financial support from us. But in November 1978 he had been so keen to fly from Darwin in the Northern Territory south-west to Broome in the Kimberley region of Western Australia that he phoned and asked for the fare. He intended to stay in Broome for a month.

The Aboriginal communities in the Kimberley knew their culture was threatened by the encroachment of White Australia on their lands. Their way of life, their security and their very survival were at risk, and they were starting to talk about what they could achieve by working together. One of these communities was the Nookanbah mob who successfully worked a cattle station 250 kilometres inland from the mouth of the Fitzroy River. The station had been leased by the Aboriginal Lands Trust, on their behalf, since 1976. Their sense of urgency was acute, as the West Australian government was encouraging an American oil company, Amax, to drill for oil on an especially important sacred site, Pea Hill, of the Goanna Dreaming. The site was integral to their sense of stewardship of the land and their dependence on it for food and spiritual nourishment.

The Aboriginal community has a respect for social order and privacy based on their law, which Steve quickly understood. They liked him and asked him to stay until the end of the year to liaise with the community to keep the media accurately informed about the confrontation with Amax. He returned permanently to the Kimberley in May 1979 and, in 1980, became the first resource officer for the group of Aboriginal communities known as Marra Warra Warra, with his headquarters at the small, regional town of Fitzroy Crossing. His salary was paid in the first year by 'chuck-in' from the Nookanbah mob. He always worked to make it possible for the community to speak for themselves, which they did very convincingly to those who would listen. But an open mind is rare in the battle of dollars and big business versus cultural and spiritual law. It became a long, drawn-out conflict. In 1989 Stephen completed a book, *Nookanbah: Whose Land, Whose Law*, about these events, with photographs by Mike Gallagher, which won national awards from the Human Rights Commission and the National Book Council (the 'Banjo' award for non-fiction).

The atmosphere in Fitzroy Crossing, at the time of the Nookanbah confrontation, was tense. The police were well aware of Stephen's identity and kept a close eye on him and others who they perhaps saw as trouble-makers. Stephen had evidence of this one evening when he went to drive a few hundred yards home from a friend's place – unaccompanied and on 'L' plates. As he pulled out of the driveway a convoy of eight police cars, on their way back from Nookanbah, drew up, and he was charged with a driving offence.

Then one night, the police got Stephen out of his bed at midnight and held him at the station until four o'clock in the morning. He was, when it was all added up, on forty-four separate charges under the Electoral Act. Four other people were similarly charged. Stephen had been involved in a campaign to make sure Aboriginal people at Fitzroy Crossing were enrolled to vote. As it happened, when election time came, a large number of Nookanbah people had gone to Lajamanu (Hooker Creek) in the Northern Territory on 'law business' and got stranded by the wet. Stephen managed to get there with postal-vote forms for them and, in the eyes of the police, had been guilty of offering them 'improper assistance' in enabling them to cast their votes.

The story of Stephen's arrest at Fitzroy Crossing got national media coverage and my telephone became busy with offers of help from lawyers, politicians and friends. As it happened, when the first of those arrested at the same time as Stephen went to court, the case was dismissed. After that, all charges against Stephen and the other three people were dropped without going to court.

In the semester break from college I travelled to Fitzroy Crossing. The trip is a reminder of just how large a country Australia is. Travelling two sides of a triangle via Perth, I covered a distance of almost four thousand kilometres each way. I saw my family in Perth, then flew on a small plane north to Derby. Steve met me there in his unspeakably decrepit Suzuki utility for the drive to Fitzroy Crossing. The vehicle made a terrible noise, and for much of the 240-kilometre drive we yelled at each other excitedly, above the din, to catch up on each other's lives. At the Crossing, I stayed where Steve had digs at the home of the local state Welfare Department officer, his wife and their two little children. I could see that Stephen loved the possibilities for family life there. He also loved the freedom of country life, the special ambience of the out-back, and the lack of bullshit. His friends were just as you found them – there were no facades. Stephen was later to meet his future life partner, Lesley Corbett, through their work there.

It happened that the day after I arrived Stephen needed to go to Nookanbah and I went with him. We went by the river road, longer and more difficult to traverse, but he wanted me to see the country. Well out on the track our dust-cloud and another slowly drew together. Eventually we came upon Nipper and stopped to share a roll-your-own smoke with him: a piece of luck for me to meet so soon a Nookanbah tribal spokesman. Steve admired Nipper and I knew something about him from transcribing oral-history tapes made by Stephen the previous year. The older man's eyes scanned the country lovingly as he talked of it being his place, where his tribal elders had 'growed' him.

The hub of community life at Nookanbah was the wool-shed, built in an earlier era when the place was a sheep station. A huge, high-roofed, concrete-floored structure, it contained the bush radio terminal and the auxiliary power plant. It was also the place where school lessons, meetings and entertainments such as occasional film-screenings were held. Here the women learned to cut and sew, or mend garments on treadle machines, and here the community cooperative store was run. Most activities were about teaching Aborigines the ways of whites, but regularly the old men took the young boys out to teach them bush lore. The women attended to the girls' knowledge. All the young were continuously nourished with the stories of their people, with the important knowing and belonging of their culture. Most meetings about community matters were held under great spreading gum trees, sitting on the ground near the river bank.

During my day at Nookanbah I met lots of the people and had cuppas with the teacher, a white, Education Department appointee up from Perth. We sat under a bough-shade lean-to off his caravan. Steve did the business he had come for and we drove home in the late afternoon. When I caught sight of myself in the bathroom mirror I was the deep burnt-orange colour of the desert dust and my hair stood on end where it had been blown back by the scorching wind. I understood the importance of 'shower stops' in the Kimberley!

On subsequent trips I made to the Kimberley, Steve arranged for me to stay at the local kindergarten. It was also an informal drop-in centre, a place where travelling friends could come for a shower and a feed, and the news exchange centre of the west Kimberley. I occupied the only spare room, so any travellers who needed a bed were dossed down on the kindergarten floor and used the toddler-sized bathroom facilities. It was a wonderful way for me to learn about Kimberley life, as people yarned on about the local news – 'local' covering an area of hundreds of kilometres square in this great, expansive land.

The white residents in Fitzroy Crossing could be divided into the Boong-lovers and the Rednecks – the terms each used to refer to the other. Everybody knew where everybody else stood when it came to respect, or the lack of it, towards Aboriginal people and their culture. My interest in Stephen's work there blossomed. I liked the unobtrusive way he and his colleagues went about supporting the Aboriginal struggle. I went to the Kimberley almost every year for the thirteen he stayed there and I became quite accus-

tomed to haphazard forms of travel. I remember one flight in particular. The tiny plane was overheated from waiting on the tarmac
in temperatures around forty degrees Celsius. I was sitting in the
bucket seat next to the pilot, who said before take-off, 'Hold the
door open and she'll cool-off'. So I did, until the plane was in the
air, then slammed it shut. That only happens in the outback!

At Fitzroy Crossing I joined in fishing and walking in the
bush. We went swimming (always on the lookout for crocodiles!)
and picnicking at the spectacular gorges and on the coarse yellow
sandbanks and waddies of the grand old Fitzroy River. I have never
been there to see it rise in flood, as it does every year in the wet. But
in the dry months, we could see the flood debris left hanging in the
trees, up to thirty feet above us. We dropped in on friends at outback stations and I observed snippets of their lives. I went driving
and swagging with Steve when he made calls on Aboriginal communities. Sometimes we would spend the night in sleeping bags on the
hard ground, after a campfire meal and strong billy tea. Once we
drove to Tunnel Creek, aptly named, as the river flows underground
for about two kilometres. Just inside the entrance to the cave-like
tunnel, two large snakes, entwined, dropped from a rock ledge into
the water below. They were startled by our presence – and we were
startled too! With a Tilley lamp held high, for it was pitch black in
here – a place where bats live – we strolled along the white sandy
beach at the river's edge until suddenly the sunlight broke in.
Through the tunnel's mouth ahead we could see the weeping
boughs of trees over a tranquil lagoon. One can easily understand
why this is a special sacred site for the Aborigines. I was not a
tourist. I saw this unique country in a privileged way, with my son,
and I will never forget it.

◆

In August 1980, Bob resigned his presidency of the ACTU and
began his campaign for the federal election as candidate for Wills.
He shared the focus of the campaign with the Party leader, Bill
Hayden, and its new national president, Neville Wran.

The funeral of George Rockey, Bob's dear friend and my

friend and confessor, was held on 7 September. I knew Bob would miss George terribly, but I believe he had no idea how much I would miss George after the counsel and encouragement he had given me, and his insistence that Bob and I should stay together.

I also made a note in my diary that September after an incident I found moving. I was sitting in a lecture in college when Noirin Malone, a lecturer in sociology with whom I had become friendly, gave me a decisive come-on nod and left the theatre. I followed her out. She was about to have an epileptic fit and needed help. She urgently instructed me what to do. We ducked into a nearby empty office where I held her in a straight-jacket grip on a chair, the way she had told me, and she went into a frightening convulsion which lasted, it seemed to me, forever, but in reality I suppose for just a few minutes. She came out of it white, limp and depleted. I drove her to my place where she rested before making arrangements to go home. I was pleased that she had chosen me and in such a businesslike manner given me a responsibility that she knew I would meet. It took my mind back forty years to when, as kids playing on the road in Coogee Street, we all knew what we had to do when the boy amongst us who took convulsions keeled over.

◆

Susan's studies were taking second place to her causes, Rosslyn was recklessly damaging her health, and a friend of ours who had suffered a head injury in a car accident and was in daily therapy, was staying at our place. I had to do six weeks of fieldwork for the diploma course and was expected to do it in the semester break. I told the department head, George Clarke, that I really wanted to go to the Kimberley. His welcome response was to suggest I do the placement up there. I jumped at the idea. I could do my fieldwork and, at the same time, have a much needed break from responsibilities at home that were making me feel like a drowning woman. I did the placement with the shire social worker stationed in Derby.

◆

On 18 October, though the opinion polls had given Labor a good chance of a win, Malcolm Fraser's coalition government was returned to power. Bob won the seat of Wills and was installed as shadow minister for Industrial Relations. Clem and I went to Parliament House on 26 November to hear his maiden speech.

We bought a flat in Canberra for Bob's headquarters and shopped together for furnishings and equipment. The monster drink had gone from Bob's life but infidelity had not. I felt extremely unsure about our future and was lonely. Now I would often drink alone, at home, with my solitary dinner, a very unwise practice. It had been a pleasure for me to unwind the dutiful daughter, wife and mother inside me with the help of wine and the company of good friends. But I knew too well the flips of personality that too much alcohol, especially when it is combined with unhappiness, can cause. I would be careful!

During this year I learned transcendental meditation and after practising it for some weeks found how useful it could be for self-management. One day at home when there was a very difficult episode to deal with and I felt myself becoming hot and speedy, I made myself withdraw and sat quietly meditating in the garden for twenty minutes. It had a magical calming affect – my pulse and breathing rates reduced dramatically and I felt a general steadying. A good one to remember, thought I.

By December 1981 I had successfully completed my two years at Caulfield Institute except that I had one more fieldwork placement to do. I began at the Moorabbin Council's Citizens' Advice Bureau in March 1982, but had been there for only ten days or so when I felt ill and had to go home. Barry Connard, our local doctor, drove me to hospital to be admitted for emergency surgery to remove an about-to-burst appendix: also exploratory surgery to check adhesions from the caesarean and hysterectomy operations of previous years. Susan came down from Sydney to care for me during my convalescence, and prepared delectable meals she had learnt how to prepare at the course she was doing in macrobiotic cooking. I attribute my excellent recovery to this nourishment and care.

I decided that I needed to get myself well and strong. I

began Tai Chi classes, did Oki Yoga and followed Sue's example and did some macrobiotic cooking seminars. I played tennis and set about major gardening projects at home. I knew that I needed to be more fit, more relaxed, a better sleeper and looked for whatever would assist me to be as steady and wise as possible. The things I learnt, and practised, in my year of 'wellness' have been of value to me ever since.

At the end of May 1982 Bob and I went overseas, via Singapore and London, to Helsinki where he was attending the Socialist International conference. We explored Helsinki, new to us, on foot, and planned to attend a symphony concert in the Finlandia Concert Hall on our first evening. But Willy Brandt, the former chancellor of Germany, asked Bob to dine with him and I went to the concert alone. I wandered along the waiting queue with the spare ticket until a gentleman bought it from me. We sat together, of course, and had coffee and a pleasant evening.

The next evening Bob and I dined with the British socialist delegation. This reminded us of an old British socialist friend in the Melbourne Trades Hall, Jack Topp. He was a caretaker there and fed the legion of Trades Hall cats. A rather solitary man who spent his time alone reading widely, Jack liked his beer, and Bob and he yarned in the Lygon Hotel. He sometimes came to our house, enjoying the domesticity and the children – in fact he baby-sat for us on occasions. But I remember him best for sharing his knowledge of the Scots poet Robert Burns, and for his gift to me of a well-thumbed volume of the complete works, which I still treasure. On this trip I was feeling good, and Bob and I were more relaxed together.

The trip was organised at very short notice and I phoned some friends before leaving for suggestions for things to do. The upshot was splendid. In Paris I met Elsa Petersen-Schepeler, a Melbourne friend of Vera's, and we took a train south from Paris to the Loire Valley for a few days in the beautiful chateau country. Then in West Berlin I stayed with Marianne and Harald Meinhold, a contact from the Brotherhood of St Laurence, who toted me around their city for an introduction to local art and theatre. I went on to New York to stay for some days with Andrew and Mary

Whist in Brooklyn. I made forays to galleries, and even rode the subway alone, feeling courageous. This holiday proved to me that I could be independent, in my denim skirt and comfy shoes, with my suitcase on a wheel. I was doing things in a way I never had before.

A brief June entry in my small diary for 1982 reads simply: 'Leadership momentum'. Bob was now an established parliamentarian in Canberra, and the Australian Labor Party was going through one of its upheavals, which was to have a dramatic effect on our lives. Bob had always kept me informed about the broad issues of his work, but I was by now thoroughly involved in my separate activities, keeping well and coping with family crises. The intricacies of the power struggle going on in the ALP largely passed me by.

I still had to complete the last fieldwork assignment for my diploma and went to work at the Ecumenical Migration Centre in the inner suburb of Richmond. I worked there with the Turkish staff member on a project to assist elderly immigrants who had come from rural areas and who felt idle and isolated in high-rise city accommodation. After several of the six weeks required, I decided I wanted to be at home for Rosslyn, who had come back to live at Sandringham again.

We did not know it then, but Christmas 1982 proved to be the last in our Sandringham house. Susan and Rosslyn were at home and Stephen came from Western Australia to be with us. Matt Dillon, who Rosslyn was later to marry, was staying with us. My year's effort in the garden had paid off and it was looking lovely – just right for an outdoor, sunny celebration with family and friends.

Then the New Year took off apace. Bob went to Brisbane for the ALP National Executive meeting. On 3 February, Ros and I had been out and as we drove into our driveway we were greeted by several journalists thrusting microphones and wielding cameras. I went inside to a continuously ringing telephone and finally spoke to Bob in Brisbane. There had been a vote and Bob was now the federal leader of the Party. Although I had known it was on the cards, when the news actually came I was struck by its significance to us, personally. It was an extraordinary coincidence that at the very time the vote was taking place in Brisbane, the prime minister,

Malcolm Fraser, had gone to the governor-general, Sir John Kerr, in Canberra to put a federal election in train for 5 March – only weeks away. The ALP's official campaign was launched on 16 February.

◆

At first I had no plan to go along on the campaign trail. But as the momentum gathered, I did join in and began to enjoy it. Campaigning was not a new experience for me but this was very different, as we were at the centre of the action. The travel, the crowds, the tactical discussions and the camaraderie of a team caught up in a hard-fought battle were irresistibly exciting. Casting my mind back, I believe the ALP organisers were not sure how I would go – how much they should build me into the campaign. But as things went on, I did more. Later, when it looked as though Labor might win, one of them said to me, 'You'll need to be able to have afternoon tea with the Queen.' He cocked his little finger as though holding a cup, then added, 'Or have a chat with my aunties.' I was amused that he thought he might have to remind me of the breadth of social graces needed by a prime minister's wife – though he was also renowned for measuring public opinion by the views of his several aunts.

I didn't get the impression, on the campaign trail, that people out there are turned off by politics. I believe that, by and large, voters understand that political decisions affect almost every aspect of their daily lives, and they know that they should be well-informed and cast their votes thoughtfully.

The official opening of the campaign was at the Sydney Opera House, where the Concert Hall was filled to capacity. As we stood in the wings, among all the 'hype', waiting to go on stage I thought my legs would dissolve but some yoga breathing steadied me. On the night of the election, we were staying at the Lakeside Hotel in Canberra, with family and just a few friends. The mood was optimistic, but quiet – even restrained. Our daughters and Bob's dad were with us, as well as Bob's long-time mate and racing companion, Col Cunningham, and his wife Gloria. We flicked channels

Photo: Herald & Weekly Times Ltd

Hazel with the children, Chindi the cat and Flash the dog in about 1971

Our house in Royal Avenue, Sandringham

During the 1972 election campaign

Birthday dinner for Hazel, with the family and Paul and Jane Munro, 1973

At a fund-raising dinner for a Labor candidate in 1978. I am wearing a silk caftan Bob brought back from Jordan.

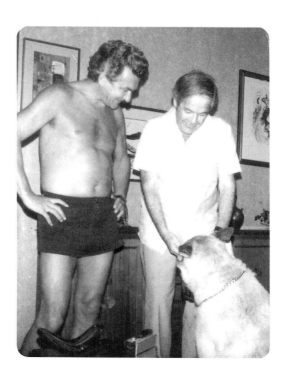

Bob and his friend George Rockey, 1978

Getting ready for a game of tennis at Royal Avenue, 1979

Bob, Ros and me
in our kitchen at
Sandringham,
1981

Steve, Susan, me and Ros with Beans the cat in the garden at Sandringham, 1982

Travelling light, Paris 1982

At the Sydney Opera House for the opening of the 1983
federal election campaign

Election night, Canberra, 1983

on the television to catch figures and interviews. Bob Hogg and Peter Barron, political advisers on the campaign, and his press secretary, Geoff Walsh, were taking calls from booths around the country and assessing the trends. At about half past eight we knew Labor had won. It remained only a matter of choosing the right moment to claim victory. In the interim there was, in that room, a feeling of deep satisfaction, and the knowledge that a huge responsibility was upon us which would take absolute priority in our lives. There was no whooping or wild celebration but quiet, affectionate exchanges, as we thought ahead to what would come next.

When the right moment came, Bob and I were driven out to the tally room at the Canberra Showgrounds and taken through pressing crowds by a wedge of security men. The huge, clattering space was packed to overflowing with media personnel and excited supporters. Being at the centre of that pulsing crowd was a heady feeling – tempered, however, by prescience of what the change would bring for us. I had watched Bob grow, from a young university student to an academically-successful scholar, from proving himself to the union movement in research and advocacy to presidency of the ACTU and the ALP, then as a shadow minister in the federal government. That very brief summary of thirty-five years hardly conveys the formidable workload and focused striving of the years I had known him. He had been written about, talked about and analysed more than any other Australian public figure – with three biographies, countless articles and television footage. His easy rapport with people was legendary. The voters knew him and chose him – and I agreed with them. I knew he would give the job his total effort – there was no doubt he was an extraordinary man, who I loved and would support in whatever ways I could in this new task.

That day, Saturday 5 March 1983, was Clem Hawke's eighty-fifth birthday and he was with us. I wondered how Ellie would have felt, had she been alive, and in my mind I sent her my love.

The next morning Bob did more interviews, and more photographs were taken. For some time Bob and I had been re-establishing our sense of partnership. There were no blinding flashes or passionate declarations, but we were more relaxed and companionable with each other as life's storms abated. We had been rebuilding – this time not the life of our youthful dreams, but a more comfortable and mature partnership, one with new, different challenges. Our reconciliation had a positive feeling of inevitability about it. I felt thankful that this was where we had got to, so that our standing together and smiling together on national television felt right. I knew we would work well together.

During the day we left for Sydney and our first night at Kirribilli House, the prime minister's official residence there, a lovely, verandahed Victorian villa on the edge of the harbour. It was towards evening when we arrived and Bob – an inveterate tea drinker – pressed a red button on the sitting-room wall. Instead of summoning bearers of teatrays it brought the security police running. Oops! Within minutes of that small error I went to our bedroom to see a housemaid bending over my case, which she had opened. At first I was offended at the instrusion but then I realised that she was doing her job: unpacking my things and settling us in. For many years I had been a little resentful at the lack of privacy in our family life and now I was facing the prospect of staff attending to our very personal needs. I was not sure I was going to like that aspect of the new job. I was afraid it would interfere with my fierce sense of independence, of being in control. Little did I know then how I would come to trust and love the staff who worked with us over the years.

One week after the election we flew back to Canberra to take up residence in the prime minister's Lodge. Kirribilli House has a homely feeling but The Lodge is not a house that settles around you. It has two storeys and is also divided down the centre by a hallway, a mezzanine floor and stairways. For a family which gravitates instinctively to a focal point – and we usually headed for the kitchen – The Lodge presents a disconcerting spread of rooms with no natural heart.

That first Sunday afternoon we explored our new home only briefly, as we were invited to dine informally with the governor-general, Sir Ninian Stephen, and Lady Stephen, at Government House, Yarralumla. What a treat it was to be with this couple of exceptional substance and warmth, as we swapped yarns about politics, the law and our families. Observing their absolute lack of formality, Bob asked Sir Ninian why he had accepted Malcolm Fraser's invitation to take up the position, when he was already an eminent judge on the High Court of Australia. To our surprise he replied, 'Well, I never really liked the law much.' The fact of the matter was that, while they didn't bring any pomp and circumstance to the job, they did bring commitment, capability and the utmost sincerity. As we drove away, Bob and I discussed our good fortune at having the Stephens to work with.

I knew, as we settled in that night, that there would be a great deal for Bob and me to experience together in the coming years. Although his family had wondered for a long time whether he would ever become prime minister of Australia, I had never been personally ambitious about it. But once the scene had been set that February, events moved very quickly and swept me along. Here I was. I was happy about that.

PUBLIC AND PRIVATE LIFE

◇

The next morning Bob was whisked off in the white car with the 'Star 1' plates and I was left wondering about life at the Lodge – what it meant for me, what I was to do. I felt, as I stood alone in the entrance hall Bob had just left, that if I suddenly disappeared, no one would notice.

After being the pivotal point of the diverse and busy household in Sandringham, it was a shock to my system and probably to my pride, to think I might be irrelevant here. The cleaning, shopping, cooking and laundry – and even the garden which had been my escape and my sanctuary at home – here were someone else's responsibility. At the Brotherhood of St Laurence I had seen how damaging to relationships it could be if people encroached on the responsibilities of others around them. In the Resource Centre careful attention had been paid to job descriptions, for volunteers and support workers as well as family members, so that everyone knew what their duties were and would not intrude beyond them. It was going to be important that the Lodge was a contented ship, so I decided to bide my time and see what responsibilities came to me – and come they certainly did!

First there was a trickle of visits to me from 'Ceremonial and Hospitality' personnel in the Department of Prime Minister and Cabinet. In just three weeks there was to be a visit, initiated by the outgoing government, by the Prince and Princess of Wales. Invitation lists, programs and menus had to be discussed and chosen. Everyone wanted the Lodge and its garden to look its best for the royal lunch party. The advisers produced swags of notes and diagrams describing the protocol and logistics of the welcome, ceremonies, functions and departures. We struck an agreement that as long as they were good shepherds and made sure I was in the right place at the right time, I would play the rest by ear. This arrangement suited my need to relax and be myself, and it lasted throughout our almost nine years in office. It worked well, except for the occasional forgotten name or office which I could usually ask for, or fudge.

Before I found myself in the job of prime minister's wife, I had been rather disparaging about protocol and ceremony, thinking it was all a bit of a carry-on. I soon saw that there was good reason for it. Visiting dignitaries come with a large assortment of rank and status. They might speak no English or have different attitudes about what is taboo and what is acceptable behaviour. For instance, ideas of suitable dress vary: some cultures require that arms and neck be covered, and for some wearing black is a mark of disrespect. If visitors of state are new in the job themselves, or from small communities, they appreciate help with introductions and advice on when to be where. Old hands have their own style. On later royal visits, for example, I was to notice that the Duke of Edinburgh preferred to range around the crowd choosing for himself which people to talk to, rather than be introduced in a formal way. At such times I would hover, smiling, and talking to different people myself. If it works, do it! In my experience, the most renowned official visitors are usually the easiest to entertain. They walk through their parts with aplomb.

After a week or two the head of the Department of Prime

Minister and Cabinet, Sir Geoffrey Yeend, paid me a visit to tell me that I was entitled to secretarial help. I said I was used to looking after myself, thank you. In his kindly way, Sir Geoffrey suggested that I think about it. It was almost no time before I realised my ignorance in assuming I could manage alone and was crying out for help, as a deluge of mail and telephone calls came in. Many were congratulatory, but there were also requests to do things, and 'help me' letters from people with problems. Sir Geoffrey told me I could appoint someone I knew, or advertise, or take someone from the public service. I decided on the public service option, in the knowledge that if it did not work well for either of us, the secretary could be reabsorbed into the department without disadvantage. That decision brought me one of my pure-gold bits of luck, in the form of Sharon Massey. She worked with me until we left the Lodge, and we are friends for life.

Ever since Bob had rocketed to public recognition in the sixties, I had to deal, from time to time, with a wide range of people who saw him as Mr. Fix-it and wanted access to him. Some had special requests or problems, some wanted to see him because they admired him – some were just curious. There was nothing between them and me but the front door or my ability to hang up a telephone receiver. At times I had some difficult situations to deal with. Once, when my mother was minding the children, she opened the door to an elderly man and invited him in because the weather was foul. He turned out to be an absolute nutter and a nuisance – I had to despatch him when I arrived home. Once when I was trying to write an essay to a tight deadline, there was an industrial dispute in progress and I counted sixteen telephone calls before I left the phone off the hook in desperation. I welcomed the advent of answering machines which let me judge whether to take a call or not.

Now, at the Lodge, all that changed as staff and security mechanisms protected us from intrusion. After a while, journalists began to comment that I had changed. I found this mildly irritating, and would point out that the essential me had not changed, as anyone who really knew me would verify. Some of the press no doubt remembered that during the seventies I had been less than cooperative – certainly not open to all of their requests. They didn't take into account that in those years I was unsure of myself, without administrative or any other kind of support as I bumbled along, the spouse of a controversial public figure and the mother of teenagers growing up in a society where there were no certainties. The support I had in these early days at the Lodge and all through our years there was wonderful for me. It redressed the feeling of having been unsupported and unacknowledged in previous years. It was clear from the beginning of this new stage of my partnership with Bob that those around us took it for granted that my job was important and that I had a contribution to make, both politically and personally. Although I had been finding my own ways of developing confidence and a sense of self-worth since the sixties, I now relaxed in the atmosphere of being regarded as a part of the team. Also, I felt a responsibility to a broad constituency, in politics, which had not been comparable in previous years.

One of the first positions I was asked to take on was president of the Australiana Fund. My predecessor, Tamie Fraser, had established this body on the model of the Americana Fund in Washington. The idea was to raise money to purchase furnishings, works of art and other objects of historic importance to be housed in official establishments. In this country the designated establishments are the Canberra and Sydney residences of the governor-general and the prime minister. I remembered, years earlier, reading press reports of the Fund's establishment in Australia and thinking that it was unconscionable to be raising one million dollars in capital for such a purpose when the people I was working with were wanting for a good meal. So, at first I baulked at the idea of getting involved. But again I realised the good sense behind an idea I had viewed cynically from the outside. After reading the background papers I saw that the Fund took the politics out of an important contribution to this very young nation of ours which had not paid enough attention to its heritage. And by now it was clear to me that the residences in some respects looked and functioned (or malfunctioned) at less than appropriate standards – for incumbents, for visitors and overseas guests and for the general public to see on open days.

The upkeep and renovation of the prime minister's residences has presented difficulties over the years. The family needs of the occupants, as well as their differing taste in different eras, has led to quite a variety of styles in decor and configuration (notably, when Joseph and Enid Lyons and their eleven children were there they needed every available space for bedrooms). I was faced with these matters early on, when the Lodge representative from the Official Establishments Trust, also implemented during the Fraser years, came to me with suggestions for upgrading the interior of the Lodge. I couldn't feel any enthusiasm for the task until I'd had time to get the feel of the house and the needs it had to meet, both for us as a family and officially. The Trust's job was to take an overview of the structure, decor and maintenance of the same four residences as the Australiana Fund. Like that Fund it was an attempt to depoliticise the work to be done. Although each incumbent is responsible for the upkeep and development of the houses, they are open to accusations from the media and the public of feathering their own nests if they undertake renovations. The Trust lacks administrative teeth and still depends on the government of the day to sanction any expenditure. But it is a step in the right direction.

We had been in residence at The Lodge for only a matter of days when Bob announced that he could not live without a cat. He always had one as a boy and we usually owned cats at Sandringham. My theory was that if you kept one cat, you kept two, for company. So I went to the local Canberra RSPCA and returned with two wee kittens, one black and white, and one black all over. We called them Whisky and Bess.

At the end of March we made a quick visit back to our house in Sandringham and I fitted in an afternoon's tennis with the Saturday girls as if nothing had changed. Back in Canberra I was briefed for the first overseas trip we were to make. Then I was off to Melbourne for a meeting of the Action and Resource Centre for Low Income People in Melbourne. Here also I was pleased to be regarded in exactly the same way as before: 'Hi Hazel, how's things!' I still harboured the notion that I would do some welfare work. Although I had finished the course at Caulfield, I still had a field-work placement to fulfil. I wanted to complete that then find a part-time job. As my hopes faded, a friend remarked dryly, 'You've been placed all right!' In fact as the years went on and I became involved with various projects, or even just one-off events, in the area of social work, I was able to keep in touch with some areas of professional practice. I didn't ever take out the diploma from college, or bring home a pay cheque from a job, but I did gain a great deal of information and satisfaction in other ways.

Official life quickly became demanding. On 15 April we held a reception at the Lodge for delegates to the first of the summit meetings Bob had called to tackle some of the urgent problems facing the country. As leader of the government, he was quickly putting his cooperative approach to the test in this larger arena, inviting representatives from unions, industry, business and welfare bodies to a series of discussions to be held in the parliamentary chamber. The concept met with mixed reactions. At the reception we hosted I asked George Polites, the shrewd and amiable employers' representative, against whom Bob had done battle during the Industrial Court years, what he thought about it. He replied with typical good humour that we were all on the same ship and it was better to talk about it than fight about it, 'Or we'll all go down together.'

On 17 April the Chinese premier arrived in Australia, on 21 April there was the opening of Bob's first parliamentary session as prime minister with all the attendant ceremony and hospitality and on 26 April we attended a legal convention in Adelaide. Then officialdom was interrupted by the momentous occasion for Bob and me of the birth of our first grandchild, David Dillon, to Rosslyn and Matt. I flew over to be with them for the birth, and this beautiful boy was born at home in Sandringham with my dear friend and nurse, Yvonne, assisting the doctor. Bob arrived a couple of days later, after the convention finished, and we were all in a state of great happiness – there is nothing like the beginning of a new life to focus the joy and hopes of a family.

As I began to get the feel of the job, it was clear that I would need to pay some attention to my wardrobe. Vera had helped me with some basic shopping before the summer election campaign, but now the winter drew near. Anyway, my clothes were geared to housework, welfare work and gardening, with just a few 'better' things. I had made most of them myself. Now I didn't have the time to sew any more, and was required to dress for grander occasions on the whole. I had urgently needed to buy an evening gown after we arrived in Canberra, and on a visit to Sydney went looking for one in a fashionable, up-market shopping centre. The next day there was a fuss in the newspapers about my indulgence – even though the goods I carried out were on approval only and I made no purchases. Thankfully, a friend introduced me to the designer Adele Weiss and my difficulties of shopping publicly, with all the hype it attracted, disappeared. Now I could go to the work-room of this established fashion house away from prying eyes, and the people there became my friends over the next few years.

In June we set off overseas to visit Papua New Guinea, Indonesia, Britain, France, Switzerland, the United States and Canada. It was all very tightly planned and filled with official com-mitments. Port Moresby was a pleasing beginning for Bob and me – we were greeted for the most part by old friends who we had first met in the sixties when they were eager, politically active young men. Now they were in parliamentary and ministerial positions – including Michael Somare as prime minister. In Djakarta the pro-gram over four days was non-stop. I had no secretary to steer me and did not always know what duties I was to be involved in. On the flight from Djakarta to London I established an aerial-sleep record which remains to my knowledge unbroken – seventeen hours straight, including a refuelling stop at Muscat, with no assistance from pill or potion. My sedative was exhaustion. I arrived bright-eyed in London while the rest of our party were strained from tiredness after the long flight.

After we got back to Australia, I went with Bob when he spoke at a National Press Club luncheon. Over the years I had always found these luncheons, where he made a speech and then took questions from assembled members of the media, a good indi-cator as to how he was performing and how he was being regarded by the 'Rat Pack', as federal politician Andrew Peacock had dubbed the political journalists. Also in that same month of June the Premiers' Conference was held in Canberra. There was a dinner for the premiers at the Lodge. I noted to myself the changed complexion of Australian politics in the eighties compared to the seventies. Now there was not only a federal Labor government but also a majority of the states with Labor governments.

In August I flew to Sydney to speak at a luncheon. I had written the speech myself but when I was told there would be about four hundred people present it put me temporarily off balance. I quietly convinced myself, before the plane landed in Sydney, that I could think of each of the four hundred as an individual. Why should their assembly in a crowd make them more formidable? The lunch was a fund-raiser for Jewish women's charities: a success for them and something of an icebreaker for me.

The calendar for 1983 became increasingly laden with public duties, and towards the end of the year I decided to establish a balance in my life. I found a teacher of Iyengar yoga, Pam Brown, and quickly discovered that she had very special qualities. I continued lessons with her throughout my years in Canberra and found the practice an endless well of strength and resilience. The other terrific thing was that I found a music teacher. My commitment to the piano had begun to fizzle out way back when I first met Bob, and social activities claimed my time. During our Oxford years, I had played the North Oxford church organ occasionally but the habit of regular practice was broken – and after we returned to Australia and married, it virtually died. Indeed, for many years I didn't have a piano until Ellie bought me one in the sixties. I used it only spasmodically and, sadly, most often when I was alone, for making music with others is the greatest pleasure. So when we came to the Lodge I decided that I could take it up again and did so with a sense of regaining something I had lost. John Bowan, Bob's Foreign Affairs adviser, was passionately interested in and formidably knowledgeable about music. He arranged for me to talk with Bill Hawkey, the deputy head of the Canberra School of Music, who agreed to take me on. Our lessons began immediately and continued throughout my whole time in Canberra, with Bill and me fitting in lessons between other commitments. I was rusty and, although I was embarrassed at my awkwardness, we soon had a relaxed way of getting through lessons. Bill encouraged and pushed me slowly. There was a fund-raising concert to be held at the School, and he shrewdly coaxed me to play duets with him as a contribution to the program. Rehearsing became great fun, as we played Dvorjak and Faure duets and rattled through Bizet's *Le Bal*, flinging the pages over our shoulders as we went. We both enjoyed these lessons and became great mates.

By the time Sharon Massey came to help me in July my workload was heavy, but things became easier with her arrival. At first I had written all my own speeches – I was keen to keep my hand in at some writing and research, after acquiring a taste for it during my two years at Caulfield Institute. But I couldn't keep it up, and it became clear that if I used the assistance available to me through the public service the speeches would be much more substantial. If, for instance, I was to speak on women's issues, the Office for the Status of Women would provide me with notes. If I spoke about encouraging young people to stay at school longer, those working on education policy would provide input for the speech. This meant that my information was up-to-date and correct – I was not just speaking off the top of my head. Sharon and I would give the appropriate department notice of my engagements, and then I would familiarise myself with their notes. I always adapted the speeches so I felt comfortable with what I was to say, and could do a bit of adlibbing if the occasion arose. I also tapped my welfare colleagues shamelessly for information.

As we settled into our busy days and nights, Bob and I were finding more ground for companionship than had been possible since those first days in Sandringham. It had always been a pleasure for us back in his student days when I could perhaps gather statistics for him or type his essays and research – I felt included and got to know something about his work. Now my diary noted Bob's commitments as well as my own – not just because it was necessary to avoid double-booking, but because this helped me get the feel of what he was doing. If he had things which interested me I could perhaps accompany him. I often went to sit in the Speaker's Gallery in Parliament House, in fact I was there on most days the House was sitting in those early years, not to appear as a good wife show-ing support for my husband – although there was an element of that – but primarily because I was very interested indeed. I found it fasci-nating to watch at close quarters the behaviour of members on the floor of the House. This meant I could form my own opinions about them and was not limited to the interpretations of Bob, other politicians or the press. So we were sharing our commitment and experience in a way which was useful and enjoyable to both of us.

Although we were often together there was little opportu-nity for privacy. Those opportunities came mostly in the bathroom or the bedroom. One private space I wanted to claim was in Commonwealth cars. When he was on his own, Bob enjoyed sitting in the front seat next to the driver – it was more comfortable and more egalitarian than the back. But when I was with him it meant that we couldn't chat quietly together. I pointed out that it looked bad too, that I looked like an add-on rather than his wife and help-mate. I remembered that years before I had felt offended, as a woman, when I saw the same practice in a previous prime minister. So Bob began to sit in the back when I was with him and we would catch up on each other's doings and on family talk.

In November we went to New Delhi, for the Common-wealth Heads of Government Meeting which extended over ten days. Security for these CHOGMs was always strict, with so many heads of state gathered together. On this occasion there was extra anxiety, as a visiting diplomat had recently been killed in India. When we landed on the airstrip at dusk there were security and baggage staff swarming about in large numbers without any appar-ent sense of order. Sharon stood over our baggage like a clucky hen, guarding it then making sure it went the right way. It was hours before some of the staff and media contingent were cleared and brought to the hotel. We had lots of laughs as we compared stories later. Next morning Bob and I found John Bowan asleep on the set-tee in our suite, curled up with the pillow he had brought up with him from his room on the third floor. When provoked by journal-ists who said the Foreign Affairs man, of all people, couldn't cope with the Third World he quickly replied no, no, it was only the third floor he couldn't cope with! Our hotel, the Ashok, was quickly re-named the 'A Shock' in contrast to the five-star accommodation at our previous stopover.

It was in Delhi that I became friendly with Elspeth Howe, wife of the British Foreign Minister. In addition to her already busy life, she was employed to watch over women's opportunities in the British workforce. I also began getting to know many of the other spouses who would attend these conferences in the years to come. Denis Thatcher was the only husband accompanying a leader. When I found myself seated next to him at dinner I asked his advice, from an old hand to a new chum, about being a political spouse. In his own inimitable way he told me how he flew the flag: 'You know, and do my own thing.' He did – and had it down to a fine art, the way he pursued his own interests but also supported Margaret. Although Mrs. Thatcher was a formidable politician, known as the Iron Lady, she was relaxed and companionable with her husband.

An incident which amused me during this first CHOGM occurred when we were returning to Delhi from Agra after visiting the exquisitely beautiful Taj Mahal. As a rather unwieldy collection of spouses, we often felt we were 'rounded up and put in holding pens' prior to the next move. We were instructed that on disembarking from the return flight we should leave the plane in the alphabetical order of our countries, as the fleet of cars would be in that order. Being 'A' for Australia I was happily at the head of the queue – and guess which car came first – Zimbabwe. The cars were, as promised, in alphabetical order, they just began at the other end. So it was me who waited longest on the hot tarmac!

I have been asked many times whether I modelled my approach to the job of being a prime minister's wife on anyone. My unequivocal reply was always a firm no. It was crucial to me to be myself and, except for routine protocol matters, I have made my own choices, with no direction from my husband or the ALP. Many invitations and requests for patronage or support came in, from a wide range of organisations, and I responded to what I felt comfortable with or could learn from. By the end of 1983, I had set up a pattern of activities which coincided with my past interests or had the potential to attract my support. They were mainly in the areas of social work, women's issues and the arts, especially music.

◆

At the end of this first year in the Lodge we went to Sydney to spend Christmas and the New Year at Kirribilli. This beautiful old house was built between 1856 and 1858. In 1920, when it was to be sold and its grounds were threatened with subdivision, it was resumed by the federal government. It was leased to private occupants until, in 1957, the government decided to make it the prime minister's Sydney residence. Its site is one of the most enviable in a city teeming with enviable sites and wonderful views. From the front verandah one looks over a great expanse of the famous harbour and the constantly changing harbour life.

The first time I stayed alone overnight in Kirribilli House, on a working trip to Sydney, I rediscovered the fascination of observing the comings and goings of boats. From my vantage point I saw the great variety of craft, from tiny sailboards, fishing boats, old ferries, modern hydrofoils, tugs and floating restaurants, to large ocean liners and ships of the Australian Navy. That night, as I sat alone having my dinner, a huge container ship headed straight for the sitting-room. It came surprisingly near, then turned suddenly to follow the line of the shore to its berth. Over the years I came to have my harbour favourites. Amongst the ferries it was the small green and yellow ones, but most of all I liked the quiet, rounded tugs. They reminded me of women. As I watched them work I saw them as kindly, no-fuss boats which patiently tend much larger, grander, more important-looking ships. They make sure these ships get to the right place at the right time, shepherding them with a pull or a push as needed. Their power is not immediately obvious but it is there – inside. I watched them a lot and never tired of seeing their unsung but absolutely essential work. The silent, strong women of the sea.

◆

In January 1984 I went to Melbourne to pack up our family home. We had fondly imagined, when we went to base ourselves at the

Lodge, that we could keep Sandringham as a retreat for weekends or holidays – but it just wasn't practical. Apart from our own expense of keeping it serviced and running, there was also a high cost to taxpayers in meeting the prescribed security requirements. We had been reluctant to face the facts, but by now it was clear that we should find tenants for it. I arranged for the packers to come, and began the tedious task of separating from the paraphernalia of twenty years of our family lives. At first I would hesitate over every object as memories flooded back – would I keep it … would I give it to a friend … would I put it in the Brotherhood Op-shop pile? Putting and taking, discarding and retrieving – I became faster and faster at building the stacks and accepting that life moves on. After two days of this I slept alone in the empty house, in a sleeping bag on the floor, with a solitary telephone sitting beside me. Next morning I walked out the door with a feeling of completion. We had been fortunate to have such a home. It had served its purpose and now our needs were different – there were no regrets. But as I walked out through the garden into which I had put so much and from which I had drawn so *very* much, I shed a tear or two.

Back in Canberra, Bob was looking forward to the cricket match between the Prime Minister's XI and the visiting West Indies Test team, on 24 January. The annual Prime Minister's XI match had been started by Robert Menzies in 1959 but, when subsequent prime ministers didn't have such a passion for cricket, the matches lapsed. Bob was eager to start them again. They were interesting sporting events, and also gave him the opportunity to indulge in his love of the game. Bob, his principal private secretary, Graham Evans, and John Bowan chose the team with great care. They wanted to pick several up-and-coming Test cricketers to join current top-class players. That first match was highly successful. Canberrans and cricket lovers from further afield filled the stands and the grounds, welcoming the resurrection of the tradition on a glorious sunny day. David Boon, who had been 'spotted' for Bob's eleven, did well and went on to a successful Test cricket career.

◆

On Australia Day 1984, I was to speak at the National Press Club luncheon. This was a first for a prime minister's wife; I was surprised and a little apprehensive at the invitation. I knew that my Australia Day speech would not be expected to be as political as the many I had heard Bob deliver at the Press Club, but I also realised that once I was there I would be fair game. I decided that it was an opportunity and challenge I did not want to let pass. In the first days as prime minister, Bob had upgraded the importance of women's issues for the government when he appointed Anne Summers to head the newly renamed Office for the Status of Women. He made the Office part of his own portfolio, giving it access to himself and Cabinet. I respected Anne Summers' writing – it was her book, *Damned Whores and God's Police*, that had helped me so much when I was sorting out my role in our marriage during the seventies – so it was a pleasure when she came to Sydney to talk with me about the speech. I wanted to write it myself, and I decided to address topics I was interested in and knew something about: women's issues, Aboriginal affairs, and my thoughts on approaches to social and community work. I was a little nervous about questions from the floor, and Geoff Walsh, a political adviser to Bob, ran through the issues we thought might arise. I also wanted to establish that I was not a conduit to the prime minister, as there are proper processes for that.

Australia Day, 26 January, dawned very hot, and I knew I would be generating considerable body heat of my own, so I wore a light, silk dress and set out for the hairdresser. He had washed my hair and I was in that bedraggled, rat's-tail state when – would you believe? – the electricity supply went off! I had timed the hairdo to fit in with going straight on to the Press Club, so perhaps my anxiety, indeed panic, as I demanded that he DO something, was understandable. Fortunately the power failure did not last long enough to give me heart failure!

The National Press Club lunch was filled to capacity when I delivered my speech. It was well received. I was relieved to find that I was regarded as a person in my own right, and not simply as my husband's 'handbag' – I had the feeling of having jumped a hurdle which would make future hurdles less daunting. As I left the

Club a memory popped into my mind, of a letter written to me in 1979 by a rival who, had things gone differently, may well have been in the Lodge with Bob. She had written that this was not her own opinion but, 'there are members of the press who say that, should he ever become prime minister, you would have to be hidden.' I had been extremely hurt and angry that she had needed to burden me with these words but now they fell away – another ghost had evaporated. As I approached the waiting car, my driver, who usually addressed me very correctly as 'Mrs. Hawke', was beaming as he cried, 'That's my girl!'

◆

I made it a practice, in this busy life, when I went to work interstate, to stay with friends, in order to maintain a thread of continuity – particularly with Vera's friendship. She was my 'Melbourne Pub'. Time often didn't permit the long meaning-of-life conversations we had always enjoyed, but a meal or even supper and breakfast on the run were worthwhile. She pampered me wonderfully, would run a hot, perfumed bath, put flowers by my bed and squeeze fresh oranges in the mornings – and chicken soup was always on tap!

One of my regular commitments in Melbourne was to attend board meetings of the Australian Children's Television Foundation. When I was first invited to join the board, I had replied that I felt I didn't have anything to offer them. All I knew of children's television was my frustration, when our kids were younger, at the lack of good programs for them. I had definite views about that! Phillip Adams, the messenger, was already a board member and he persuaded me that this was enough. My first meeting demonstrated the vision and commitment of the Foundation and aroused my gut feeling that here was something very exciting – a feeling which has been vindicated as the work has blazed on with success upon success.

Just one month after my first board meeting, I was asked to speak at a meeting of the Australian National University Women's Club. I decided to try to convey my enthusiasm for the work of the

Foundation and its research into the effect of television on today's children. I based part of my speech on Neil Postman's book *The Disappearance of Childhood* and many of his conclusions are borne out by my own experience. He writes, for example, about the lost tradition of children's street games and how they have been increasingly replaced by games needing umpires and organisers, venues and equipment – all leading to expenditure and the necessary involvement of adults. And in this century, children have no protection from the harshness of life. They have lost the opportunity to learn about life for themselves – slowly, through observation and the absorption of experience. They are hit with everything at once – and it can overwhelm them. Violent stories and fairytales have always been told to young children, but before television there was the moderating influence of the reader's – often the mother's – voice. Television drama tends to reinforce all kinds of misconceptions, including: death is not permanent; violence is fun; violence is normal; the goodies always win; people are either good or bad; the baddies deserve to die; revenge is justifiable; instant gratification of all desires is possible; things can be acquired without hard work, planning or waiting; men and women should have particular roles in life if they are to be happy and fulfilled; girls must be pretty and sexy; boys must be rough and tough.

My work with the Foundation, though regretfully limited by the rest of my workload, has continued for eight years and my excitement about it has not waned the slightest bit – on the contrary, it has been reinforced!

At the risk of implying that the Lodge is like Fawlty Towers, I will tell of an amusing incident that day on my way to speak to the Women's Club. Someone needed some photographs and Sharon had arranged to have them taken before I left for the University. I dutifully cooperated, posing as requested (for me, the hardest part of the job!) in the front garden, looking, I hoped, my best when … Pow! Whirr! and a cascade of water! With uncanny synchronisation the camera and the sprinklers had blasted into action. It was so funny that I could not be cross with our gardener, Mark Carmody, who had been thrilled with the installation of a computerised, automatic watering system – but it did mean a rapid change of clothing and dabbing of hairdo before I scrambled off to the women's meeting.

◆

Even though public life was taking up a lot of my time, the family remained in the foreground for me. Susan was continuing her study of macrobiotic cooking and yoga in Sydney. On 1 August Rosslyn's second child, Paul, was born, a dear little brother for David. But Ros's health was poor and I travelled to Melbourne whenever possible to see her. At that time I was smoking so much it was reducing my fitness, and I felt self-contempt at not being in control of it. So I was really ready to stop and, finally, at the end of August, set an afternoon aside to go to Manly for a mixture of hypnosis and aversion therapy. It worked, and I never smoked again.

Sue went off to Japan to continue her study of yoga and wrote to us saying that she had met her future husband there, Jan Pieters. They planned to marry on 7 September in Antwerp, since Jan was born in Belgium. I was not sure until almost the last day whether or not I could travel to the wedding. Sir Geoffrey Yeend told me that the Belgian government would want a security person to accompany me and that I should also take a secretary. I wondered if all the arrangements would be worthwhile, so I phoned Sue to find out whether there would be an opportunity to spend any time with her, since I could only manage to arrive the day before the ceremony. She and Jan had already discussed that probability and suggested we should all go off for a short break together after the wedding. The upshot was a honeymoon for six – Sue, Jan and I along with Sharon, a Dutch government driver and my security man who doubled as the second driver. We drove through Brittany and stayed for a few days in the quaint and ancient fishing village of St Malo. We had lots of seafood meals, did a great deal of walking, and then drove back via Paris to Antwerp. I have fond memories of that time and the laughs we shared. My happily married security man, Graeme Sindel, still nominates it as his second-best honeymoon! It was special for me to be our family representative there, and to meet Jan's extended family.

On the way home I went to the Kimberley to see Steve, Lesley and our second grandson, Kelly, born while Bob and I were in Japan earlier in the year. I had the pleasure of taking the baby for walks in the pusher on the red-dust tracks. In Perth I caught up, as always, with Alan and Pat Barblett, then brought my mother, now aged eighty-eight, back with me to stay at the Lodge. She especially wanted to see Ros.

The year was bringing an escalating round of functions and meetings but I was also establishing a regular schedule of music practice, tennis with friends I had made at the local Forrest club, and yoga classes. It might seem odd that I was spending time on these therapeutic pastimes when I was so busy – but for me they were a necessary respite from my mounting concerns about Rosslyn and her family. Bob and I and the whole family had been shattered by her doctors' pronouncement, after Paul's birth, that despite her struggles against it, her addiction to heroin had become life-threatening. For Bob, that debilitating sadness together with his political responsibilities had been eroding his legendary resilience – to the point where he was seen weeping on the television screens of the nation as he responded to an intrusive question about the family.

We felt that we should do something about the furore caused by Bob's obvious distress. It was a difficult situation for all of us, and making some kind of public statement seemed the best way to put an end to the escalating rumours. Together we decided that I should do an interview on national television with Terry Willesee on 24 September.

In this interview our aim was to 'clear the decks' and to counter the misinformation that was current in political and media circles in Canberra about our family. We wanted to put a stop to the innuendo that was not only unfair, but which also interfered with appropriate treatment for Ros and her own family. It provided me with an opportunity to explain that Bob's distress had been due to anguish about our daughter's health which, coupled with his work-load, was causing chronic exhaustion.

I was also aware of the possible side-benefit of opening up public discussion of a subject that was almost taboo in our society – private distress being made worse by the fact that drug abuse by a loved member of a family involved them in illegal and covert actions.

My remarks also touched on another taboo: men crying in our stiff-upper-lip culture. I would rather a man who can show what is a natural expression of grief, rather than suppress tears in order to be manly. Bob has, over the years, demonstrated an astounding capacity to return to strength after grief or defeat, and perhaps it is because he *can* cry.

Happily, as I write this in 1992, it is in the knowledge that those traumas have been dealt with. We count our blessings. Many of Ros's and Matt's friends did not come out of that dark tunnel. The initial response to my television interview was dramatic, but it confirmed the positive outcome of going public. It brought many, many hundreds of letters, most of which expressed appreciation of an opportunity to open up. Drug users and their families were caught in the bind of needing to be protective, while at the same time needing to be open, in order to obtain medical or counselling assistance. The stigma attached to drug addiction is another inhibiting factor. In my private agony I had spoken with doctors and psychologists that I felt safe with. The organisation called DUPA (Drug Users' and Parents' Aid) which provided information and counsel, had been a great help to me. But it was like walking on eggshells, and the heartache was unspeakable.

Only a few days after my television statement, my mother became ill and we had to take her to hospital for surgery, an ostectomy. She was put into intensive care. She is such a strong woman that she defied the prognosis and some weeks later I took her home to Perth, her place, her family.

A JOB WORTH DOING

◇

On 14 October 1984, the Department of Prime Minister and Cabinet was playing the press gallery in a social cricket match when Bob created a wonderful photo opportunity! He already had a reputation for cooperation with the media – he understood that becoming recognised and accepted by the public is part of politics – but he hadn't planned, this day, to help the photographer Peter Wells of the *Canberra Times* win two award categories for 1985 National Press Photo of the Year. Bob was at the crease when he hooked the ball into his face and staggered from the blow. The photograph even captures the flying bits of his shattered spectacles. He and I were quickly into the car and on the way to the hospital, picking fragments of glass out of his eye as we went. Thank goodness there was no permanent damage.

The next day I wrote in my diary, 'Here we go again. Election campaign meeting!' The date was set for 1 December, just six weeks away. It seemed no time since February 1983, but in fact

Bob had been prime minister for nearly two years. My program was stepped up: on top of all my existing commitments there were campaign meetings, extra travelling and interviews to be fitted into my schedule. On election day we were in Melbourne to vote in Bob's electorate of Wills, and that evening he again claimed victory for the Australian Labor Party.

As well as demanding considerable emotional fortitude, the year, one way and another, had been extremely busy. Even in my weary state, I looked forward to a board meeting of the Australian Children's Television Foundation on 5 December where we had a screening of its spectacularly successful series, 'Winners', which went on to win several awards both in Australia and internationally. Then, on 15 December, Bob and I escaped to a holiday house on the coast of northern New South Wales. We sat in the sun, explored the beaches and read books for a few days before returning to Sydney for Christmas at Kirribilli House with the family.

In January 1985, Ros and Matt made a big decision. They had tried so hard to keep their family together, but it is a devilish business to bring the mind and body to rights after they have been in the grip of heroin. For the sake of their sons, they found the strength to do what was necessary to make themselves well. They felt they needed to be apart to succeed in their cures, and Ros went off to a rehabilitation centre in America. We took our two grandsons to the Lodge and privately engaged a young woman to take care of them. The effort and resolve of both parents allowed them to go on to rebuild their health and their lives with courage and success.

◆

The round of official engagements continued in the new year, including a two-day visit by the Japanese prime minister, Mr. Nakasone, and his wife. On 2 February Bob and I left on another overseas trip. We had a few days in Belgium and then went on to the United States to visit Washington, New York and Los Angeles. Public life was fascinating and enjoyable – but you can imagine how we had almost no time to spare, with the onerous daily responsibilities of government for Bob, and for me the answering of mail, the continuing involvement in family matters and the preparation necessary for events and travel. The premier event for us, in mid-February, was the birth of our grand-daughter, Sophie, to Sue and Jan.

On 21 February the parliamentary session began, with the attendant hospitality, including afternoon tea in the Senate gardens and lunch at the Lodge for spouses. Although I knew most of them enjoyed the tradition of these lunches, it never seemed to me to work entirely satisfactorily. Awkward timing was the biggest problem, so I tried an early start, which let those who wished go off for question time at Parliament House. This was an important glimpse of the working life of parliamentarians for spouses who travelled far, and rarely, to Canberra. Old hands stayed on and chatted long into the afternoon at the Lodge – we always got on well, cutting across party-political allegiances. The first time I hosted such a lunch, in 1983, we had a buffet in the house while it teemed with rain outside. Everyone perched on the arms of chairs, sat on the stairs and huddled in crowded groups juggling plate and drink. Oh dear! thought I. But I must say it broke down any new-chum nervousness about ceremony or decorum. There were some male spouses there for the first time and a couple of the wives picked me up on this, on the grounds that it had always been a ladies' lunch. But I felt strongly that 'political spouse' was the only qualification for attendance. After all, for every man attending the lunch, there was a woman in the parliament. In 1983 there had been thirteen female senators and six female members of the House of Representatives, now in 1985 there were fifteen senators and eight members. But the total numbers were seventy-six senators and 148 members: just over ten per cent, we still had a long way to go.

I was beginning to get a feel for the official residences by now, and I asked the government's Fine Arts adviser, Margaret Betteridge, to show me the work she had supervised in Sydney, restoring the historic buildings of the Parliament Houses and Hyde Park Barracks. I was impressed with what I saw and felt that restoration was the right way to approach the maintenance and decor of the prime minister's residences. When I said to Margaret, 'This is the way to go,' she was delighted. We would have a philosophy to follow and could perhaps avoid the personal 'decor statements' of the past. I wanted the residences for which we were answerable to live up to their roles in national life and their part in Australia's heritage. During the first half of 1985, I had a meeting with those involved to discuss my thoughts: Sir John Bunting from the Official Establishments Trust, Bryan Hoffman of the Department of Prime Minister and Cabinet, Lady Parkinson from the Australiana Fund and Margaret Betteridge. I also asked James Mollison, director of the Australian National Gallery, to come along and contribute his thoughts. We agreed on an approach, and decided to seek professional advice on restoring the Lodge and Kirribilli House as historic buildings. The Lodge was built in 1926 and I asked James Mollison to lend the house some Australian paintings that may have hung in rooms of that period. To my delight he agreed, and let us have works by Arthur Streeton, Tom Roberts, Frederick McCubbin, Grace Cossington Smith, Grace Crowley and, later on, some by Rupert Bunny. I loved living with them!

I knew the Lodge had once housed a piano made in 1926 by Beale, Australia's only professional piano-builder ever, one of a limited number of its kind. It took some time to locate it, but eventually Bill Hawkey tracked it down and we went to see it, hidden away in a back room at the School of Music. It was looking absolutely unloved and was not even in good enough condition for use as a practice instrument. That became a project. At first the quotes we got to repair it were too high, but then we found the ideal solution at the Preston Institute of Technology, in Victoria. They had recently begun to teach the making and maintenance of musical instruments, and in their workshop the dear old Beale was dismantled into its hundreds of parts for restoration. I went to visit it there, spread over the floor and benches of the workroom, and saw the loving care it was receiving. The Yellow Room at the Lodge now became the Music Room and, over the years of Bill Hawkey and me playing it, the Beale was 'run in' to become a very respectable piano – as well as a little bit of history and heritage. One particularly pleasant memory of the Music Room is of a Sunday afternoon when Geoffrey Tozer, the eminent Australian pianist, and Walter d'Espasj, the world-renowned Yugoslavian cellist, were about to begin a concert tour of Australia. They rehearsed together, for the first time, at the Lodge. John Bowan and I were ensconced in two armchairs for a musical treat as we watched them go through that first practice run – playing, then discussing, each passage; feeling the music together.

During 1985, the inaugural Sydney International Piano Competition was held in Sydney. This was quickly to become a musical event of international prestige, attracting top-line talent and up-and-coming pianists. I was invited to present the awards and had the pleasure of meeting the candidates and the adjudicators on the night of the finalists' concert. It was a particular thrill for me to meet Eileen Joyce, one of the judges, because of a tenuous link I felt with her. She was born a West Australian, and my dear teacher, Mr. Bastian, had taught her for a time during her childhood. Meeting her, I told her how, on a cold winter's night in Oxford in 1954, I had gone to one of her recitals in the town hall. There was a lighting failure which plunged the hall into darkness before she began to play, and I was mortified to think that this could happen to her – my childhood idol. My admiration had increased when I saw the grace with which she handled the mishap.

Early May saw the annual general meeting of the Australiana Fund at the Lodge. There was a variety of reactions to our approach. A few members lacked enthusiasm because we proposed a return to the style of the 1920s, a period they considered to be at best architecturally questionable and at worst, just awful. I admit I'd had a touch of doubt myself about the period, but the more I learned the more interesting and attractive I found it. Of course we took some licence for comfort against pure authenticity – we were not prepared to be without modern-day heating, lighting and plumbing! But there was no compromise where the integrity of the building itself was concerned – its structure was renovated and all the wiring and piping was concealed. This sometimes meant inconvenience and delay – we had to wait for funds to become available before doing even quite minor repairs because we were determined to do everything properly and in accordance with our plan. I remember that I had to resist the repainting of the Lodge dining-room before a royal luncheon because I knew if it was done out of context with our plan it would only have to be changed later. One of the biggest jobs undertaken was the restoration of the wood panelling in the entrance hall and stairway. It took weeks of smelly, messy work to burn and sand off the white gloss paint. My hope is that the work we began, with the Department and the Trust, will be taken up by those who follow us, enabling continuity of restoration for a residence which, in the nature of things, does not usually have long-term tenure – and certainly not family inheritance! What is really needed is a new Lodge, built on the site reserved for that purpose.

At about this time there was a staff change and we were fortunate indeed in our new house manager. The Lodge had previously had a morning-suited butler in the English style. But Bob said he didn't want to be 'butlered'. Gordon Mair brought just the right mixture of good humour and professionalism to the job. On hearing his broad Scots accent, Bob exclaimed jokingly, 'We've got a bloody foreigner!'

◆

On 15 August 1985, Steve and Lesley's second son, dear little Sam, was born. Now we had five grandchildren.

At the end of August, I took on an unaccustomed role as compere of the high-rating daytime television program, 'The Mike Walsh Show' – I was to stand in for Mike while he was on holiday. The format of the show was an hour of interviews interspersed with music by guest entertainers, and I was asked to select some of my own interviewees.

For one spot, I chose two members of a team of young Australians who had returned in October 1984 from an expedition to climb Mount Everest without oxygen. Their achievement had provided one of those splendid 'Australia can do it' stories for the nation's press. Bob and I had invited the whole team to the Lodge for a celebratory lunch at the end of 1984. As we gathered after lunch in the sitting-room for coffee, we had felt privileged to listen, still and silent, with a sense of awe, to the taped voice of the leader of the expedition, Tim McCartney-Snape, as he stood alone on top of the great mountain. Through his laboured breathing he forced out the words to express his feelings about being there, and about our responsibility to our planet. It was a very special experience for every one of us present in that room.

Now, my guests on the show were Andy Henderson, who had sustained serious frostbite and whose hands were still bandaged heavily, and Simon Balderstone who had one arm in a sling after the resetting of a finger broken during the expedition. I had also invited the Aboriginal and Islander Dance group to appear and after the show, when we were all having a drink together, there was amusement all round as we noted that Simon and Andy could not open a can of beer between them!

I had prepared the night before the show as though I were swotting for an exam! I quickly had to read a book for an interview with its author, feeling it was a desperate cram (Susan helped me). A singer from the Australian Opera about whom, to my shame, I knew nothing was also to be on the program. So my homework was serious business. I arrived early at the studios the next day and was taken through the system of cue boards, camera positions and so on. I then proceeded to enjoy myself enormously as things got under-way – although it requires total concentration to act as compere for a whole hour. Back at the Lodge, family and staff had watched the program and, though they were too kind to say so, my guess is that they sat with fingers crossed that I would not make any gaffes!

The Commonwealth Heads of Government Meeting was held at Nassau, in the Bahamas, in October that year. I had come to regard leaders' meetings such as this to be the nearest thing to a holiday I would get, so I made it my practice to pack bathers, tennis racquet and golf sticks. There were always formal ceremonies to attend, but otherwise my time was my own. In the Bahamas we stayed in a modern hotel on the beachfront and most days I swam, sunbaked, and played tennis. One afternoon I went out in a catamaran with John Bowan and Bob's principal private secretary Chris Conybeare. They were dab-hands at sailing and it was great to be out on this wide bay in the fresh wind. Our security squad came out, too, on a separate catamaran – all in the name of duty, of course.

We were at first concerned and then highly amused when we three had sailed safely back to the beach but they had capsized and the rescue boat was speeding out, sirens screaming – very embarrassing for those who were supposed to be looking after us! I relate this story with the best of goodwill, as they were really very good at their job.

The Queen, as head of the Commonwealth family, always attended the CHOGM. It was her practice to give a formal dinner for the heads of government and their spouses – and when she had travelled to the conference on her yacht *Britannia*, the dinner was on board. In Nassau, we received a message, just before leaving for the Queen's dinner, that guests would not proceed by car but by boat. Bob guessed the reason immediately – to avoid the host prime minister's embarrassment at street protests along the car route – and he was adamant that we would proceed by car as arranged. So we arrived at the yacht on time, with a few other guests who had come in cars, but the boats were delayed by engine trouble and rough seas. We stood and chatted with our hosts, then sat about for over an hour until the rest of the guests arrived. Her Majesty and Prince Philip were not amused! But still, her speech embraced the concept of family, the Commonwealth family. My understanding of the goals of the family from my grandmother, my parents, and my own experience was that the stronger members help the weaker, that those who need more help receive more and that all members, hopefully, give and take with tolerance and understanding. I could see it working through these meetings to which the Queen is so strongly committed, in the Commonwealth of stronger and weaker, older and younger nations.

During these meetings Bob took the lead in working close- ly with the prime ministers of Canada (Brian Mulroney), India (Rajiv Gandhi) and Zambia (Kenneth Kaunda) for the continuation of the use of sanctions in the struggle for equal rights for black South Africans. Their shared cause helped to consolidate the friend- ship between Rajiv and Bob. The British prime minister, Margaret Thatcher, was adamant in putting the case for lifting sanctions against the apartheid regime, but this group dug in. They prevailed, and Bob was the spokesman for their position in the closing media conference.

◆

By now Bob had been prime minister for almost three years. Although our work and leisure were often separate, we had much more of a sense of a shared base and of working in tandem. Apart from our common commitment to the job we were doing, our family had grown to include David, Kelly, Paul, Sophie and Sam. Studying psychology at Caulfield I had looked at patterns in partnerships – I used to go to the psychology section in the library and read extracts from research into relationships and families, simply because I was interested. I believed the strong early passion and certainty in each other that Bob and I had experienced would carry us through hard times. But no matter what emotional riches a marriage stores, it needs nurturing. Even though it may be a hackneyed image, I can think of no better analogy than a garden. If you do not water it, nourish it, pull out the weeds, and protect it from the rabbits you cannot expect it to flourish and bring you pleasure – and you should not be surprised if it dies.

On our first official trip to Washington I had asked about the size of the city's population, and was given two figures – one for when Congress was sitting and another for when it was not. The explanation was that members and their families live in Washington during the sittings, which coincide with school terms – so children go to school in Washington. For the rest of the time the families live at their home bases. This was only conversational information but it appealed to me, considering the similarity in the geographical dimensions of our country and the USA. There are obvious difficulties in introducing this idea to Australia. The expense of acquiring the stock of houses which would be required in Canberra would be enormous. Also, it is less than ideal for any family to live in two places. But I can't help wondering whether a schedule like this wouldn't be a good investment in the sanity of political families: sanity which may be reflected in the stability of marriages and the quality of the contribution politicians make. Back in the forties there was criticism of John Curtin's wife for not being by her husband's side, especially in wartime. It should be remembered that she had home and family in Western Australia, and that the journey overland took several days each way. Elsie Curtin also worked hard on the political front while she was in Perth. There were no electorate offices for politicians in those days and she dealt with all the mail that arrived for her husband.

When Bob was elected in 1980, I found I was entitled to return airfares to Canberra six times a year. Now, of course, spouses often have careers of their own and are not free to come and go. Some find there is no joy to be found in infrequent visits to Canberra anyway – they feel like outsiders in that incestuous scene. Whichever way you look at it, the political family's life is not an easy one. And such families are aware that their private lives are under public scrutiny, with high expectations of community service from spouses, particularly wives. There are rewards for those who are interested in the political process and feel a personal allegiance to their partner's political party – it would be intolerable to feel hijacked to the cause. In my own case I felt fortunate that Bob was involved with the ALP, the party that best represented my own aims and hopes, the values I had absorbed as a child and in my youth.

The stress of political life takes, perhaps, its greatest toll on the parliamentarians themselves. I travelled a great deal on commercial flights in the Lodge years, and repeatedly saw the stress on federal members from far-flung electorates. Western Australians, for instance, had to cope not only with one, or even two, changes of flights to and from Canberra, but also a time adjustment of two hours in winter and three in summer. They may catch up with essential reading on the plane and in transit lounges, if they can escape the distractions of company and the socialising that results. Many have to travel by road for long distances from home to the Perth airport. Imagine how politicians, especially those with heavier workloads, ministers or committee members, arrive at the family hearth with their long day even further extended, dropping in like aliens from space. Perhaps a frazzled wife and tired children are waiting for them or – worse – a family all bright and lively and expecting the same of an exhausted 'visitor'. There are constituents' messages waiting and matters to deal with the next morning at the electorate office, as well as public events to attend over the week-end. On Sunday night, if members stay for a function or the evening meal with the family, they must catch the 'red-eye' at midnight, arriving in Melbourne at 5.20 a.m., and wait there for a connection to Canberra at about seven o'clock – and thus to the office. It is too hard! How can we expect so much of them and their families?

◆

On 14 February 1986, Bob's Uncle Albert died, the one with the engaging personality, the love of sport and the political career. From childhood, Bob had regarded him as something of a mentor. We flew across to his funeral in Adelaide, where his niece Beatrice, who had looked after him in his ageing years, told me how he had said to her, wearily but not without humour, 'It's very trying, Beat, this dying.' Soon after that he pulled out the tubes that were sustaining his life. I thought to myself, 'How very courageous and sensible.'

This year, as usual, I travelled all over the country opening projects and speaking. There was another visit by the Queen and the Duke of Edinburgh in March, then an official visit by the president of Korea and his wife. In April, I went bush with a television crew to make a video designed to encourage the planting of trees for the greening of Australia. But between all this I was preparing for a lieder concert at the Canberra School of Music on 9 May. This was my most ambitious musical undertaking in Canberra. Bill had introduced me to one of his advanced students, the singer Teresa Rosendahl (now Raynor), and coached us in many songs from which the program would be selected. This is just what I adored doing – making music with others. On the night of the concert, to be held in the recital room at the School, Teresa and I were extremely nervous. While we were waiting in the wings we told each other it would be like walking down Bourke Street naked. But once we were out there, that awful fear of exposure faded and we enjoyed it immensely. Five days later Bob and I left on a trip to China and Japan.

In June, I attended a reception at Parliament House to mark the publication of a report, appropriately called *Women's Business*, from an Aboriginal women's task-force. In 1985 Australia had sent a delegation to the United Nations End of Decade for Women world conference in Nairobi. One of the resolutions was to encourage participating countries to develop forward-looking strategies for women, establishing specific goals over the coming decade. Some nations had given their women more support than others, and it was a matter of some satisfaction to me that the Hawke Government had taken the conference seriously and funded task-forces to research and establish national agendas for various groups of Australian women. It was a delight to see the evidence of strength, support, frankness and sisterhood which had blossomed for Aboriginal women throughout the process. The agendas were researched and established in a variety of ways, including interviews and good old networking. I could see that already positive results had emerged simply through women talking to each other and with task-force members about their lives and their needs.

For two consecutive weekends at the end of June and the beginning of July, I attended a personal development seminar in Sydney with my daughter Sue. We had done this sort of work together at one stage in the early eighties, and Sue was keen for us to do more. The seminar encouraged participants to identify and deal with both difficulties and goals in their lives. It reinforced the idea, if there was ever any doubt, that we are responsible for our own decisions, successes and failures, that there is no room for 'if only' or 'being the victim'. I knew all that, but the course did offer suggestions for working through the bits that one gets stuck on – and it was good to do it with Sue. Communication and companionship flows from discussing these things together – as we still do.

On 1 August little Paul's second birthday party was held at the Lodge. I was spending as much time attending to the delights of being a grandmother as I could, in between official duties. There is a smattering of entries like 'H mind boys' or 'take boys to playgroup' in my diary.

In September I undertook to host Mike Schildberger's current affairs radio program in Melbourne. This, in my view, is more difficult than television, because you have to sit in a sealed studio with only a microphone and learn to press the right buttons – quickly. For my telephone interview guests I chose Professor Sir Gustav Nossal, head of the Walter and Eliza Hall Institute and a world figure in immunology; Norm Spencer who headed up the 'Australian Made' campaign, and Dick Smith, businessman and adventurer. The phone-in questions were much easier to handle than you would think – most questions are pre-selected by the producer, and the topics are usually predictable because of the subject under discussion. So that was another new experience.

Later that month I travelled to Ballarat, in Victoria, to launch a book called *Girls Can Do It*, a collection of the stories of women who had pursued unusual careers. This book became a favourite gift of mine for those who doubted we could do it! Or for girls, young or old, who doubted their own courage to do out-of-the-ordinary things.

Shortly after the *Girls Can Do It* launch, I was in Adelaide at the 'Speak Out' seminar, for women of all ages and occupations, funded by the South Australian government. There were expert speakers on a wide range of issues and I delivered a speech prepared by the Office for the Status of Women. Then a week later I went to Melbourne for the opening of 'Maia Place', a hostel for young drug-dependent mothers where they could live with their babies while they rehabilitated. The hostel was developed and run by one of my fellow students in the welfare course at Caulfield Institute, and it made me feel proud to know her.

I feel extraordinarily fortunate to have had so many opportunities as the wife of the prime minister to follow interests and priorities I had developed myself, and to participate in so many projects highlighting the warmth and dynamism of Australian women.

◆

On 24 November 1986, Pope John Paul II arrived in Australia – a man of undoubted presence. His church's policies affecting women, especially women in poor, overpopulated, Catholic countries and particularly in the area of family planning, are unfortunate, I believe

– but meeting him for the second time I observed again the special gentleness of his manner, and his insatiable interest in current affairs showed itself in his lively discussions with Bob.

In December Bob and I flew north to Noosa, in Queensland, for the Jack Newton Golf Tournament. We had known Jack and his wife Jackie for years. He had sometimes called in at our Sandringham home with Col Cunningham, for billiards and a beer – of which he was fond! At the height of his career as a world-class professional golfer, he was involved in a ghastly accident resulting in the loss of his right arm and his right eye as well as severe internal injuries. Not to be stopped, he can still hit a golf ball a country mile, does golf commentaries for radio and television, and works tirelessly for junior golf. His is yet another of the 'irrepressible Aussie' stories which are so inspiring.

♦

It was important for both me and Bob to maintain our personal friendships in the peculiar framework of public scrutiny that came with life at the Lodge. The idea is sometimes put about, wickedly fuelled by a few journalists, that personal friendships should somehow be kept within ideologically pure bounds. People on both sides of politics have, from time to time, deplored Bob's closeness with friends they believe aren't appropriate for a Labor prime minister. Bob has always found friends across a spectrum of interests and incomes. Of course he had constant dealings with employers and businessmen – and celebrities – through his work with unions and the Labor Party. The swapping of ideas often leads to the building of friendships, and Bob valued this as part of broadening his view of how the world works – we need to understand each other. The most publicly criticised examples of Bob's friendships are those with Peter Abeles and Frank Lowy. I remember the first day Bob met Peter, when he came to our house in Sandringham with his partner Ken Thomas. It was a routine call to establish a working relationship in the area of industrial affairs, and so began our friendship with Peter and his wife Kitty. I have watched ever since how Bob's friendship with Peter has deepened – they enjoy and respect each other's minds, and talk endlessly, mostly about international affairs and national affairs, but also about their children and grandchildren. And even how to succeed at blackjack! Peter is like a loving teddy bear with our kids and envies Bob his grandchildren. Frank and Shirley Lowy are friends for life who have shared some of our most difficult moments. They have been guardian angels to our Ros, especially while she was in America becoming well, and we love them for that. The fact that these men are successful in the world of business is irrelevant – as is the fact that Bob's closest mate, Col Cunningham, is just like a character out of a Damon Runyon story, and a dedicated family man.

Rosslyn, with her two infant sons, and Sue and her family who lived nearby, came to spend Christmas with us at Kirribilli House. The warmth of Sydney, the peace, the sun on the water and the sloping green lawns enveloped us all after another busy year. As we sat in our bathers, sunning ourselves, reading, and talking, and playing with the kids, we waved back from time to time to the calls of friendly holiday makers on boats, or Sydneysiders commuting on ferries, 'G'day Bob, good on yer', 'ow yer going?' And 'Hi, Haze'. In what other country could that happen? Happy Christmas!

THIS VAST ELECTORATE

◇

We had a happy holiday for two weeks that summer, before launching into the new year of 1987. Bob and I went to a performance of *The Mikado* at the Opera House with my sister Ede (neither of us young enough now for her to be 'Sis') and her husband Ron, over from Perth. Bob took Rosslyn and her boys out to visit a friend's horse stud, and one day Bob, Ron and the little boys had a fishing trip with Peter Doyle, Sydney's fisherman raconteur-restaurateur.

Another day Bob went to visit Ted Noffs, who had become an invalid after suffering a severe stroke. Ted, a Methodist pastor in the sleazy, Kings Cross end of Sydney, had set up Life Education Centres after he became more and more distressed at burying young drug addicts. Believing passionately in the individual worth of each and every human being, he felt that self esteem was the best defence against such tragedy, and developed the Centres to prevent young people getting involved with drugs. The Life Education model was designed to make sure they were well-informed about their bodies and how drugs distort perceptions and behaviour. It was totally positive and full of fun – kids loved it. The work of the Centres has continued and spread, even after Ted's illness. Bob was saddened to see the severity of his disability when he visited him that summer.

Another day Dick and Pip Smith and their daughters came for lunch and a swim. We had got to know them through our mutual interest in the Life Education Centres. Once Dick had made money, through his successful electronics business, he set about adventuring, and encouraging and funding others to adventure, as well as supporting causes he believed in. One of his driving maxims was that he would work against anything he wouldn't want his young daughters to do, and he became an invaluable patron of Ted Noffs' activities.

Then, holidays over, it was back to Canberra and work, preparing for another short overseas tour at the end of January which took us to Davos, in Switzerland, where Bob spoke at an international economics symposium, then on to Jordan and Israel. We returned to Australia, via Perth, in the first week of February and took up the round of local duties again – but I managed to fit in some bridge lessons and some golf before the year really gathered pace. Our old friend Yvonne, who had been desperately ill with cancer but defied all her doctors' predictions, came to stay at the Lodge for our grandson David's fourth birthday party.

In April, I took part in the launch of a fitness program called 'Walk for Pleasure'. I walked the route through Canberra with the prime minister – but not Bob. It was the actor Paul Eddington, famous for playing the part of the British prime minister in the comedy series 'Yes, Prime Minister'. I could never persuade my own prime minister to walk just for the pleasure of walking – for Bob there must be a reason: you walked to gather mushrooms, or to play golf, or very fast for fitness, but never just for the pleasure!

The next week I was one of the speakers at a seminar in Frankston, Victoria, on 'Women, Work and Health', organised by the local Commonwealth Employment Service staff who had become concerned at the low and limited horizons of girls leaving school after year ten and finding only unfulfilling work. The seminar was attended by about five hundred girls, their teachers and some local dignitaries. There was also a screening of 'STDs – Not Just Phonecalls' a state-government-funded film about sexually transmitted diseases. One of the speakers, a young woman doctor, was inundated with questions from the girls. The whole morning's program just flew and I was very impressed by the creative approach taken to addressing the lack of information and ambition among girls of that age. Over my remaining years in the Lodge I attended and spoke at many more of these seminars. They became very popular as the word got around and the model was adapted for a range of young women needing to equip themselves for an increasingly complex future – where they could not count on getting married and living happily ever after.

That evening in Melbourne I launched a video for a friend, Carmel Hurst, to help another good project along. Carmel, a nurse, was matron at a hospital for elderly patients located over the road from a boys' high school. She had involved the boys in visiting the old people and had worked to encourage the establishment of real friendships between the old and the young. In Australia, many children don't know their extended families (as I had, so happily) because they are migrants from overseas or interstate. Carmel's work reminded me of the SPAN program developed by the Brotherhood of St Laurence while I was there. Among other things, SPAN encouraged retired people to help school children with reading practice or school projects, in turn providing the helpers with enjoyable company – and maybe a game of snooker. It is gratifying to watch relationships grow and deepen in such programs, demonstrating over and over again how effectively community social work can match people who have something to offer each other.

On my next visit to Melbourne I had a Children's Television Foundation board meeting, and then did some publicity for Headway Victoria. When a request from Headway first came to me I was interested because I knew of their work from our friend who had stayed with us in 1980 after he had sustained head injuries. He lived with us for several months and attended Coonac Rehabilitation Centre every day. On most evenings we would have a bit of a talk over our meal. It has been a profound pleasure to watch his determination and complete recovery over the ensuing years. Headway was set up to draw attention to, and raise funds for, the care of sufferers from what they call the 'silent plague' – the alarming number of people, especially young men, who sustain such injury. By this stage Headway was becoming increasingly effective in assisting victims and their families. Mike Willesee was doing a segment about its work on his current affairs television program, and I was to be a part of it. The victims of head injury, who may suffer a multitude of symptoms – lack of motor-control, memory loss, involuntary muscular spasms, and more – were wonderful interviewees. We finished up with an eight-minute segment which brought widespread attention to their predicament and their needs.

Next day, Bob and I left for Western Samoa for the South Pacific Forum. I took my bathers and my golf sticks again and had the fun of playing on a course carved from dense tropical rain forest: picturesque but rugged. I still have a snapshot of my security man balancing his way over a log across a deep, fast-flowing stream, with my bag of clubs, in their buggy, clutched in his arms.

At the beginning of June it was on again – a federal election called for 11 July. We decided to have three days of rest and sun at Port Douglas, in Queensland, before Bob hit his straps for the campaign. But for the whole time it was cloudy and raining, and he vented his frustration on the skies, his staff and me! But it was still a rest: sitting still can be a great bonus, especially as a counterpoise to perpetual motion.

My job made me constantly aware that Australia is a very large electorate. Tropical rain forests, dusty outback, hardwood forests, green pastures, broad beaches, cities and country towns – it is immense and varied. But in a federal election campaign my sense of its vastness was heightened, as we raced the clock to cover as much of the country as possible. The Hawke Government was returned to office once more, with eighty-six seats to the combined opposition's sixty-two in the House of Representatives, in spite of the doomsayers – even in our own party.

At this stage of our lives we were both running hard and keeping fit. But Bob, especially, had a backbreaking workload. Most mornings at the Lodge we woke at around seven o'clock and proceeded to devour a stack of national and state newspapers. Bathroom, dressing and breakfast were completed in minimum time. Bob's day would rarely finish before eleven or midnight. If there was no function to attend at night, there was always the reading, the endless reading! Even at weekends his staff brought three stout briefcases full and he diligently addressed himself to the task of reading *all* of it and signing correspondence. He always took special interest in letters from children, and read bits out to me sometimes when he was amused or moved by them. I must say he surprised me endlessly with his capacity to absorb, retain and use voluminous amounts of information. It was a skill and discipline he had developed years before, and one which remained an important tool of trade. On Saturdays, unless there was something of importance he had to attend to, he made phonecalls to racing friends to work out the afternoon's punting. He enjoyed these calls which often became chats about politics and families as well as horseflesh. Afterwards, he would sit making minute and complicated notes on the racing-form, before placing his bets. That done, he could concentrate for ten minutes on lunch and maybe me! Then he would listen to those races in which he had an interest – and count his winnings more often than not. Over the years he had become a very successful punter! Maybe then a short nap or some exercise, or sometimes we slipped out for a quick nine holes of golf. We ate dinner from trays by the fire in winter, or in the garden in summer. The reading of documents, which was threaded throughout the day, then continued uninterrupted.

Bob continued to surprise people with his energy and fitness. On being questioned about it he used to say, 'Hazel keeps me on Pritikin.' This is not quite accurate, but near enough. My interest in macrobiotic food, developed during our last year in Sandringham, had not dwindled. At the Lodge, it seemed too kinky to ask the staff to use ingredients like kombu, nori or mirrin – or to present guests with such food. The Pritikin way of eating offered us some of the same principles, so I adopted it as much as possible without being finicky. No salt, no sugar, foods in season, wholefoods, limited meat and fat, no alcohol. It may sound draconian but when done well, as it was, it offers delectable meals. This practice attracted some mild ridicule, but we did keep fit and had plenty of energy. People could refer to Bob as 'the old fella', and allude to his silver mane, but he could keep up a cracking pace at work and sport – and his mane was still thick and curly.

Paul's third birthday, on 1 August, was celebrated at the Lodge. He was proving to be an absolute dear, and enjoyed a special rapport with the extended family of house staff, gardeners and security staff. It always gave me exquisite pleasure to see the little ones pottering with the gardeners, playing in the swimming pool, or in the sandpit we had made, or on the swings we had hung from two stout trees. From my office I could catch glimpses of them even when I was busy, as my windows looked out over the garden at the back of the Lodge. In fact my office was well placed in many respects – it was at the centre of the house with its door facing the front entrance. I could see comings and goings to and from the house and within the house from the service side to the entertaining side. With my windows facing west, I saw wonderful sunsets in Canberra's clear, mountain air. As well as the desk, bookshelves and filing cabinets, the typewriter and later a computer, I had a couch to flop on, a couple of chairs for visitors and a small TV to watch newscasts. Oh, and my CD player, of course, for music. I spent most of my waking hours in the Lodge there, and truly felt I had the best room in the house to call 'a room of my own'.

◆

In mid-August, I delivered a speech at the Sydney Opera House, written by John Bowan. The occasion was to announce a major corporate sponsorship by Qantas for the Australian Youth Orchestra and, among other things, they played *Waltzing Matilda* from *The Swagman's Promenade*, arranged by Michael Hurst, which never fails to raise goose-bumps of pleasure. And the morning sun streaming in through the huge harbour-front windows onto the rich purple of the carpeted stairs added to the atmosphere of excitement and enjoyment, as this excited and exciting orchestra prepared to leave on a five-week Grand Tour overseas.

James Mollison invited me to open a Margaret Preston exhibition at the Australian National Gallery and I happily accepted. She was a woman before her time – in some ways she reminded me of Bob's mother, Ellie, as she pursued her goals with such single-mindedness and thoroughness. When Margaret Preston was in her seventies, she went on a marathon trip around the Australian outback to *feel* it, and paint it. She collected rocks on her travels and was seen dragging them from her utility truck into the respectable Mosman Hotel in Sydney, where she and her husband lived. She ground the rocks into powder, then used the pigment for her outback pictures. Her paintings are so strong and so feminine – they are unmistakable.

On 2 September, I visited an Aboriginal Women's Birthing Centre at the red centre of Australia. This is a community house where the women can give birth with care from other Aboriginal women, and according to traditional practices. The old woman, who talked with me there, demonstrated in the most graphic way how as a mid-wife she held the mother and lovingly welcomed the new baby and 'made it safe'. She was as dry and ageless as the desert she had grown in, and so wise, humorous and lovable that I wanted to hug her. But this was a group project and I would have had to hug everyone!

Next, I was out of my cotton frock and sandals and into suit and stockings for a Women in Management conference in Melbourne – it could have been a world away, but there too, I felt the caring of women for each other. The women at this conference had defied the odds by making it in a man's world. I may well have felt intimidated by these successful women – after all, I was there because I was someone's wife. But in fact I felt at ease. It pleased me that women who had broken the traditional mould still remembered to share their strengths and problems with each other.

Later that month, Bob and I were off overseas again, to San Francisco, Vancouver (for another CHOGM), Dublin, Geneva, Belgrade and Dubrovnic. I must relate some incidents which will help to convey something of the flavour of our visit to Ireland. When our aircraft had touched down in Dublin and we had assembled ourselves on the tarmac for the ceremonial welcome, the band struck up *Advance Australia Fair*. At one such ceremony in America the band had played *God Save the Queen*, to our dismay. So Bob raised smiles when he thanked them in his speech, noting that such a mistake would *never* be made by the Irish! It was a raw, cold, rainy evening as we arrived at our hotel and were asked by the protocol officer what she 'could be doin' for us.' Having come from the American continent where they seem unable to make tea, Bob and I replied in unison that we would like a cup. It came in quick time – silver tray, teapot with cosy, tea-strainer, all the trimmings. When she returned later we enthusiastically expressed our appreciation, and were highly amused when she replied in a rich Irish brogue, 'Ah, that's foine. Y've got to be havin' a good hot cup-o-tea, and it's got to be strong enough to trot a mouse across!'

Many of our travelling party were of Irish stock, and took the opportunity to track ancestors while we were there. I investigated possible links with Paddy Masterson, the President of Dublin University when we were there for Bob to deliver a speech. We got as far as agreeing on a physical resemblance – and Paddy told us that one branch of his family had a Bartholomew, the proper name for 'Bat'.

◆

Australia's bicentennial year, 1988, was upon us, with all the extra activity that would mean. On New Year's Eve Bob and I were in Melbourne, at Station Pier, to see the fleet of sailing ships – the Tall Ships – assembled for the celebrations. So the bicentenary dawned for Bob and me in Melbourne, and from there we flew before breakfast to Albury-Wodonga with Jim Kirk, the chairman of the Bicentennial Authority and his wife Jean, whose company we were to enjoy on countless occasions throughout this busy year. Bob was to open the enormous Bicentennial Exhibition, housed in a series of tents, that would travel the country all year, taking the nation's history and a celebration of it, to even the most far-flung outback towns. We gathered on a podium for the inevitable speeches and, though we were in a patriotic mood, I have to admit there were rather too many local and state and federal officials and parliamen-

Photo: James Renner

Election day in Bob's electorate of Wills, 1987

Guest at a women's lunch while in New York for the Sydney
Symphony Orchestra's 1988 tour: with leading feminist Gloria
Steinem and 'Doctor Ruth', sex therapist, writer and broadcaster

Dancing with women, Yeundumu, 1988

Launching a campaign against domestic violence, Canberra 1989

Enjoying our joint sixtieth birthday party, 1989

Meeting the press at the Lodge with Down's Syndrome children and their parents, 1990

Photo: ACTF

With Patricia Edgar, director of the Australian
Children's Television Foundation, on location in a
Melbourne park for the filming of an early episode of
the television series 'Lift Off'

Photo: Sue Spence

Sue Spence, me and Vera Wasowski
waiting for results on election night,
1990

My last run through the music, at
Kirribilli House, before dressing for the
Mozart Triple Concerto concert at the
Opera House, 1990

Photo: T. Schramm

Photo time after the Mozart concerto: with Bob, Rebecca Chambers and
Duncan Gifford

In Istanbul after visiting Gallipoli for the memorial service in 1990. With some of our favourite colleagues: Sandy Hollway (Bob's principal private secretary), Craig Emerson (Economic adviser), Kim Beazley (minister for Defence), Graham Freudenberg (speechwriter cum philosopher)

In Delhi for Rajiv Gandhi's funeral, 1991. Emerging from Teen Murti Palace with Sharon Massey (left), and Gareth Evans (minister for Foreign Affairs)

My study at the Lodge

Relaxing during a day of picnicking and fishing with Steve and Lesley and the boys, Fitzroy River, 1991

Brothers: David and Paul, Canberra, 1987

Yvonne, with Sophie and Benjamin, Sydney, 1989

Kelly and Sam, Derby, Western Australia, 1990

tarians strutting their stuff. I found my own diversion, as I often did, by scanning the crowd for anything that took my interest. A bevy of local teenage girls had danced barefoot, and squelched the mud from recent rain through their toes with delicious satisfaction. I amused myself by watching them through my small binoculars, while the speeches began in what was to become a year of speeches and ceremonial procedures. But this special year in our young nation's history presented Bob and me with extraordinary opportunities to get to know even more about the achievements and characteristics of its people.

I had, however, an uneasy feeling about the excitement and pride of our bicentenary because of associated guilt and shame at the history of European treatment of our land's first inhabitants. They have lived here for at least forty thousand years, whereas we had chalked up a mere two hundred! On the night Bob became prime minister it occurred to me he might still be in that position for the year which celebrated the coming of the white invaders to a land which was declared to be uninhabited – the people here being classed as savages and of no account. That the Australian Aboriginal race has an intelligent culture very much suited to their country, with the qualities of compassion, responsibility, community organisation and discipline built into everyday life, has been better understood in recent years. The Bicentennial Authority had given special consideration to this difficulty – of celebrating a white invasion, and the establishment of a new, dominant culture, while also acknowledging the inherently fine qualities of the culture which we progressively undermined for the same two hundred years. I had harboured some qualms, but I was hopeful that the year would enable more recognition of and justice to the original Australians.

After the speeches, and viewing the exhibition, we had breakfast in a huge marquee with two hundred school children, then flew on to Sydney for an hour's drive to Homebush to attend the dedication of the Federation Pavilion by the governor-general. That afternoon at Homebush, I was struck by the extent to which our cultural heritage has diversified over the years: the enthusiastic audience was made up of Australians whose families had come from 142 different nations.

We flew back to Canberra that afternoon to host a New Year's dinner, in the Lodge garden, for a very large gathering representing all walks of Australian life. The staff had taken it on as a professional challenge and their work brought them great credit. Our gregarious Lodge cat, Whisky, always attended garden parties, but this was a special one for him, as there was a prevailing aroma of fresh seafoods. He caused more than one surprise as he roamed under the cloth-skirted tables, with his strong, furry tail tickling the ladies' stockinged legs!

That we had spent the first day of the year in three states, flown and driven hundreds of kilometres, stood for hours and talked with hundreds of people was indicative of the rest of the year to come.

Australia Day, 26 January 1988, dawned clear and sunny, much to the relief and joy of the Bicentennial Authority, who had organised the most spectacular event ever held in Australia. Bob and I were taken by barge across Sydney Harbour to join a harbour cruise followed by a state luncheon. The harbour is breathtaking on any day, but on this day of days it was just sparkling, decked-out and looking its best. All of Sydney, it seemed, was out to celebrate and those Australians who weren't there were watching their television sets in every part of the country, to enjoy it the next best way. Bob and I were on the forward deck of the flagship, HMAS *Cook*, with the Prince and Princess of Wales and a bevy of admirals and guests to view the parade of Tall Ships. In full rig and sailing formation they were a grand sight indeed. Throughout the day everyone felt the sense of watching a once-in-a-lifetime spectacle, as we drew each other's attention to constantly changing vignettes of high-spirited Sydneysiders in small craft of all shapes and sizes, out to fill the day with fun. I felt I should pinch myself to see if it was real, young Hazel from the West, forty years down the track. One never knows what life will bring!

In the evening, back at Kirribilli House with family and friends, we watched the fireworks over the harbour and swapped stories about the remarkable day we had been a part of.

It proved to be an extraordinary year. I kept up my interest in women's issues, Headway, children's television, Life Education

Centres and other sustained commitments alongside the special events of the bicentenary – and I carved out spare moments for golf, bridge and music. The year was too full to do justice to here, but I have picked out a few occasions which were of significance for me.

◆

The opening of the new Parliament House in Canberra took place in May. The old Parliament House was opened in 1927. By the eighties it had become so overloaded that members and staff worked in conditions which interfered with efficiency. After an international competition in 1978, a design for a new parliament had been chosen by an all-party committee. Canberra had been planned, as the result of an earlier international competition in the 1920s, by Walter Burley Griffin. His plan had been faithfully adhered to and I believe it has been extremely successful in meeting the needs of the citizens, as we had experienced in the fifties – and Griffin showed surprising foresight in the way he took environmental considerations into account. In his plan, a site was reserved for the new parliament on Capital Hill, one of the three hills dominating the basin in which the city lies. The winning design, by an American architect, entailed burying the new Parliament House in the hilltop, covering the slopes with spreading lawns and placing an enormous flag on top to announce its presence. When Bob and I were taken to see the building in its half-finished, raw-concrete stage, I was upset to see its inward and downward cast. Bob is a fellow who loves the sun, preferring to look outwards and always to the light – here his office overlooked a courtyard with no view beyond. I found that virtually all the offices were denied a view. Since my daily walks to and from work in 1956, the ever-changing blue of the hills surrounding Canberra has always reminded me of the sea, with variations in colour and mood. It seemed to me that people engaged for long hours in the worry-scurry of political life would find it inspirational to have expansive views over those blue hills, but the die was cast – in concrete and for ever.

But my negative reactions receded as the building and its furnishings took shape. The office suite of the prime minister, for example, contained beautifully crafted timberwork and tapestry. Now that the House has been lived in, it has become a place of considerable stature, containing many exquisite objects of art and craftsmanship.

On 9 May 1988, the Queen opened the new Parliament House at a ceremony in its Great Hall. The last sitting day in the old building took place on 26 May and the new House became the home of the national parliament. Since its opening, a constant stream of buses has brought visitors to see the new building, and there is a very strong feeling of the people of Australia identifying with the building, and owning it with pride. After the move, I still went to Parliament House for special occasions and occasionally for question time, but I missed the intimacy and accessibility of the old building – the rubbing of shoulders, the accidental meetings in the corridors that were so enjoyable. There I had sat in the Speaker's Corner on the floor of the chamber, where I felt in touch with what was going on. In the new place I felt like a distant observer.

◆

I was in Sydney on 5 June to welcome home Kay Cottee, the young Australian who had sailed alone around the world non-stop, the first woman in the world to achieve this feat. The winter's afternoon managed clear sunshine as she sailed up the throat of the harbour from the Heads, to Darling Harbour where she would dock. Her yacht was appropriately named *First Lady*, and Kay's arrival was acknowledged by thousands of cheering, proud Sydneysiders, some on the water in small craft and some on land, all welcoming her and claiming her as their own. This was yet another privilege my job offered me – to be first to hug Kay as she stepped onto the shore after her marathon voyage.

◆

In mid-June I had a wonderful visit to Yuendumu, four hundred kilometres west of Alice Springs, to open a gallery housing the art work of the Aboriginal women of the community there. The project had been funded by the Bicentennial Authority. We were unable to fly out of Canberra to make our Sydney connection because of heavy fog and took a six-seater aircraft instead, direct to the Northern Territory. With me were Sharon Massey, the federal member, Warren Snowdon and his wife Elizabeth with a nursing baby, and John, our security man. We flew, and flew, begging some fruit for sustenance at a stopover in Alice Springs – no cabin service on this flight! Finally we landed in fading light on a dirt strip, the edges of which had been hurriedly marked out by tins filled with burning newspaper. Our welcome was extraordinary, and excitement levels were high for the occasion. We shared a barbecue, then donned layers of warm clothing against the cold, desert night, and sat in the sand to watch a corroboree by the men, followed by some women's dancing. The men had been practising their dances for several days, and must have spent most of that day smearing their bodies with fat and decorating themselves with feathers and ochre. Their dancing is very vigorous and we were not surprised, but highly amused, when they told us after a while that they could not go on, 'Too much practice, proper buggered!' We moved over to where the women were dancing, in quite different style, accompanied by the continuous, mellifluous chanting of those sitting in the sand around them. The women, too, had painted their bodies with the circles and lines of ceremony.

Early next morning we were out at the stockyards to see the work done on this community's cattle station. The mercury was already up high, and the heat helped make me just a touch squeamish as I watched the steers' testicles being cut off and thrown to the waiting dogs – expert catchers of such delicacies! But the highlight was the ceremony for the opening of the art gallery which would bring tourists and income to the community. The women took me in (no men allowed here), explained their work and taught me the steps to dance. We linked arms as we sang and danced our way around the gallery. They fixed feathers in my hair, and my dress and arms were smeared with the painted colours adorning their own bodies. We emerged, laughing, to the bright sunshine, the cameras and the crowds. This visit was turning out to be great fun. The rest of the day was filled with seeing the children, doing media interviews and talking with the people over tucker. I hadn't had time to fit in an interview with a writer from the American magazine, *Time*, and told him he could come to Alice Springs on our flight so we could do it on the run. When we were seated on the small plane he exclaimed, 'If this were Nancy Reagan it would be a 747 and there would be comforts and a phalanx of security.' I told him I had security and pointed to John sitting next to the pilot, trying his hand at the art of flying. 'That's him.' The reporter from the USA, where everything is big, just couldn't believe it! I attended a seminar on childcare in Alice Springs then flew on to Canberra. What a wonderful couple of days they were!

◆

In September, I had breakfast with the Sydney Symphony Orchestra at the Opera House, before they embarked on a playing tour of the United States. I was to meet them over there, to act as hostess and undertake publicity for their tour. I had a great product to 'sell'. The conductor, Stuart Challender, and the players had forged a great musical voice, written about as the 'Australian Sound'. There was also a winning trifecta in this band: the players were one-third female, one-third immigrant Australians and one-third under thirty years of age. The orchestra was to play at a star event in the main chamber of the United Nations, an acknowledgement of Australia's bicentennial year. A commercial television network was sending a team, led by Chris Masters, to do a profile as I took part in the tour. It was such a privilege to be involved, I couldn't believe my luck! After the orchestra had done some concerts on the west coast, I flew with Sharon, John and our media man Grant Nihill to meet them in New York. I was to narrate a film presentation of the United Nations concert and my part needed to be recorded as soon as I arrived, to be combined later with the video of the performance. I was heavily jet-lagged but struggled on through several delays caused by noise interference – we were recording in the large auditorium of the United Nations. But, with that behind me, it was roses all the way.

In Washington the orchestra's concert in the J. F. Kennedy

Centre received a standing ovation. At the orchestra's rehearsal on the morning of the UN concert I witnessed Stuart Challender's frustration as he 'chased the sound' in that round, imposing but acoustically dreadful venue. It was very difficult for the orchestra to work in and, I am sure, for Dame Joan Sutherland as she sang with them that night. But it was still a great occasion, with a gala reception to follow.

During my time in Washington I stayed with our ambassador to the United States, Rawdon Dalrymple, and his wife Ros. Rawdon was a Rhodes Scholar at Oxford when Bob and I were there. After his marriage he and Ros lived in Canberra when we did, in the fifties. Ros and I enjoy a friendship in which we pick up the threads between postings and by letter, so this was a good opportunity. In Washington, she showed me the stunning silver and opal jewellery she was making, and we talked about our families. For years I have observed the dilemmas faced by diplomatic spouses often with children at school, and parents, half a world away. The rounds of tea and cakes and good-works are not always acceptable to the new generation of wives, but the option of an independent job is not often available in foreign posts. Each spouse must work out his or her own way of adjusting to a way of life for each posting.

The greatest concert of the tour was on a Sunday afternoon in New York's Carnegie Hall, that historic mecca for great musicians making great music – I felt I was treading hallowed ground here. When the orchestra played and Dame Joan sang, the critical New York audience showed their enthusiasm with another standing ovation. On the program was Peter Sculthorpe's orchestral piece, *Mangrove*, which brought the sounds of the Australian outback to this sanctuary in the middle of New York. I stayed privately in New York with Jim and Elaine Wolfensohn. It was Jim, an expatriate Australian, who had rescued Carnegie Hall from the wreckers when he brought off the seemingly impossible feat of raising the funds, then driving the refurbishment, day and night. One day he took me, quietly beaming with pleasure, to glimpse the small, unassuming plaque bearing witness to his achievement – then quickly hurried me on.

In between concerts I visited a large hospital where head

injury was treated and researched, an experience which made me feel thankful for Australia's medical benefits system (I believe it is the best in the world) and went to an annual Foreign Affairs forum which had made Australia its focus for our two hundredth birthday year. There, in Mount Vernon, which was described to me as a typical Midwest town, I also visited social work projects and attended civic events for two days. In Chicago I visited Life Education Centre programs and talked with David Noffs, Ted's son, who ran them there.

Wendy McCarthy, now general manager of communications for the Bicentennial Authority, dreamt up a publicity event with a difference, for the US tour. I was to open a day's trading at the New York Stock Exchange. We were entertained to a champagne breakfast by the chairman, and then proceeded to the Exchange, where the four percussion players from the orchestra, with their tin whistles, vibraphones, triangle, tam-tam and cymbals were lined up along the catwalk balcony overlooking the trading floor. The floor was in its pre-trading frenzy but when the Aussies struck up with *Waltzing Matilda*, *Click Go the Shears* and other Australian songs they were a hit. The chairman showed me how to ring the starting bell, telling me strictly that the timing must be exactly right, to the split second. It was something of an experience to stand high up there and see the remarkable antics of this ritual. When I rang the bell the noise exploded and the pace quickened. A fast-forward circus … cannibalistic money chasing … how to describe it?

◆

One of the strengths of the Bicentennial Authority's plan for 1988 was its community program. It was conceived as an Australia-wide series of events and activities to celebrate and commemorate the scope and diversity of modern Australian society. There was a national education and youth program; multicultural, interfaith and union programs; a local government initiative grants scheme; programs for women, Aboriginal and Torres Strait Islanders, people with disabilities and older Australians. I'm sure that initiative grants for community work are a sound investment, although they are hard to evaluate. Any society is diminished if it ignores the benefits of a self-help approach to community development.

Bob and I gathered a great deal to remember during this special year. My friendships with Wendy McCarthy and Quentin Bryce, head of the Human Rights Commission, grew – two 'good woman' friends. The Bryce house has become my 'Brisbane Pub'. I stay there on any Brisbane visit and if Quentin is not at home her delightful family welcomes me and spoils me. So I am grateful, in many ways, for all that 1988 gave me.

WHAT'S NEXT?

◇

In January 1989, Vera and I were thinking about a touch-up to the cosmetic surgery we had in 1977. When I told Bob, he gave me the best possible response: he didn't think I needed it, but it was OK by him anyway. My main problem was to put aside some time, but finally we made arrangements for March. Although we went about it as quietly as possible, the press picked it up and ran a spate of sensational articles, the object of which seemed to be to ridicule the practice, and me. But at least this opened up a public discussion about the merits or otherwise of cosmetic surgery.

When we came out of hospital, Vera and I went for a few days to a farmhouse at Woodend, in Victoria, where we read, rested, cooked and walked. Then, back in Melbourne, I had some small surgery done to repair an old tennis injury to my knee. So now I had not only a bruised face, but was also on crutches and looked as though I had been in a first class box-on. I felt well, however, and

Vera and I rather enjoyed a few extra, secluded days at her place, pottering in her magical garden and cleaning out cupboards, while her boarder, a young Israeli fellow just out of the army, fielded intrusive phonecalls and visitors.

The amount of mail I received on the topic of cosmetic surgery, after the press had run their stories, surprised me. I still get a trickle, three years later, all positive and often seeking advice. I can only support the right of each individual to make up his or her own mind. I don't see why there should be any stigma attached to a procedure which may lift a person's self esteem – or even improve job opportunities. The main prerequisite is to seek expert advice and to be certain that the measure is taken for reasons right for the individual and not to please someone else. The figures at that time showed that the largest percentage increase in elective cosmetic surgery over the past five years had been for men, not women.

My problem was how to get back to Sydney without being chased through airports by cameras. But I had a very special incentive, to meet our new grandson, Ben, born at their home in Sydney to Sue and Jan. Yvonne and her second husband, Harry McGain, offered to rescue me and we did the journey by car. When we stopped along the way, I would don dark glasses and a Garbo hat, take up my crutches and avoid curious eyes as much as possible. I stayed in Kirribilli House in Sydney, working from there, and swimming each day to strengthen my knee and having physiotherapy for my knee and face. I wanted to be presentable again in time to return to Canberra for a long-standing commitment to a cause close to my heart, Neighbours.

Neighbours is a project begun by two Canberra health-centre sisters who saw the difficulties of young mothers, mostly without partners, struggling with life in government housing. Their accommodation was usually in places where their children had nowhere to play, and which were not safe from vandals, discarded syringes and traffic. I'd had contact with Neighbours from its inception, as the health sisters and the women worked together, creating a cohesive community, offering each other support and friendship, and learning new skills. I was its patron and the people involved were my friends.

I was keen for the project's progress to be acknowledged by the local press, as there had been considerable community interest and support. But on its special day the media went into a feeding frenzy on – guess what! – my face. I was appalled, and did my best to redress what I saw as an insult to Neighbours, but not very successfully. In the long run, though, Neighbours has won the recognition it deserves. Not long before Bob and I left Canberra in 1992, there was another Neighbours birthday celebration, where I saw what I like to see most – life's possibilities enhanced and horizons widened for people who need and deserve a break.

In a lighter vein, I did get some positive encouragement from Peter Bowers, a political journalist who had been around for years and was a bit of a Hawke-watcher. He wrote a piece in the *Sydney Morning Herald* discussing Australia's longest-serving conservative prime minister, Bob Menzies, and the possibility that Bob Hawke might become the longest-serving Labor prime minister. He wrote about the next federal election, saying, 'Timing will be everything. If Labor is to have any chance of winning a fourth time, Hawke will need to have a lot more going for him than he has now. Above all, he will need lots of luck.' Bowers rambled on – and I quote some of his observations, which amused me. I wonder if in other countries journalists make such light-hearted comment on political leaders – a bit of micky-taking!

Still on the subject of luck ... Hawke's biggest slice of luck, demonstrably, is that he married – and stayed married to – Hazel.

She is his front-row prop and there must have been times when she thought marriage was one long scrummage. The prime ministership brought a measured, homely pattern to Bob Hawke's life.

The bunker grandpa uses to practise wedge shots also serves as a sandpit for plastic toys. The footpath is a fast-track for trikes and other things that go bang, crash.

Off the booze, and with his own car, driver (and a security escort), and with the Lodge within cooee of Parliament House, finding his way home at night is no longer an improbable adventure for Bob Hawke.

Arrrhhh, well arrhh in respect of Bob and Hazel, it's time to say congratulations, happy anniversary.

Yesterday they celebrated 33 years of marriage, 42 years of togetherness. They had a little party at the Lodge on Thursday night with Ros and grandchildren David and Paul.

Hazel, who is into yoga ('it can be meditative and settling or dynamic and energising') has taken charge of her husband's fitness program. She installed an exercise bike on the landing, put a phone beside it so he can keep pedalling while talking and a Walkman to listen to (wait for it!) Bruch's violin concerto.

On overseas trips she makes sure there's an exercise bike in the hotel so that no matter how fraught the round of duties, he gets 20 minutes' exercise a day. The occasional nine holes of golf is a bonus.

The diet she describes as a mix of Pritikin and macro-biotic: 'good plain natural foods'.

If I were Paul Keating I would be worrying about more than the economy. Bob Hawke looks fit enough to do at least five more years as prime minister. Electorate permitting, of course.

◆

In April I had the thrill of launching the naval vessel HMAS *Melbourne*, wrapped against the cold in woollen suit and a black hat of Vera's. I tightened the inner headband for my smaller head and the hat looked very swish until it came unstuck and dropped to rest on my ears, making me look more like Chico Marx than a prime minister's wife. It was a thrill to see this sleek ship slide down the slipway – silently and ever so elegantly cutting an almost unrippled path into the sea. Later that year I launched *Aurora Australis*, a ship built in Newcastle to service Australian research in the Antarctic. On a howling windy day I stood on a small, high platform and triggered this spectacular sideways-flop launch. This is a breathtaking sight: the ship lurches into the sea and slowly rights itself in the wake of the great wave it creates. I always feel a special relationship to the ships I have launched – something like a grandmother! It was perhaps two years later when Bob and I were driving past the docks in Tasmania that I spied the outrageously bright orange of the *Aurora Australis*, and cried, 'There's my ship.'

This was the year of my sixtieth birthday and Bob and I spent that day, 20 July, travelling in three states while he launched the government's environment policy. I enjoyed every minute of it. We inspected work that coincided with my own interests as national patron of Greening Australia – a non-profit organisation established in 1982 to provide a focus for action by the whole community to increase tree cover in rural and urban areas. There were of course lots of trees planted that day, which I can identify as being sixty years younger than I am! On the RAAF flight home, the crew broke out the champagne and served a wonderfully gooey, chocolate birthday cake.

There was another special day for us on 6 September when Stephen's book, *Nookanbah*, was launched at the National Library in Canberra by Manning Clark. A little later in the year, I was presenting Human Rights Awards for the Human Rights Commission and indulged in a little quiet pride as one of them went to Stephen for his sensitive and telling account of the struggle of the Nookanbah Aboriginal community to save a site, of high significance to them, from oil drilling.

Bob had his sixtieth birthday, too, in 1989, and we celebrated our milestones with a joint party in December. Having considered various ways of doing it, we decided, for ease of privacy and security, to have it at the Lodge but pay for it ourselves. This was the only home we had, and we wanted the once-only gathering of family and friends to feel homely. That decision made, our daughter Rosslyn, who lived nearby, undertook the considerable task of planning and implementing it. She did a superb job! It was the party of our lives for me and Bob, and the time flew. Old friends from union days, Perth days and Melbourne days, sports friends, music friends, political colleagues and family gathered on a night of foul weather which put the marquees to the test. Adele Weiss had made me a pink party dress and our Scots Lodge manager, wore his dress kilt and jabot. Lionel Bowen made a toast to Bob and Wendy

McCarthy made one to me, then Bob and I responded separately. Peter Logue and the bush band played all night and we danced and sang until breakfast time – then re-lived it all the next day.

As Christmas drew near, I sent off a dress to my mother and a Christmas cake to Bob's father. But on 23 December Clem died, aged ninety-one, and just two days after Christmas we flew to Adelaide to his funeral. Bob loved his 'Pop' and was always appreciative and affectionate towards him. He felt the loss acutely. When Clem was away during the war, Bob, aged about eleven, used to tell Ellie he couldn't live without him. I believe that Bob also felt a particular kind of aloneness when his father died. With Neil, Ellie and Clem all gone, he was the last of the family. Our children and I trod softly as he grieved, and got on with the things that need to be done when there is a death in the family.

◆

The day after Clem's funeral I was sitting in an easy chair in the bedroom at Kirribilli House, peacefully reading and occasionally looking up from my book to the garden and the harbour beyond, when I had the curious feeling of the chair moving – or did it? We don't think of Australia as an earthquake country, although there are tremors from time to time, but I soon knew from a newsflash that what I had felt was indeed a tremor from an earthquake at the city of Newcastle, 170 kilometres away. As Bob was officially on holiday, Lionel Bowen was acting prime minister. Bob instructed his staff to keep him informed, and we went off to the Lakes Golf Course. We had played only seven holes when he received a radio message through his security men – this was more than a tremor, Newcastle was hurting. We left the course and boarded a helicopter at the foot of the Kirribili House garden to fly up right away. At that time I was writing a weekly column for the *Telegraph* in Sydney and I wrote, in part:

It was shocking to see a city in such trauma. We visited the SES operations centre where we saw workers, volunteers and service personnel applying themselves to the task with total commitment and concern. Many anxious citizens stood tired and drawn, waiting for news of loved ones – it was only a few hours after the quake and it was not clear what had happened to whom. The mood was tragic as brick-by-brick the painstaking task of searching the rubble went on …

Acting prime minister, Lionel Bowen, had accompanied us to Adelaide the day before to attend the funeral and service for Bob's father. Early next morning he attended the service for the Kempsey bus victims and flew straight to the Newcastle tragedy. He looked, as we met him on the beach where the helicopter landed, ashen-faced and weary. As I commented what sadness he had witnessed that day, someone told me it was his birthday …

Nine lives were lost in the Newcastle Workers' Club and the total toll of the earthquake was thirteen.

◆

A few days after the Newcastle earthquake, I went to Adelaide to pack up Clem's flat, sifting through the remnants of his everyday, earthly life. I set aside some furniture for the kids, or the Salvation Army, and collected his books and papers to take back to Canberra. He had lived simply and modestly, just meeting his needs, no frills. Then I had to fly on to Perth for an official function. This last year had been a busy one. The pervading sadness of Clem's death and the earthquake tragedy, along with the extra travelling of the last two weeks, made me feel the summer holiday had disappeared without having been one at all.

Bob had given me an overlocking sewing machine for Christmas, and for the next two weeks, back at the Lodge, I enjoyed making small tracksuits, bibs and dresses for grandchildren aged from one to six. It was a peaceful time, and sewing was a therapeutic labour of love for me as well as being practical. At last I had a place in the Lodge where I could set out, and leave, my sewing things. It had been a walk-in wardrobe but now it was fixed up with a bench for my machine, an ironing board and drawers so I could make use of snatches of time to sew for the kids and do the mending for

Rosslyn and her two sons: then shut the door on my mess, until next time!

We were gathering energy for another election campaign. On 24 March 1990, Bob led the federal Labor members to the treasury benches for the fourth time, the first Labor prime minister to achieve this. He had defied the early odds. He was a great campaigner, rising to the challenge and loving being out amongst people on the hustings. I thought he was clearer and more consistent in this campaign than I had ever seen him. I joked that it was because he was not smoking those fat cigars, but I seriously believed that it really did help.

I recently asked Bob to recall the occasion that most moved him during our years at the Lodge, and he said without hesitation, 'Gallipoli'. This was the seventy-fifth anniversary of the bloody and devastating campaign fought by the Anzacs on the beaches at Gallipoli, during the First World War.

The trauma of the Great War was still very real for my family when I was growing up in Mount Hawthorn. My uncle had been killed in France in 1917 and my Aunty Maud had remained a spinster, as did many of her peers, because of the heavy toll of young men. My mother told me once that Maud had loved a soldier who did not return and Mum felt sad that she had 'missed out'. Dad had been too young for that war and it was clear to me how much Mum appreciated her own marriage. She felt lucky to have got Dad, and once said, 'You know, Gladdie could have had him.' She was baffled that Glad had not responded to the possibility, when they were all in the church group together, and had remained unmarried all her life. The lot of a spinster of that generation was usually a long working-life and care of ageing parents.

The cost of Gallipoli was hideously high, with so many killed and so many more wounded. Those who lived would measure their lives 'since the war', as it was a monumental experience of adventure and tragedy never to be forgotten. Ever since then, there have been criticisms of the fact that Australia rallied to the British flag, and of the strategies of the British War Cabinet during the campaign. But the undeniable fact remains that the Anzac experience forged a new ideal for the Australian national character: adventurous, inventive, resourceful, larrikin, loyal – mates.

Surviving veterans were now in their nineties and a contingent of them was flown to Turkey to join in a commemorative service at the site of the battle on the beaches of Gallipoli. Extraordinary care was taken of them before, during and after their journey, even down to looking after their pets and gardens at home while they were away. For those of us who went with them, it was a poignant experience. We were at the beach at dawn on Anzac Day for the service, each person there in his or her own way contemplative, attending to our emotions. When the service was complete and people began quietly, hesitantly moving amongst each other, I looked about and noticed a veteran – capped and scarved and with rug about his poor old legs – sitting all alone just looking out to the hills in the growing light. I went and sat beside him, saying nothing. A minute or two must have passed when he moved his hand to mine and murmured, 'My brother's out there … somewhere … '

The incorrigible veteran, Jack Ryan, still full of beans and with a twinkle in his eye, was not slow to plant a kiss on my cheek. At the luncheon which hundreds attended, we saw with high delight mixed with tears of emotion, old Jack and an equally wizened Turkish veteran hugging each other. Part of the legend of Gallipoli was the mutual respect of the Anzacs and the Turks – and here, seventy-five years later, these two were free to express it.

◆

Amongst my usual round of duties, I was preparing for an unusual one. After Bob and I returned from Gallipoli, I had gone to one of the Sydney Symphony Orchestra's winter concerts. Backstage, the conductor, Stuart Challender, astonished me by asking if I would play Mozart's Triple Concerto K242 with the orchestra, at two public performances. I hooted with laughter, thinking it a ridiculous idea, until he explained that it was not a demanding part, and the plan was to draw attention to the ABC's annual awards for Young Performer of the Year. This was worth doing! After Bill Hawkey had reassured me that the concerto was within my range, I agreed to do it. Bill coached me and, as the concerts drew near, he gave me a run-through with two other pianists at the Canberra School of Music.

Then, on 29 October 1990, I went to Sydney for the first of three rehearsals. Duncan Gifford who had won the 1989 Young Performer's award took the first part, Rebecca Chambers the second, and I took the third. At rehearsal, the television camera crew determined the position for the three Steinway grand pianos, Duncan took centre place with Rebecca on the right and me on the left, all of us facing the conductor and the orchestra. Making music with others – and how! I was confirmed in my opinion that we shall see more of these young performers, as their musical careers develop.

Duncan and I did interviews together to publicise the concerts, which were at the Sydney Opera House on consecutive Friday and Saturday nights. It felt like star treatment when I was given a practice piano in my own dressing-room. Flowers and gifts arrived.

As I waited in the wings, on the first night, the orchestra members – friends of mine since our American tour – wished me warmly to do well. I was nervous before the packed concert hall and played with total concentration – for my entries, especially. In the second movement, however, I played a chord one bar too early, fortunately in the same key so it was hardly discernible. The conductor, John Hopkins, slipped me a wink under his raised arm when he next swung my way, as if to say, 'We can get away with that one.' In 1991 I was to hear the opera singer, Joan Carden, speak at the National Press Club. One small part of her talk was about stage fright and how the best way to calm performance nerves was to put concern with one's own anxiety aside and to 'serve the music'. It is wise advice.

On the second night I was more relaxed and, as we played the last movement, I was wishing it wouldn't end. I could have played all night! But there was a supper to attend, with Bob there to share my pleasure and, happily, a sponsor announcing its intention to continue support for the Young Performer's award. After the second night's concert Mary Vallentine, the manager of the Sydney

Symphony Orchestra, hosted a memorable dinner at the Opera House where she and I, Sue Spence, Sharon, Wendy, and Quentin 'got through a few words', as Bob would say, and had a great time. The opportunity to play these concerts with the young performers and the orchestra remains one of my life's most enjoyable bonuses.

◆

After a Christmas break spent playing lots of golf, Bob and I returned to the Lodge on a Sunday evening in the middle of January. Our holiday mood quickly evaporated. At ten minutes to eleven in the morning on 17 January, US president George Bush phoned to inform Bob of the coalition forces' proposed action in the Persian Gulf – the beginning of what became known as the Gulf War. In another of my moments of contemplation back in March 1983, when Bob had first become prime minister, I had earnestly hoped he would never have to make the solemn announcement, as prime minister Menzies had done in 1939, that his country was at war. In 1952, when we were so young, with the world at our feet, I had been grateful that Bob was not needed to go to the Korean War. And when Australian troops were sent to Vietnam in 1965 we had marched in moratorium protests and opposed the government's committal of troops. War was the big, black, NO! And now we had come to this – that Bob must commit Australian personnel and three of our warships to war in the Gulf. They were part of allied forces made up of 533,000 US and 200,000 coalition troops.

Bob took briefings from defence and foreign affairs officials, and intelligence agencies, at all hours. Like much of the world, we watched America's CNN television coverage of the war, turning it on during the nights when we woke, wondering. It was an extraordinary reporting feat, as modern technology brought events to television screens with such immediacy. At that time I thought the one hopeful factor in this war was that the United Nations, after all its ineffectual years when such conflicts have broken out, might at last become relevant. The suffering and devastation in war seems even more shocking than great natural disasters: to think that we do such things to each other. The Gulf War lasted for forty-three days

– the Iraqis capitulated on 28 February – with no Australians lost, to our great relief.

◆

On the home front, I went to Melbourne to launch a magazine supplement with a difference. Here was Cleo, a glossy magazine with a contemporary image, targeting young women with a supplement about unionism in the workplace. If anyone had dreamt up such an idea in 1958, when Bob and I first came to Melbourne, it would never have got past the male-dominated union movement. But to its credit the ACTU was now endorsing this project, which its women officers brought to fruition. I was delighted.

Four days later, I was on 'The Midday Show' with Anne Sargeant, who works to promote women's sport, her own speciality being netball. Over and again, those working in the Women's Sports Promotion Unit of the Australian Sports Commission have pointed out how women have won more gold medals at Olympic Games for Australia, as a percentage of their participation, than men – without equal opportunity. Women, and not a few men, have been chipping away for years at the comparative injustice of the resources available for women's sport. It is gratifying to see, gradually, a fairer approach being taken and more balance in the funding from the Australian Sports Commission. There is also a begrudging but nevertheless increasing proportion of women's sport being reported in the media. I attended a board meeting of the Women's Sports Promotion Unit at the Australian Institute of Sport where the main agenda item was a campaign directed at twelve to four-teen-year-old girls. The aim was to encourage them to play sport and to stay in it through their awkward, pubescent years. The Women, Work and Health seminars for year-ten girls also promote this cause. Sport can be a great asset in the lives of girls and women – I have seen this in operation at a community centre in the suburbs of Perth. The babies are in the creche and the toddlers in the childcare centre while the mums play netball. They all have a great time over lunch and a cuppa afterwards. This sort of break from the daily grind brings friendship and fitness to the young women – and, importantly, self-esteem and all that flows from it.

Two other groups deserving special support in sport are the physically and the intellectually disabled. And the rewards are not only for the participants themselves. Families who have been socially tentative, even isolated, in caring for disabled members, come out to start a race or hold a stopwatch and go on to make friendships, travel around and open up their lives. Australian paralympians are making a great name for themselves in international competition.

Bob and I went to Barcaldine, a tiny outback town in Queensland, on 3 May 1991, to celebrate the centenary of the origins of the Australian Labor Party. It seemed unlikely that this great, national, political party had begun in such an out-of-the-way place. But history makes it understandable. There had been a confrontation there between pastoralists and rural labour. When the government sided with the pastoralists, the workers and their families suffered considerably – it was clear to them that they needed representation in government. And so the first state labour parties were formed, with the federal Party being founded at Federation in 1901. I enjoyed the look back into history this visit gave us. I also enjoyed seeing Bob's easy affinity with these men and women. He understood the labour movement, its heart and guts, as well as anyone in the country – and they liked and respected him.

◆

On 21 May, in the lead up to an election in India, widely expected to return Rajiv Gandhi to power, he was assassinated. I was in Newcastle the next day, in the local radio studio with host, Terry Willesee, when I was called out to take an urgent phonecall. It was Bob – would I go to India to the funeral? When? Probably that night. Bob was unable to go, and because of our friendship with Rajiv and his wife Sonia, he suggested that I accompany Gareth Evans, the foreign minister, to India. I finished the radio chat; visited the good steamship *William IV* that I had launched in 1987; spoke at a large fund-raising lunch on another boat (where I had the amusing compliment of two passing ships hooting messages to me); and on the way to the airport I used the telephone in the car to make arrangements for my departure. By then it was clear that we would not leave for India that evening, but the next. That made it much easier for me, but I still shopped on the car telephone for a suitable dress to wear to a ceremony where white, not black, would be worn – and where the temperatures would be in the forties. Friends came to my rescue, and Jean, a Lodge staffer who could sew, altered the frock to fit me.

The next evening, Sharon and I joined Gareth and his staff on the plane. We chatted over a meal and a glass of wine, took a sleeping pill each, put out the lights and woke up in New Delhi at about six o'clock the next morning. The city was besieged by dignitaries from all over the world for the hurriedly organised state funeral. I was grateful for the resourcefulness of our high-commissioner in Delhi who had quickly booked suites in a good hotel. When he was pressed to relinquish my booking for the Prince of Wales, he moved staff in. Possession is nine-tenths of the law, they say!

That morning we went to Teen Murti Palace, the spacious dwelling and gardens where Jawaharlal Nehru lived when he was prime minister of India, which is now a museum. This is where the body of Rajiv Gandhi was lying in state, and mourners gathered. People milled about in a great confused crush, and Gareth and I joined a long queue as we entered the palace. In these rooms it was dark, noisy and there were flies floating about in the heat. A protocol person came unexpectedly with a message from Sonia Gandhi saying I might speak with her. I appreciated her thoughtfulness in allowing me to convey our sympathy personally. I was taken to the room where she sat with her daughter Priyanka. Small, elegant, and beautiful, swathed from head to toe in a simple, white sari, Sonia spoke to me in her quiet way. She was the epitome of love, tragedy and quiet strength.

After lunch we travelled by bus to the funeral site, a large, open parkland, and were shown to our places. I was seated in a small enclosure for dignitaries, on a plastic chair about five rows from the front. Gareth, Sharon and our security man were whisked on somewhere else. It was a long, *very* hot wait in the sun. I felt grateful for the advice I had followed. My white mourning dress was cooler than black would have been, loose-fitting and made of linen which is also cooler than synthetic fibres. I wore friendly, old, black court shoes with stockings to keep my feet comfortable, and a large, white stole which I could drape over my head and arms as I needed to. A sunshade or hat would have been useless in the gusting wind. I was comfortable for the whole afternoon.

When the truck carrying the funeral bier drew near, there was at some stage an almost indefinable sound – as if a murmuring, but one was not quite sure – until it slowly became the recognisable sound of tens of thousands of people walking respectfully behind it. I wondered what would happen if the crowd in its emotion broke the flimsy post-and-rail barriers around the park, but this didn't happen. For perhaps an hour before the beginning of the cremation ritual, Hindu elders chanted at a microphone placed quite near to where I sat, and when the bier was placed on the raised platform in the centre of this huge crowd, the ceremony began.

There were special responsibilities: Rajiv and Sonia's twenty-year-old son, Rahul, placed the first timbers for the fire. Incense was sprinkled, chanting continued. All the while nineteen-year-old Priyanka was close by her mother's side, sometimes holding her, for hours. As I watched these children, so young, I recalled our discussions with their parents some years earlier about where they could be educated, safely away from the known security risks. We had wondered whether it might be in Australia. Now their world had suddenly changed with the ghastly assassination of their father, and they were doing what had to be done. Eventually the funeral pyre was lit and the flames rose up, before dying away into the charred pile with its stark images. This long, gruelling ritual was difficult for the family, but perhaps it is better than our way of quickly and quietly burying our dead. We inherited a culture which denies that display, the catharsis of grief. My dictionary says, 'Catharsis: outlet to emotion afforded by drama.'

◆

On 31 May 1991, deputy prime minister and treasurer Paul Keating went to the prime minister's office and made a blunt demand that

Bob resign, in accordance with a verbal understanding between them, reached on 25 November 1988. Paul was anxious to have the top job and he needed lead-time in it to improve his low popularity with voters before the next election: due by May 1993. I knew that, in the meantime, Bob had wrestled within himself and with advisers about it, as since their agreement two factors had changed: the political climate was more difficult for Labor, electorally, and the relationship between the two men had changed. Paul Keating had made a speech to journalists at a press gallery dinner in which he claimed that he was the Placido Domingo (the best) of Australian politics and that Australia had never produced a great leader. Bob's most immediate reaction was to deplore Keating's deprecation of John Curtin, Australia's wartime prime minister whom Bob admired so much. But of course the real implication was unavoidable. That was it.

On 3 June, to settle the matter Bob took it to a Caucus ballot, where the vote was forty-four for Keating, sixty-six for Hawke. Both sides declared that was the end of it: the treasurer resigned his portfolio and retired to sit on the back benches.

That last weekend in May before the vote, Rosslyn and I had just carefully chosen a pattern and wool for me to knit her an Aryan jacket. As I sat knitting away at the Lodge during the number-crunching, we joked that I was Madame DeFarge knitting the numbers in. But for some of the time I was also busy on the telephone arranging to bid at an auction for a house in Sydney, for our retirement. Bob had not yet seen the house we were consider-ing – for a politician under pressure to be seen preparing for retirement could be the kiss of death, a good story! Two weeks later he and I went to see it and I was delighted with his reaction to the site. Each room of the existing house had windows that looked through and beyond the native bush to the still water below, where little boats lay anchored. He was entranced. As we walked out he said how peaceful it was, just a short distance from a convenient freeway, yet here we could hear no traffic. Bob was spontaneously responding to serenity and nature. Very good, thought I.

It is not easy to get the timing right in the business of poli-tics where so many factors are beyond one's knowledge or control. I was quietly puzzled about when Bob's exit from politics should be. If he did lead the Party to the next election he would be called a lame duck if he didn't undertake to stay on for some time. I was beginning to rather like the idea of moving on before too much longer. But I kept my thoughts to myself – the political agenda took precedence over my own vague wonderings. I was feeling tired, though.

◆

On 22 June Bob and I attended the opening of a new building for the Australian Broadcasting Corporation. I remembered this great institution with affection from earlier years when I was a full-time housewife and mother. 'It's my lifeline to the world,' I used to say. The talks were interesting and there was always good music on ABC radio. When I didn't get around to reading the newspapers I could listen to the current affairs programs 'A.M.' or 'P.M.' and later there was current affairs television too. One can only try to imagine what a blessing the ABC has been to Australians in the outback – including, importantly, the School of the Air. The symphony orchestras established by the ABC – in Sydney and Melbourne in 1926, and all other states since then – were a commitment to the arts of astounding proportions, considering our small population. I was so glad to see the organisation housed in specially designed headquarters rather than its previous scatter of make-do premises. One feature of the new complex is a state-of-the-art concert and recording hall which the Sydney Symphony Orchestra can now call home.

My diary was still crowded, and I was mostly doing the things I loved. CHOGM in 1991 was held in Zimbabwe, a country neither Bob nor I had visited before. As the plane was making its approach at Harare, the capital, we saw great swathes of jacaranda blooms at their best. On some mornings we slipped out early for a few holes of golf, on a course carpeted with fallen purple petals. I shall always associate jacaranda trees with Zimbabwe.

When we flew out by helicopter to see projects in remote areas funded by aid from the Australian government, we were appalled at the lack of medical facilities and water supplies, and at the meagre resources on which so many must live. We saw how much the gift of a few cows for a dairy herd, or help from Australian aid workers to construct a village water-pump, at the small cost of two or three metres of PVC piping, could mean. We visited a clinic, held once a fortnight under a baobab tree in the bush, to which some women had walked perhaps twenty kilometres carrying their babies: that in itself is a measure of what the clinic means to them. Life in Zimbabwe is not easy. The major, encroaching tragedy is AIDS, difficult to arrest because of custom and family structure. I visited an AIDS centre for women, run by Irish nuns, and a hospice for AIDS victims counting out their last months and days. Seeing the condition of their lives is deeply distressing, perhaps even more so because the Zimbabweans are an inherently vital people. Their spontaneous dancing is wonderful, and the schoolchildren's yard games, where they 'called us in' to join them, were irresistible.

It was suggested to me that I visit Beaulah Dyoko, a mbira player. I drove out with Sharon and our high-commissioner's wife to Chitungwiza – a backblocks township described as the Soweto of Zimbabwe. When we arrived, Beaulah unexpectedly invited us into her house. It was about two metres square with a single cot-bed, a bench and some shelves. We perched on the wooden bench while she sat on the floor, talking in the most captivating way about the meaning of life, sickness and health, what we are, what our future might be. There was a little of the gipsy about her – dark eyes, wisdom and wit.

I realised that her hospitality had been a compliment, but I wondered if she was ever going to play her music. People like Beaulah don't go by the clock, but eventually she made a move. The mbira is an instrument made from a hollowed gourd, or pumpkin, with finger-keys inside it. She sat on the ground and began to play, and slowly people from around the village came to dance. Nothing was said. The music was continuous and mesmerising. As it went on, others came to join her, some with drums. It rained but that didn't matter. The dancers joined in and stepped out as it pleased them. Many were young mothers with babies tied in shawls hanging on their backs. They flopped gently with the motion of the dance, some awake and some sleeping. Some of the dancers were old women, some were children. No men were dancing – this was obviously the women's realm. I felt that Sharon and I were witnessing something special in that township, and we stayed long beyond the scheduled half hour. We were told that they would play and dance for hours after we left – possibly all night.

During our stay in Zimbabwe the Commonwealth leaders were taken for lunch to the famous old hotel at Victoria Falls. Bob and I were first off the bus and walked on ahead of the rest of the party, coming to stand at the edge of the garden looking across to the fragile railway bridge that spans the Zambesi Gorge from Zambia into Zimbabwe, passing almost through the spray of the great waterfall. As we stood there, a figure came up behind us and laid an arm on each of our shoulders. It was Robert Mugabe. This was the man who had been jailed as a political agitator by the white-minority government of Rhodesia (as Zimbabwe was then called). He had been set free during a period of detente in the mid-seventies and joined a seven-year guerilla war to achieve majority rule for his country. Bob and I were moved as, quietly and with anguish, he shared a moment in history with us. He described how during the war he had met with Ian Smith, the prime minister of Rhodesia, on a train mid-way across the bridge over the falls. It had been a failed attempt to negotiate an end to the struggle that eventually cost nearly thirty thousand lives. Zimbabwe finally become an independent republic within the Commonwealth in 1980, with Robert Mugabe as its first prime minister.

At the CHOGM meetings, there was a particular surge of interest and admiration when Nelson Mandela arrived. He had visited Australia not long after his release, on 11 February 1990, from twenty-seven years in jail for his anti-apartheid activities. That year he went on a world tour to seek support for the African National Congress and its leading role in the liberation of black South Africans – still his life's mission. He knew he'd had Bob's support for the last twenty years – since that first strong, stand, in 1971, in opposition to the Springboks tour on behalf of the ACTU. I had met Nelson Mandela in Australia and had a discussion with him over lunch. He had the same rare quality that I had observed in Rajiv Gandhi. When he was talking with you he gave you his whole attention. He communicated with his steady eyes as well as his quiet, earnest voice. When Sonia Gandhi had said of her husband that she saw in him an 'inner beauty' I had known instantly what she meant, and I saw it also in Nelson Mandela.

◆

We had been warned that the high altitudes in Zimbabwe would make us tired, but I was exhausted by the day's end and needed to rest for an hour each afternoon in readiness for the CHOGM dinners which sometimes provided interesting conversations. Such lethargy was unusual for me, and it was almost two years since I'd had a medical check. So I asked Sharon to make time for a doctor's appointment when I was next in Sydney. Two weeks after our return to Australia, that check-up found I had an ovarian cyst which would have to be removed, and a biopsy done. The only good thing about this news was that it explained my tiredness – I had tried to rationalise it by telling myself, 'After all, you are in your sixties.' The surgery was performed as soon as we could make the arrangements, and I left hospital on 28 November, minus the cyst and feeling lucky that it proved to be benign. There was a lesson for me in the experience which I pass on to other women – the cyst would not have been discovered if I hadn't had an internal examination.

I rested and slowly built up my daily walking exercise in the peaceful gardens at Kirribilli House. I spent a lot of time reading: *The Road from Coorain* by Jill Ker Conway, *An Unfinished Woman* by Lillian Hellman and *The Change* by Germaine Greer. Greer had written *The Female Eunuch* more than twenty years earlier and I had read it at the time. It was an important book that moved women on – with a bit of a shock. In *The Change* she is in a much mellower mood and it is a sensitive and instructive book, which I felt was again timely.

The rounds of Christmas parties began. I was sorry to miss the Glee Club night for the staff of the prime minister's office. As a group they had a camaraderie of very special quality. It gave me pleasure that such attention was paid in Bob's office to friendship and support. Everybody there worked exceptionally long hours with skill and responsibility, right through the ranks. Bob always made sure that their modest celebrations of comings and goings or special occasions fitted into his itinerary.

◆

But all the activity in Canberra was not festive. The challenge Paul Keating said, back in June, would not happen, had indeed re-emerged and was approaching at full gallop. I watched news bulletins and read the newspapers to keep informed, and Bob phoned each night. He came to Sydney, and then I returned to the Lodge with him on 15 December, the soonest I could travel. Every day and night the number-crunching continued. I felt that Bob should take it to the vote rather than walk away in resignation. We discussed it, of course, but I stood back from any attempt to influence his decision. It was exhausting for him. The talking, lobbying and head-counting needed to be fitted in to his already full diary. One morning he must have been thinking about it while he was dressing, and after he asked me, 'Which tie?', as he often did, he went on, 'It's tempting to piss off and live in our little bit of magic isn't it.'

After my return to the Lodge with Bob, the challenge dominated our waking hours. Sleeping hours were at a minimum for him, but I was still convalescing. Colleagues came to discuss the options: the factor which was paramount for Bob was his belief that he could lead the Party to another term in government, because of his established record. Bob would have considered resigning after winning the next election – probably about halfway through the following term, contesting an election therefore being justifiable, and giving the Party time to make its decision properly about the succession.

What was not generally understood about Bob was the purity of his deep sense of mission, the commitment to public service which had come in his blood from both mother and father, reinforced by twenty years of hearing his father's sermons and his Uncle Albert's political philosophy. He had, as I have observed earlier, the personality characteristic of being without caution, and this showed in his relationship with the public. Often his projection of his own qualities, of his aims and achievements was taken as conceit and arrogance. But I would argue – knowing him as I do – that it has an innocence about it, and is an honest, straightforward request for people to use his talents and join him in his aims – their aims. He wanted power so he could DO those things. I believe anyone in political life needs an element of that in them to be effective. It's no use having something to offer if you cannot convince the people you will serve of your worth. I would put the critics' argument the other way around: it is arrogant to expect to be accepted into political public service if you don't make the effort to reach out and inform the electorate of your belief in yourself and your potential to work for them.

The Party was going through contortions, and the media was undoubtedly favouring Keating. At about four o'clock in the morning on 19 December, Bob and 'Grunter' (Grant Nihill, his media adviser) came and sat on the end of my bed and we 'read the writing on the wall' together. Then Bob snatched a bit of sleep before an eight o'clock caucus meeting. Bob was advised that the roll was relentless and Keating would not be delayed, so he took it to the vote himself, calling a meeting for half past six that evening.

The atmosphere in Parliament House was electric. The media were clamouring – one might say of some that they were baying for blood, ready to pronounce, 'The King is dead, long live the King.' The vote was taken: fifty-one for Bob, fifty-six for Keating. Six months later, Peter Hartcher of the *Sydney Morning Herald* wrote: 'Only in retrospect is it clear how close Hawke came to surviving. If his supporters had not despaired, if the Left had not freed its members to vote as they pleased, and if Hawke had decided to recall Gareth Evans from Singapore, the ballot would have been tied at 54 votes each.'

After the vote, Bob made his way back to his office, where Susan and Ros and I were waiting. We were all emotionally exhausted, and Bob carried the extra exhaustion of the struggle. I still felt sore and weak but neither Bob nor I had entertained, for one moment, the thought that I would not be with him at this time, which was curiously private though played out in public. There was, however, no wailing or crying, but rather, a quiet acceptance. This was not the way he would have chosen to finish his prime ministership, but that's life.

Then we walked back from his office, together, through the corridors to a press conference which was to be televised live to a national audience. He fielded questions with a dignity and directness which won him respect from all over the country: it was the impressive exit of the statesman he is.

◆

Now, we had to pack up and move both office and home. His dedicated office staff were in a mood approaching mourning, as they went about the task. I shrank from the thought of life without Sharon, without the extraordinary band of staff and friends around us. At the Lodge I faced packing up our only home for almost a decade – helped by the department's packers working in a professional and thoughtful manner. I needed to be thinking clearly, organising to pack some things for the archives, some for the government store, some for an immediate holiday and some for use in the medium term until our house in Sydney was ready. But we left all that until after Christmas – first things first!

I had set in train a Christmas gathering of family and friends as usual. This year we would be at the Lodge where there is more room than at Kirribilli House, and where the swimming pool and gardens are safe and wonderful for the grandchildren. This time we also had Jan's parents with us, out from Belgium, Vera with her infant grandson, and Col and Gloria up from Melbourne. The staff at the Lodge could not have been more considerate – which was no surprise, as under Gordon Mair's leadership they had developed a friendly and professional competence. It was a warm and happy time, with the children playing in the garden, and the constant coming and going of friends – singly and in groups or families. We reminisced and thought about the future – ours and theirs, especially staff whose jobs had come to a sudden end. On New Year's Eve we had a party, with the Bush Band playing again until the early hours. Then the last stayers sang 'golden oldies' to Peter Logue's squeeze-box until nearly breakfast time. Our years in the Lodge had given us even more very good friends, as well as nine years rich in memories.

THE HOME STRETCH

◇

When Bob was abruptly – but by then not unexpectedly – evicted from the prime ministership and decided to leave parliament, he announced his intention of looking after me and his family. Among other things that meant earning a living and he quickly got on with it. Some feelings of hurt lingered, and he remained convinced that his leadership would have given Labor its best chance of staying in power. He had also wanted to consolidate the reforms his government had achieved and put in train. But any feelings of rejection were quickly swept away as offers poured in to him. He said to me one day that he couldn't believe it. My reply was that these opportunities weren't just falling out of the sky, but were an acknowledgement of his accumulated abilities and experience – his reputation in the world of politics, business and the broader community, both in Australia and overseas.

John Singleton had kindly lent us his house in Sydney for the month of January 1992, along with a home-help. It was pleasant there, at the water's edge. The children visited us and I was resting. And yet I could not make myself feel well again – in spite of the fact that I was eating good food and walking in the park every day. I was eager to get on with planning the new house we had decided to build on our beautiful block of land – and with writing this book.

The possibility of writing my story had been slowly developing over perhaps two years. In March 1989, I wrote myself a note:

Today my friend Lois Miles brought Ruth Park to meet me, after I expressed admiration of her book, *Poor Man's Orange*. The conversation began rather hesitantly but gathered interest and direction as we (I suppose inevitably) discussed our experience as women. I raised with her the possibility that I might one day write my autobiography, seeking out her wisdom, as she is a woman of formidable writing achievement with an interesting life story of her own to tell. It is as yet unwritten and she is pondering the idea. [The first volume of her autobiography, *A Fence Around the Cuckoo*, was published in September 1992.]

I said that if I wrote my autobiography I would feel defeated if it read as a tract. Ruth described just such a book: 'When you cut out all the "I"s there is nothing left.' There are many reasons for writing an autobiography, Ruth said. Sometimes a motive is vindictiveness, which is unforgivable, especially when it is aimed at someone who cannot defend the case, for instance the dead. Self-justification or even self-promotion may be another – this would quickly become clear to the reader, although some of it always sticks and becomes part of the public's perception.

Autobiography is, by its nature, subjective: its potential for objectivity is a matter of degree. This can be a conscious or unconscious thing on the part of the writer. Lack of objectivity can come from using incomplete, inadequate or biased sources for information and research. So one is at the mercy of the readers' judgment about motive or – more daunting if one is honest – at the mercy of one's own judgment.

A powerful reason to tackle autobiography is the need to

understand one's own experience better and to use any resulting insights for future growth and hopefully wisdom.

That was my record of our conversation, but I went on in my note:

Keeping diaries (or scribbling episodes and memoirs on bits of paper as I often have) can be a way to further relish some special moments too good to let fade. But it is also a useful way of talking things through without involving anyone else: sometimes an upset is too intimate and requires a lonely solution. At difficult times I would write it all down, for myself. It made me feel better just to distil it to words.

When I did this in perplexing times much emotion and trauma would flow onto the pages, usually late at night when the children were in bed and I was tired, feeling isolated and vulnerable. When I read them at a later date, I would see starkly from my writings that it was counter-productive to blame someone or something else, as things are never that simple. It was also useless to attribute unwarranted guilt to myself: self-deprecation does not equip one to be clear headed.

When it had served its purpose – and I probably felt chastened by the dimensions I had given my upset – I burned it in the incinerator at the bottom of the garden, standing over it until the last words disappeared in the ashes, for these were my unsharable thoughts.

I'd had requests, in recent years, to write a book and had always put them to one side. But in the summer of 1990-91 I got to the point of writing some pieces and showing them to an agent and a publisher. Bob encouraged me unequivocally, and the idea began to take hold. As you can imagine, time was not easy to find, and I scribbled pieces on my knee in cars and aeroplanes, or occasionally late at night when I was alone in my office at the Lodge. During 1991 I began to use a computer and to unravel its mysteries, loving the speed at which my thoughts rolled onto the screen as my typing skills came into play. Before long I thought the word processor a magical thing. A happy by-product was that my grandsons could amuse themselves playing games on it.

Writing about my own life, I can express my appreciation of the warmth which Australians from all walks of life have shown me. Perhaps it's that the things I have spoken about and supported are those which interest many people, but I am sure much curiosity, (particularly evident in interviewers' probings) has really been about my husband and my family.

My own story gives some insights into a life and a marriage. None of it is extraordinary, but rather it is in its essence typical of the experience of many women of my own generation.

The writing has for me prompted sweet reminiscences, while also reinforcing the imperative to move our lives on. There is a place for nostalgia, just as there is for adjusting to the times as the world changes around us – lest we are left behind and become strangers to those who come after us. Our grandchildren will grow up to live in a world unrecognisable from mine in 'a street at the edge of the bush'.

◆

Now, in Sydney, I was making lame attempts to get on with writing. One day my friendly physician, Ron Penny, phoned to see how I was coming along after the removal of the ovarian cyst. I found out later that Bob had organised the call – he was worried about me.

After seeing Ron Penny and consulting specialists, I was diagnosed as having a pituitary tumour at the base of my brain. It took me some days to accept that this was a brain tumour. Bob and I discussed the prognosis and the possibility that the tumour may be malignant. Superb medical and nursing care, consideration from everyone around me, many hundreds of letters, countless gifts and flowers kept me buoyant. But most importantly, Bob and the children's closeness sustained me. I counted my blessings, once again, that the tumour was benign. Yvonne came to Sydney to nurse me through convalescence in her own competent and compassionate way.

But: Oh, dear! Only three months later another operation was required – most simply described as taking a bit from my thigh muscle to plug up a slight leak of spinal fluid in my head. I had undertaken to launch the Madelaine Foundation in Sydney which was to raise funds for research into the draining of spinal fluid in the condition, suffered most commonly by infants, called hydro-cephalus. It seemed uncannily appropriate and my surgeon told me this was a project worth supporting, so I timed my return to hospi-tal to suit the event. At six o'clock in the evening of 3 June I made the launching speech, spoke with some of the guests, then went to St Vincent's for admission. The next day I had a spinal fluid drain myself. Another twelve days in hospital, this was getting boring! Although I felt lucky to be safe and so well looked after, it didn't diminish my frustration at not being able to get on with my life. My new life. Our new life. Life after politics, as there indubitably is!

◆

Now that Bob and I are through more than four decades spanning an extraordinary variety of experiences, and living life in all its aspects to the full, I can see that we have both grown in the process. Had I not, with and through Bob, been exposed constantly to the world far beyond Mount Hawthorn, to all manner of things and people and places, I would have missed most of what I now treasure. My development as a woman began at the moment Bob and I set out together, and has proved to be beyond anything I could have dreamed of forty years ago. My greatest relief, after making some mistakes as parents, is that our surviving children are in close com-panionship with us and with their own children, and demonstrating a strong commitment and determination to make a good job of raising them. My greatest joy is that the six grandchildren are all healthy, lively, loving and lovable and showing a keen interest in the world that will be theirs.

There is, in this phase after politics, another kind of con-tentment. We have been there, done all that, and now there are new horizons, more expansive perhaps than ever – but soundly based on what has gone before. We can enjoy a less demanding, more comfortable and comforting life which is not driven for months ahead by crowded diaries.

Our house will hang on the slope of the hill, a dangle of rooms embracing the northern sun and the view of sparkling blue water. The sounds are the birdsongs of the bush and the clinking of rigging on the masts of boats. The rocky hillside below is spread with old gums and tree-ferns, where grandchildren will play. We two sexagenarians have gathered just a touch of moss, but not nearly enough to stop us rolling busily, contentedly, on – with each other, our children and theirs – in our little bit of magic.